Digitalization in Industry

"This excellent book provides a refreshingly nuanced account of the impact of digitalization on industry. Rejecting the standard binary accounts of digitalization as driving either domination or emancipation, the authors offer a detailed explanation of the possibilities and pitfalls of socio-technical developments for both workers and consumers. The book deserves to be widely read by anyone interested in the future of work."

—Judy Wajcman, *Professor of Sociology, London School of Economics, UK*

"This collected edition treads a careful path between prevalent utopian and dystopian accounts of digital disruption and manufacturing 4.0 to offer a careful examination of struggles to reshape production and distribution processes and their consequence for those operating (as workers or as users) digital industries. It avoids unhelpful generalisation by theoretically-informed empirical investigation of the configuration of producers, consumer and digital tools in a range of specific settings."

—Robin Williams, *Director of the Institute for the Study of Science, Technology and Innovation at The University of Endinburgh, UK*

"Whoever is of the opinion that digitalization in industry is a key component of contemporary societies should read this book. Why? Because it provides a serious and multi-faceted contribution to analyze and theorize the empirical triangle of digitalized working practices, smart fabrication, and the novel implications of users—way beyond the commonly cherished visions of hypes and horrors as regards 'Industrie 4.0.' To this end, the authors capitalize on a rich repertoire of concepts and methods made available by

- science and technology studies, focusing here on the impacts of digital technologies on society,
- organization studies, emphasizing here on processes and effects of organizing technological change,
- as well as their mother discipline sociology, bringing, among other things, the thorny question of (new) power relations to the table.

Their distinctive perspectives notwithstanding, all disciplinary perspectives are united by the notion that (digital) society and (digital) technology shape each other thoroughly, and will continue to do so. In order to make sense of ongoing changes and (alleged) challenges, and to configure them responsibly, this book alerts us to the many frictions and ambivalences entailed in digitalizing industry, work, users, us, hence: society, its dynamics constantly moving between the poles of emancipation and domination."

—Professor Sabine Maasen, *Director of the Munich Center for Technology in Society, Technical University of Munich, Germany*

"This volume is a very important contribution on the discussion around the power effects of digitalization. It is hard to find any analysis on the subject as differentiated and profound as the texts assembled here."

—Professor Oliver Nachtwey, *Professor of Social Structure Analysis, University of Basel, Switzerland*

Uli Meyer · Simon Schaupp ·
David Seibt
Editors

Digitalization in Industry

Between Domination and Emancipation

palgrave
macmillan

Editors
Uli Meyer
Technical University of Munich
Munich, Bayern, Germany

Simon Schaupp
Technical University of Munich
Munich, Bayern, Germany

David Seibt
Technical University of Munich
Munich, Bayern, Germany

ISBN 978-3-030-28257-8 ISBN 978-3-030-28258-5 (eBook)
https://doi.org/10.1007/978-3-030-28258-5

This Palgrave Macmillan imprint is published by the registered company Springer Nature Switzerland AG
The registered company address is: Gewerbestrasse 11, 6330 Cham, Switzerland

Contents

Notes on Contributors

Attila Bruni is Associate Professor in the Department of Sociology and Social Research at the Trento University, where he teaches Sociology of Technological Phenomena and Sociology of Organizations. His research interests regard particularly the intersection of technological phenomena, work, and organizing practices.

Florian Butollo is a researcher at Berlin Social Science Center and head of the research group "working in highly-automated digital-hybrid processes" at the Weizenbaum Institute for the Networked Society, an interdisciplinary research institute exploring the relationship between digitalization and society from multiple perspectives. He is also an advisor to the Study Commission "Artificial Intelligence Social Responsibility and Economic, Social and Ecological Potential" of the German parliament.

ginger coons is educator, researcher, and designer. She studies and intervenes in the intersections of individuality, mass standards, and new production technologies. She is interested in the place of the user in the production process and how individuals take control of the goods they use. She has a multi-disciplinary educational background: a BFA (2009) in design from Concordia University (Montreal) and an MI (2011) and Ph.D. (2016) in information from the University of Toronto, where she was a member of the Critical Making Lab and the Semaphore Research Cluster on Mobile and Pervasive Computing. She is currently Course Leader in the undergraduate Graphic Design major at WdKA.

Fabio M. Esposito currently collaborates as a researcher at the University of Napoli "Federico II" after obtaining a Master Degree in Sociology and Social Research at the University of Trento, discussing a thesis on the role of users in digital platforms. His research interests mainly regard the study of the relationship between technology and new forms of work and organization.

Philipp Frey is a doctoral researcher at the Institute for Technology Assessment and Systems Analysis, Karlsruhe, with a background in critical social philosophy and theory. In his research, he deals with the future of work and utopias of automation. He is co-founder and board member of the Zentrum Emanzipatorische Technikforschung (ZET), a progressive technopolitical think tank based in the German-speaking countries.

Ulrich Jürgens is professor at the WZB Berlin Social Science Center where he is member of the research group "Globalization Work and Production." His research interests include labor and labor markets, work organization and human research management, as well as systems of innovation and corporate governance.

Yannick Kalff is a postdoctoral research assistant at Osnabrück University, Germany, at the Institute of Social Sciences. Currently, he conducts a research project on industrial group and teamwork in digitalization processes, funded by the Federal Ministry of Education and Research. His research interests cover forms of organizing and organizations in alternative economies, power and sovereignty in labor processes, and digitalization effects on organizations, work as well as economy.

Martin Krzywdzinski is head of the research group "Globalization Work and Production" at the WZB Berlin Social Science Center and Director at the Weizenbaum Institute for the Networked Society. His research interests are in the relationship between technology and work (in particular in the context of digitalization), production systems, innovation processes, and global value chains.

Felix Maschewski is currently a Ph.D. candidate at the German Department of Humboldt University in Berlin, where he is a member of the Research Cluster "Das Wissen der Literatur" and a research assistant at Institut für Wirtschaftsgestaltung Berlin. Most recently, he was a visiting scholar at Princeton University, where he did research on cybernetic realism. Alongside academic articles, he regularly writes essays for, among others, *Neue Zürcher Zeitung* and *Die Republik*. He is co-editor of the journal *engagée*, a journal committed to political and philosophical interventions.

Uli Meyer is a research group leader and head of the Post/Doc Lab Reorganizing Industries at the Munich Center for Technology in Society, Technical University of Munich. He is acting professor for the sociology of digital work at the Ruhr Universität Bochum. He was a visiting scholar at Stanford University, USA, as well as the University of Bologna, Italy. His research interests include organization studies, innovation studies, the impact of sociotechnical visions, and the interplay between science and economy. He is a member of the board of the organizational sociology section of the International Sociological Association (ISA) as well as the German Sociological Association (DFG).

Andreas Möllenkamp is a research fellow at the University of Hamburg, Germany. His main fields of research include the history and culture of digital media, music technology, online communities, the digitization of cultural heritage as well as open science. He received a Ph.D. scholarship from the department Knowledge–Culture–Transformation at the University of Rostock, an award of the German Society for Popular Music Studies for the best German article in the field of popular music research 2016 as well as a scholarship of the Open Science Fellows Program 2018.

Anna-Verena Nosthoff is currently a Ph.D. candidate at the Institute of Sociology of the University of Freiburg and a lecturer at the University of Vienna, where she teaches in the Politics Department. Her academic work has been published in various edited volumes and journals, including *Cultural Politics*, *Culture, Theory & Critique*, *Thesis Eleven*, *Behemoth*, *Jahrbuch Technikphilosophie*, and *Critical Research on Religion*. She also works as an essayist for, among others, *Neue Zürcher Zeitung* and *Die Republik*. She is co-editor of the journal *engagée*, a journal committed to political and philosophical interventions, and will be a research fellow at the Weizenbaum Institute for the Networked Society from August 2019.

Simon Schaupp born in 1988, studied sociology, law, and economics at Bielefeld and Vienna University. He was working as a research associate at the Post/Doc Lab Reorganizing Industries at the Munich Center for Technology in Society. Currently, he is the assistant of the chair of social structure analysis at the University of Basel. His research focus is on the sociology of technology and work and critical theory. His current Ph.D. project concerns the techno-politics of algorithmic management.

Christoph Schneider holds a Ph.D. in sociology and runs a consultancy for digital-social innovation (www.zukuenfte.digital). He has worked at the Institute for Technology Assessment and Systems Analysis, Karlsruhe, and at the Munich Center for Technology in Society, Munich. As an engaged Intellectual, he has co-founded FabLab Karlsruhe and he coordinates the technopolitical agenda for the Democracy in Europe Movement 2025.

Janosch Schobin born in 1981, is a sociologist. He currently leads the BMBF funded young researchers group DeCarbFriends at the University of Kassel in Germany. His research interests include sociology of technology, friendship sociology, and sociological network theory.

David Seibt born in 1989, received his B.A. in Social and Cultural Anthropology and Politics from the Free University of Berlin in 2013 and his M.A. in Sociology from the Technical University of Berlin in 2015. Currently, he is working as a research associate at the Post/Doc Lab Reorganizing Industries at the Munich Center for Technology in Society, Technical University of Munich. His research focuses on the relationship between digital technologies, industries, and the human body, with a special focus on participatory methodology. His Ph.D. project focuses on the introduction of 3D printing technologies to the prosthetics industries.

Philipp Staab born in 1983, is a sociologist. He is a professor for sociology of the future of work at Humboldt University in Berlin and the Einstein Center Digital Future (ECDF). His research interests include sociology of technology, political economy, sociology of work, and social inequality.

Gunhild Tøndel is currently working as a researcher at NTNU Social Research, Unit of Diversity and Inclusion. She has earlier been a Ph.D. student and a postdoc researcher at the Norwegian University of Science and Technology, at, respectively, the Department of Sociology and Political Science and the Department of Interdisciplinary Studies of Culture. Her Ph.D. thesis (2014) was a qualitative study about numbers as a tool of governance in the Norwegian municipal health and care sector. In her postdoc project, she explored how welfare technology, care, and old age combine in Norwegian elderly care services. Together with colleagues, she has also explored social processes related to quantification, digitalization, and technology in other contexts than health and care, e.g., the performative role of performance metrics in the academy and the digital norms of smartphone use in urban settings.

Klara-Aylin Wenten is a Ph.D. candidate at the Munich Center for Technology in Society at the Technical University of Munich. Her research focuses on practices and discourses around the transformation of industrial labor and questions of emancipation. She has a background in Science and Technology Studies, as well as in the History and Philosophy of Science and Technology. Her current research project is funded by the Hans Böckler Foundation. She is also part of the Center for Emancipatory Technology Studies.

List of Tables

CHAPTER 1

Toward an Analytical Understanding of Domination and Emancipation in Digitalizing Industries

David Seibt, Simon Schaupp and Uli Meyer

Does digitalization reinforce, or even strengthen, structures of domination? Or does it instead foster social emancipation? These questions are as old as digitalization itself.[1] Various disciplines and fields of study, including sociology, organization studies (OS), and science and technology studies (STS) continue to engage in debates as to how the political qualities of digital technologies play out under different circumstances. Weaving together some of the threads that constitute those conversations, the present volume assembles theoretical perspectives as well as detailed empirical investigations that shed light on the relationship between current forms of digitalization and new dynamics of

D. Seibt (✉) · U. Meyer
Technical University of Munich, Munich, Germany
e-mail: david.seibt@tum.de

U. Meyer
e-mail: uli.meyer@tum.de

S. Schaupp
University of Basel, Basel, Switzerland
e-mail: simon.schaupp@unibas.ch

U. Meyer et al. (eds.), *Digitalization in Industry*,
https://doi.org/10.1007/978-3-030-28258-5_1

emancipation and domination. However, our contribution distinguishes itself from the larger discussion on digitalization by homing in on a subject that has, regrettably, moved out of focus in the social sciences: industry. While the reorganization of industry and industrial production was at the very heart of classical discussions of social emancipation and domination (e.g., Blauner, 1964; Braverman, 1974; Mackenzie and Wajcman, 1985; Marx, 1976), over the last 30 or so years, it has receded from the limelight. The topic of industry has fallen out of favor both as an empirical phenomenon in Western societies and as a subject of scholarly interest. On the one hand, attention has shifted to processes of consumption and use (Bourdieu, 1984; Featherstone, 2007 [1991]; Miller, 1987; Oudshoorn & Pinch, 2003), on the other hand, to processes of knowledge production (Jasanoff, 2004; Knorr-Cetina, 1999; Latour, 1987; Latour & Woolgar, 1986) and knowledge work (Drucker, 1993; Orlikowski, 2002; Star, 1995).

Only with the most recent wave of digitalization has interest in industry and industrial production been rekindled among politicians, social scientists, and the broader public. Industrial robots have returned to the covers of major newspapers and magazines; governments are negotiating strategies for dealing with the "next wave of digitalization," and scholars are quick to compete for public and private funding as well as for grandiose claims in journals, at conferences, and in popular monographs. Out of this growing body of scholarship, we have selected the issues of *work*, *digital fabrication*, and the *configuration of users* as the focal points of the present volume, with separate sections of the book dedicated to each of these topics. We chose these themes because they point us to three ongoing debates which strike us as particularly relevant with regard to the dynamics of emancipation and domination in digitalizing industries, and as particularly contested in their analyses of these processes.[2]

Concerning the dynamics of *emancipation and domination in the workplace*, for example, hopes emerged that industrial automation and digitalization would lead to a "postcapitalist" society (Mason, 2015; Srnicek & Williams, 2015). They were quickly rebutted, however, as a fetishization of technology (Fuchs, 2016; Thompson & Briken, 2017). Some authors see networked communication technologies, coupled with the ubiquity of private computers, as a material precondition for democratic organizations (Sattelberger et al., 2015). Others point to the ubiquity of digital sensor technologies in production, warning that it may lead to a revitalization of classical Taylorism and a radicalization of surveillance (Zuboff, 1988, 2019).

Promises of emancipation through digital fabrication are frequently connected to this discussion, but often point beyond the confines of the workplace. Technologies like 3D printing are hailed as tools which will democratize production and innovation, encouraging the spread of peer production infrastructures such as shared machine shops, as well as enabling grassroots movements and open source communities (Ferdinand et al., 2016; Gershenfeld, 2005; Raymond, 2001; von Hippel, 2005). Other accounts focus on the instrumentalization of these movements by large firms (Dahlander & Magnusson, 2008; Jensen & Krogh Petersen, 2016) and emphasize the intimate relationships between digital fabrication technologies and the capitalist logic of value production (Braybrooke & Smith, 2018). Moreover, it bears mentioning that grassroots communities have themselves given rise to profit-oriented corporations (Ferdinand & Meyer, 2017).

One related question is how the digitalization of contemporary industries contributes to *emancipating, configuring, and infrastructuring users*. In this area, developments such as digital mass customization platforms (Pine, 1993; von Hippel & Katz, 2002; Piller, 2004) and the increased speed of design iterations have sparked optimism when it comes to escaping the perils of mass production. Yet, critical scholars have pointed out that computer-aided design is also threatening traditional trades and crafts (Sennett, 2008). What is more, mass customization is a long haul from true custom production (coons, 2016). The growing ubiquity of the digital means of production has been said to foster user- and community-based innovation (Benkler, 2006; von Hippel, 2005). More recently, however, it has been argued as well that companies increasingly "produce" users (Hyysalo et al., 2016) or configure them to become sources of unpaid labor (Drewlani & Seibt, 2018; Johnson et al., 2014; Ritzer & Jurgenson, 2010).

While we welcome and, to some degree, participate in this newfound enthusiasm surrounding the promises and pitfalls of digitalization, there are three reasons why we find large parts of the current debates to be somewhat unsatisfactory. First of all, many popular contributions subscribe to a simplistic linear logic of industrial development, labeling current dynamics as the *second machine age* (McAfee & Brynjolfsson, 2014), the *third industrial revolution* (Rifkin, 2011), or even *Industrie 4.0* (Kagermann, Lukas, & Wahlster, 2011). Often driven by an implicit technological determinism, these accounts frequently miss historical continuities, ironies and, above all, the myriad opportunities that actually exist for companies and users to make a difference in the design, implementation, and use of technologies. Second, many contributions take either an alarmist or a techno-optimist stance toward digitalization in industries. New sociomaterial configurations are either hailed as the forerunners of a technologized utopia (Mason, 2015) or demonized as a new level of domination by states and multinational corporations (Zuboff, 2019) as well as an impending age of mass unemployment (Frey & Osborne, 2017). What these polarizing characterizations miss, however, is the more intricate, and often ambiguous, dynamics that happen between total domination and total emancipation. Third, critical social-scientific analysis is hampered by the vague and indiscriminate use of its central concepts. While notions such as digitalization and industry seem to be everywhere and their relationship with dynamics of emancipation or domination are commonly asserted, these terms are rarely defined or subjected to any scrutiny. Yet, as long as we do not know what we mean by industry, digitalization, and emancipation/domination, any attempt at analyzing the relationships between these concepts is bound to fail or, at the very least, remain incompatible with other analyses.

The remainder of this introduction is therefore dedicated to sketching out how the present volume attempts to tackle these shortcomings by laying some of the foundations for an analytical understanding of digitalized industries and the dynamics of domination and emancipation. While we will introduce the contributions to the volume at the end of this introduction, the most important task that we have set out for this chapter is to provide some conceptual clarity as to how the terms *industry*, *digitalization* and *domination/emancipation* may be understood. As we described above, the extensive debates surrounding these topics suffer from a variety of misunderstandings which are largely due to highly disparate understandings of these terms. Of course, we encourage the development of multiple analytical lenses, as these allow scholars to highlight different aspects of the same topic. However, we would also like to insist that conceptual heterogeneity must inevitably lead to misunderstandings whenever concepts lack clear definitions. Thus, in the following paragraphs we suggest concepts of industry, digitalization, and domination/emancipation which we believe to be useful as a common framework for reading the heterogenous approaches assembled in this volume.

Between Domination and Emancipation

We will begin our discussion by clarifying what exactly we mean by the terms domination and emancipation. While there is a wide range of different approaches to these topics (e.g., in actor-network theory, feminist theory, political science), in the specific context of digitalized industries it seems useful to take a closer look at the corresponding discussions in the sociology of work. Most contributions to this subfield approach the issue of digitalized industries with a strong focus on domination in the form of managerial control. For instance, in the 1970s and 1980s scholars found that computerized production technologies materialized Tayloristic management principles (Braverman, 1974; Cooley, 1980). With a similar focus, more recent studies have repeatedly pointed out that digital tracking enables increased managerial control over the workforce (e.g., Briken et al., 2017; Staab & Nachtwey, 2016; Zuboff, 2019). While these accounts rightly emphasize the extended reach of digital control, they miss an important point concerning the relationship of domination and emancipation: By restricting their analysis to managerial strategies of control, they often do not take into account strategies of agency "from below." These, however, often present practical critiques of domination and therefore point toward emancipation (Boltanski, 2011). Therefore, in the following, we formulate an analytical perspective that is capable of grasping domination as well as emancipation. To do so, we will start by differentiating between the concepts of domination and control.

Social action is closely linked to control. The essence of control, according to Emile Durkheim (1982, p. 45) lies in the fact that "collective ways of acting and thinking possess a reality existing outside individuals, who, at every moment, conform to them. They are things which have their own existence." In this sense, control is the basis of expectable behavior, and therefore of cooperation and coexistence as such. This does not exclude individual freedom. Even language-based communication would not be imaginable beyond a mutual set of grammatical rules and their constraints. Language is likewise the basis for social interaction and thus at the same time for individual freedom (Berger, 1967). This general concept of social control must, however, be differentiated further to enable insights on the topic of this book: domination and emancipation. The first differentiation is between internal and external control. The internalization of norms is the prototypical example of internal social control. External social control, on the other hand, may take the form of positive or negative sanctions for a certain behavior. The second form of control is only possible if there is another factor in the equation: power.[3] It is only through power that other actors can be influenced in their behavior. The most widely acknowledged definition by Max Weber (1968, p. 53) understands power as "the probability that one actor within a social relationship will be in a position to carry out his own will despite resistance, regardless of the basis on which this probability rests." This definition also covers, among others, the extreme cases of power that can be described as a zero-sum game of competing wills. However, in most cases, power simply manifests as influence over other people's actions. Indeed, a society not pervaded by power, as conceptualized in the latter way, would be unimaginable, as reciprocity and reciprocal influence over the actions of others are necessary preconditions for cooperation. Reciprocal influence, however, is not the same as acknowledging an omnipresence of domination, the latter being preliminarily defined here as the *structural asymmetry* of power relations (Haude & Wagner, 1999).[4]

Many social scientists deduce directly from the universality of social control to the universality of domination and therefore see the latter as a fundamental aspect of all social action. Ralf Dahrendorf was among those especially eager to naturalize domination in this way. According to his definition, domination, in its encompassing form, can be understood as the authority to set, apply, and enforce norms (Dahrendorf, 1964, p. 96). However, even one of these factors would be enough to speak of domination in some shape and form. Thus, for Dahrendorf any kind of institution that is concerned with the securing or maintaining of norms is enough to indicate the existence of domination in the society in question (ibid., p. 98). But with this conceptual maneuver, society, and domination are tautologically defined and, for all intents and purposes, indistinguishable, as the absence of norms would indeed equal the absence of society as such. It is only in this way that Dahrendorf (1967, p. 334) arrives at his final postulate that "society simply is domination." This definitional bypass serves an explicitly political end. It is meant to prove the "futility of political utopias" and of "Marxist dreams of society" (Dahrendorf, 1964, p. 84). But other sociologists, including those who are probably less ideologically motivated, have taken the same path. Even Anthony Giddens, who elaborated one of the most sophisticated theories of power, claims that domination has "to be recognized as inherent in social association (or, I would say in social action as such)" (Giddens, 1984, p. 31f.).

From our point of view, the problem with defining domination as an integral element of all social action is that it runs the risk of brushing over the all-important differences in the *forms* and *degrees* of domination. In order to use domination as a category in empirical analysis, rather than one of the basic elements of an ontology of the social, one needs to take into account the immense differences in the extent of domination, which is precisely why we prefer to speak of domination as structural asymmetries of power relations. This argument does not depend on the proof of the complete absence of domination at a certain place and time. Even if domination were an inevitable element of the social world, a focus on structural power asymmetries allows us to see that there are still extremely important differences between different forms of domination. Such differences include the varying degrees of repression, internal and external human costs, interests and content, and basis for legitimation. Moreover, once we reject the notion of domination as a universal constant, we are able to identify forms of social action that cannot be explained within a framework of domination, such as solidarity, mutual support, and all forms of critique and resistance aimed at the structures that secure and legitimize power asymmetries. From this point of view, we are also able to see that there are not only differences in the form, but also in the degree of domination, which makes it possible to empirically identify social constellations that are structured to a greater or lesser degree by domination (Narr, 2015, p. 95).

Defining domination as structural asymmetries in power relations also implies that situations which are less structured by domination are not necessarily void of institutions. The reduction or absence of domination, if it is to be enduring, instead always rests on an institutionalization of non-domination. This means that such contexts are not simply characterized by the absence of certain institutions of domination, but by the explicit institutional inhibition of domination—as, for example, in council-systems, collective justice or the redistribution of material wealth (Haude & Wagner, 1999). To deny these institutions and to naturalize domination on the other hand, as Boltanski (2011, p. 116) notes…

> pretty much comes down to supporting overarching theories of domination which, by unmasking underlying effects of domination in any political order whatsoever – this boils down to regarding domination as ubiquitous – have virtually the same practical consequences [...] as positions that definitively exclude the issue of domination.

Narr (2015) therefore suggests a scalar approach for the identification of domination mechanisms. Such an approach would see domination not as a universal constant but also identify instances where it is reduced. These processes of the reduction of domination would then be synonymous with processes of emancipation. In suggesting such a negative and procedural definition of emancipation, we would like to emphasize two of its aspects. Firstly, we are cognizant of the fact that, as domination itself cannot be reduced to one principal social contradiction, the same is true for emancipation. Because domination consists of several intersecting lines of social oppression (Hancock, 2016), emancipation also cannot be thought of as liberation in only one of these dimensions, e.g., a postcapitalist economy. The analysis of emancipation, like domination, should be explicit about the specific kinds of structural power asymmetries it addresses and, where possible, should be mindful about how different such asymmetries relate to one another. The lessening of domination in one kind of relation does not necessarily imply a similar reduction in other regards. Secondly, defining emancipation as the reduction of domination allows us to foreground the dynamics that unfold between these two poles. States of emancipation and domination are rarely, if ever, absolute and remain in need of concrete action. It is in this sense, that domination can be contested and emancipation must be achieved and defended.

While, the contributions assembled in this volume diverge with regard to their definitions of control, power, and domination, they can be framed by these two principles. All of them describe dynamics that play out *between* domination and emancipation and all of them specify the particular *dimensions* in which they are concerned with these. In addition, the chapters are also linked by the fact that they situate their studies in the particular context of digitalized industry. In the following two sections, we will therefore sketch out what we mean by industry and digitalization, and how these may relate to processes of domination and emancipation.

Industry

Few would contest the fact that industry is a central feature of modernity in Western societies, where it has historically been linked to ideas of progress and prosperity. Yet, both the term and the phenomena it is meant to describe have had a complicated and contested career. For one thing, industrial production in the classical sense has shifted from the countries of Western Europe and North America to what economists now refer to as newly "industrialized countries" such as China, India, Indonesia, Mexico, Brazil, South Africa, or Turkey. At the same time, self-characterizations such as "industrial society" or "industrial capitalism" have been replaced with the idea that we are living in a "postindustrial society" (Bell, 1976; Touraine, 1971). Starting from the 1970s, Western sociologists observed that the focus of economic activity in their countries had shifted from the production of goods to the production of services, that white-collar work had become more prevalent, and that knowledge was now the most important form of capital (Drucker, 1993; Moulier-Boutang, 2011). This change also came with a clear shift in the valuation of industry and the places in which it was located. Where industrial production had long been an emblem of progress, it was gradually stripped of its symbolic value and physically "offshored." Following a logic of linear technological development within countries and a binary division between them, the division was no longer drawn between industrialized and non-industrialized nations, but between those that were newly industrializing and those that had already moved to a postindustrial state. However, in a somewhat ironic reversal of this trend, discussions around the most recent wave of digitalization have moved the topic of industry back into the public eye and into academic circles. Companies, governments, and social scientists have heralded (and analyzed), among others, "the second machine age" (McAfee & Brynjolfsson, 2014), "the third industrial revolution" (Rifkin, 2011), and the "Industrie 4.0" (Pfeiffer, 2017). In this newly emerging discourse, promises of smart economies based on decentral, networked, and—above all—digital technologies are linked to burgeoning political programs that aim to reinvigorate industrial production in Western countries.

To make sense of these apparently contradictory dynamics and to understand their connection to digitalization and social emancipation, it is necessary to have a clear understanding of what we mean by the term *industry*. Yet, for all the current discussion about industrial transformation, the term is rarely defined and does not feature in any of the more prominent sociological dictionaries (Abercrombie et al., 2006; Bruce & Yearley, 2006; Marshall, 2003; Turner, 2006). In search of a definition, the inclined reader is instead presented with a list of related notions which refer to industry and its related dynamics on at least three different levels.

Of these related notions, first of all, there is the term industrialization. It refers to a change in the modes of production, a concept which, even though it is often thought of as a society-wide development, encompasses a specific relationship between the means of production and the organization of work. In its narrowest sense, industrial production is marked by the large-scale use of machines and their integration into machinery within a factory system (Marx, 1976, pp. 492–642). As Marx noted, the shift to an industrial mode of production entailed a dramatic reversal in the organization of work: "*In manufacture the transformation of the mode of production takes labor-power as its starting-point. In large-scale industry, on the other hand, the instruments of labor are the starting-point*" (Marx, 1976, p. 492). Even though technology has changed tremendously since the time of Marx's writing, the relationship between technology and the organization of labor is still at the heart of industrial sociology. Digital technologies in particular were central to the controversy around the consequences of automation that developed in the 1960s and 1970s. Inventions such as computerized numerical control machines became a touchstone in the debates around de- and upskilling (Blauner, 1964; Braverman, 1974), the organization of work (Blau et al., 1976; Woodward, 1965, 1970) as well as industrial relations more generally (Burawoy, 1985; Noble, 1984). Today, technologies such as 3D printers, the Internet, or artificial intelligence are equally important for a new round of debate over the relationship between digitalization, the future of work, and the dynamics of emancipation and domination (Frey & Osborne, 2017; Mason, 2015; McAfee & Brynjolfsson, 2014; Srnicek & Williams, 2015). Thus, we can say that on this first level, industry refers to a mode of the large-scale production of goods and services, in which work is to a large degree organized around machines.

Yet, beyond the shop floor, the term industry is also used to refer to higher levels of aggregation and therefore includes the (power) dynamics within larger sets, systems, or networks of organizations. For instance, in economics, industry is understood as the system of production on the macro-level of an economy. On this level, it is broken down into different "industry sectors," each of which is concerned with the production of a different kind of products. Most famously, Jean Fourastié differentiated between the primary sector of extracting raw materials, the secondary sector of the production of products and the tertiary sector of providing services (Fourastié, 1949). In the shift toward the provision of services, he saw "the great hope of the 20th century," predicting the reduction of toil as well as a general increase in social security. A similar distinction can be made on the meso-level of analysis. Here, industries, this time in the plural, are sets of companies producing similar products or services, such as the automobile industry. Economists have usually modeled the dynamics within these sets in terms of competition (Dosi, Teece, & Chytry, 1998; Nelson & Winter, 1982). In contrast, sociologists have employed the concept of "organizational field" to focus on the interaction between firms as well as the institutional order which shapes and is shaped by these interactions (Wooten & Hoffman, 2016). Again, one explicit focus of these studies has been "the emergence of sharply defined interorganizational structures of domination and patterns of coalition" (DiMaggio & Powell, 1983, p. 148).

Finally, it should be noted that the organization and reorganization of industries have always been found to be of wider significance for processes of domination and emancipation in society at large. Changes in industry were never merely discussed as confined to the realm of production. Instead, they were seen as connected to processes of increasing rationalization (Weber, 1968), social fragmentation (Tönnies, 1957), identity formation (Marcuse, 1964; Miller, 1987), changes in gender relations (Bell, 1976), or as the harbinger of a utopian society beyond the toils of manual labor (Blauner, 1964). It is on this level that it made sense to speak of specific societal formations as, "pre-industrial," "industrial" or "post-industrial" societies, even though it should be kept in mind that such terms often take on a performative quality as normative categories used to constitute a difference between "us" and "them." It is on the same level, and with similar normative implications, that digitalization in contemporary industry touches upon larger societal developments. Users and "crowds" are transformed into a central source of unpaid creative labor, while, on the other hand, they may themselves become innovators (Hyysalo et al., 2016; von Hippel, 2005; Wexler, 2011) and engage in user or open source communities (Benkler, 2016; Raymond, 2001). Digital fabrication technologies afford opportunities for private fabrication and commons-based peer production (Benkler, 2016; Gershenfeld, 2005) as well as the extension of industrial automation, which may be leveraged to increase control over workers *and* engage in political struggles over national identities and the "reshoring" of production.

In sum, the transformation of industry is connected to the dynamics of social emancipation and domination on three levels of analysis. These include the organization of work relative to the instruments of labor on the micro-level, the organizational field around the production of similar goods and services on the meso-level, and the (self-) description of specific forms of society on the macro-level. As this brief overview has shown, processes of ***digitalization*** have frequently been thought of as being at the center of important transformations on all three levels of analysis. Yet, just like the term industry itself, the notion of digitalization is in need of clarification. As things stand, it is merely a buzzword, which is deprived of both technical content and analytical value. In the next section, we attempt to introduce some clarity.

Digitalization

Even though digital technologies are by no means new, digitalization has become one of the buzzwords of the early twenty-first century. With the proliferation of the term, however, any clarity in terms of its meaning has all but evaporated. Originally, digitalization was used as a synonym of digitization, describing the transformation of analog data into a digital format.[5] Most of the time this means that some form of input is transformed into an array of zeros and ones which are stored in a way that makes them readable by computers. This can include everything from digitally scanned files, to transferring an automotive design to a CAD tool, to converting work time sheets into a digital database.

More recently, a distinction between digitization and digitalization has been made. Digitization still describes the transformation of elements from the analog world into a digital form. Digitalization, on the other hand, describes "the way in which many domains of social life are restructured around digital communication and media infrastructures" (Brennen & Kreiss, 2016, p. 556). This is not a distinction widely represented in dictionaries.[6] Instead, it is applied in business contexts, public debates, by the media and in scholarly articles. In the business world, for instance, the restructuring of social life through digitalization is reduced to "the use of digital technologies to change a business model and provide new revenue and value-producing opportunities; it is the process of moving to a digital business."[7] With this delimitation of the two terms, digitalization loses its more technical aspects to digitization while maintaining the vague ideas of restructuring social life or business, and all the normative connotations they entail.

Ironically, at the same time the discussion of concrete technological processes is lost, digitalization takes on an air of technological determinism. More often than not, digitalization is used to describe all kinds of changes in society brought about by all kinds of technologies. In this context, digitalization often becomes synonymous with the introduction of digital technologies into new settings. Even where digitalization is perceived in a more limited sense as the introduction of new technology into companies, the variety of phenomena the term is used to describe is immense. It refers in some cases to the introduction of enterprise resource planning (ERP) software in companies—a process which began in the 1970s, or even earlier. In other cases, it relates to the use of artificial intelligence, for example, by human resource departments, or the use of collaborative robots in production—both technologies which have been promised for decades but only on rare occasions have left the prototype or demo stage.

In addition to subscribing to a techno-deterministic logic while simultaneously being emptied of concrete technical content, common usage of the term digitalization also frequently confuses sociotechnical dynamics on various levels of analysis—a finding that corresponds to what we have said about industry in general. As examples such as the introduction of ERP, collaborative robots, or smart factory solutions show, digitalization frequently refers to changes in the organization of work within single organizations. However, digitalization is also frequently used to foreground phenomena of cooperation and competition between firms, which we would situate on the meso-level of analysis. These include, for instance, the increasing ubiquity of digital infrastructures between organizations, as well as the changes in the organization of specific industries, such as the shift to "mobility as a service" in the automobile industry. Finally, there are concepts like the "platform economy" which delineate transformations of large sections of the economy and society more generally.

An example illustrating all of the above problems in the discussion around the digitalization of industry is a debate which, in Germany and other countries, got labeled "Industrie 4.0":

> Industrie 4.0 combines production methods with state-of-the-art information and communication technology. The driving force behind this development is the rapidly increasing digitisation [sic] of the economy and society. It is changing the future of manufacturing and work in Germany:

> In the tradition of the steam engine, the production line, electronics and IT, smart factories are now determining the fourth industrial revolution. (Plattform Industrie 4.0)[8]

From this perspective, the digitalization of industrial production takes place because technology is changing on a societal level. However, this debate does not stop there. Organizations and nation-state which do not conform to the narrative of increased digitalization driving a fourth industrial revolution are considered to be in danger of losing their competitive edge. Consulting agencies have therefore started to offer programs to evaluate the "digital readiness" of companies, and states provide funding to companies that want to catch up.

For decades now, STS and OS have argued that such a reduced linear perspective cannot account for the complex and intricate interplay between ongoing technological, societal, and organizational developments (Bijker et al., 1987; Bijker & Law, 1992; Collins, 1983; Jasanoff & Kim, 2009; MacKenzie & Wajcman, 1985; Meyer & Rowan, 1977; Meyer et al., 1983; Perrow, 1986). In this tradition, the contributions in this volume suggest that current developments cannot be explained simply by the advent of new technologies. In order to reclaim the notion of digitalization as an analytical category, it is necessary to acknowledge the enormous empirical complexity of the phenomenon, while analytically disentangling the different relations and influences it encompasses. A first step in this direction is to differentiate between the different levels at which digitalization takes place. Corresponding to the different levels of the notion of industry described above, we propose to distinguish between digitalization on three different levels, for each of which we suggest a specific analytical focus. In this analytical schema, we differentiate between (a) the actual routines and practices observable in contemporary industrial organizations on the micro-level, (b) the strategic planning and decisions by collective actors, such as companies or governments on the meso-level, and (c) societal discourses and debates on the macro-level (Meyer, forthcoming). This framework provides a starting point for a more differentiated understanding of digitalization in contemporary industries.

Returning to the example of industrial digitalization in Germany, it allows us to see that the massive debate on "Industrie 4.0" (level c) has not led to the implementation of smart factories (level a) on a larger scale (Meyer, 2019). But it has triggered a debate on the future of work (level c). Under the heading "Arbeit 4.0" (work 4.0), state actors like the Federal Ministry of Labour and Social Affairs along with labor unions, works councils, and companies have come together to discuss what work could and should look like in the future (Meyer, 2018). This confluence has led—among other things—to an initiative (level b) where, within a variety of organizations, so-called experimental spaces ('Experimentierräume')[9] have been created, within which companies endeavor to test a wide range of ideas about the future of work—often in close collaboration with works councils and labor unions. So, in this case, our perspective enables us to discern how the debate on new technologies and their impact on society triggered a very different debate which by now has probably had a greater impact on organizational practices than the introduction of new technologies, i.e., the original claim and starting point for the debate.

In this spirit, one of our main suggestions throughout this book is to take a closer look at the different levels on which digitalization unfolds. One goal of this edited volume is to question the prevalent view of technological determinism in relation to digitalization. More specifically, we want to push past a perspective that characterizes digitalization solely as an expression of rationalization and increases in efficiency and competitiveness. Instead, this volume addresses the digitalization of industries starting from its wider social context, and specifically from its various relationships to processes of domination and emancipation.

The Contributions

With these conceptual clarifications in mind, the present volume aims to contribute to a growing body of critical scholarship that seeks to deepen analysis, complicate binary logics, weave together disparate strands of arguments, and demonstrate the embeddedness of current developments in larger, often ambiguous or ironic historical developments. While our authors have chosen widely differing subject matters as well as analytical approaches, their contributions converge around three of the major dynamics linking the topics of industry, digitalization, and domination/emancipation in contemporary Western societies. In particular, they present thoughtful theoretical arguments as well as detailed empirical investigations around the three core issues of *work*, *digital fabrication*, and the *relationship between industry and users*. As we have sketched out above, each of these issues strikes us as offering particularly rich opportunities for exploring the intricate dynamics of social emancipation and domination in digitalized industries, not least of all because they intervene into three deeply embattled strands in the recent literature.

In all three of these sections, this volume aims to contribute to an analytical understanding of the complex relationship between industry, digitalization, and domination/emancipation. Despite the different perspectives assembled here, all of the contributions subscribe to two analytical principles. First, they do not subscribe to a logic of linear technical development and subsequent social change. They challenge the idea of a string of technical or industrial revolutions as much as they are critical of the idea that the introduction of new technologies unidirectionally produces specific social relations. Rather, they carefully analyze specific technological developments as part of the social arrangements out of which they are born and on which they in turn have—sometimes contradictory—effects. Secondly, the volume questions understandings of the relationship between industrial digitalization and domination/emancipation that are based on a simple binary logic, i.e., either postulating digitalization as the technical realization of emancipation or as the final victory of domination. Instead, the contributions emphasize the ambiguities and contradictory potentials of the sociotechnical apparatuses of digitalization (Schaupp, 2017).

The overall thrust of these articles is not to reject all that has been written on the relationship between social emancipation/domination and the ongoing digitalization of contemporary industries. Their approach is rather to deepen, complicate, weave together, and add perspective. The articles do so by tracing the genealogy of current management techniques and technologies (Nosthoff & Maschewski; Schobin & Staab). They investigate the continuities in seemingly revolutionary changes (Butollo et al.; Kalff). They study the complicated relationships between classical industry and the maker movement (Frey & Schneider; Wenten). They lay bare the reshuffling of global inequalities so deeply entwined with the rhetoric around de- or re-industrialization (coons). Finally, they offer a more complicated picture of how digital tools and platforms are connected to specific forms of emancipation for (some) users, while simultaneously materializing new patterns of discrimination, precarization, and exploitation (Bruni & Esposito, Möllenkamp, Tøndel & Seibt).

The first part of the book addresses the relationship between *digitalization and current working practices*. Going against the grain of popular rhetoric about a *second machine age*, a *third industrial revolution*, or an

Industrie 4.0, these contributions take a somewhat genealogical approach to the topic, tracing how the dynamics of emancipation and domination have been constructed throughout the long and complicated history of digitalization in industrial work. Opening this section, Yannick Kalff provides a painstaking analysis of the connection between "work 4.0" and the promise of new digital forms of democratic participation in the German context. By tracing how ideas of democratic participation continue to be shaped by well-established hegemonic discourse positions, he shows how its emancipatory scope is limited and turns into a vehicle for increased flexibility and agility in production. Florian Butollo, Martin Krzywdzinski, and Ulrich Jürgens also take issue with the idea of a fourth industrial revolution by pointing out the continuities and discontinuities between the practices of lean production and those of *Industrie 4.0*. They demonstrate that, in contrast to the dominant discourse of greater autonomy for employees, current implementations of Industrie 4.0 inherit from lean production elements of increased standardization and control, while neglecting more participatory approaches to the organization of work. Anna-Verena Nosthoff and Felix Maschewski span an even longer timeframe by showing how current management practices draw on ideas first popularized in classical cybernetic theory and practice. They analyze how freedom and control are interwoven in classical cybernetic concepts and show how the renaissance of these ideas in contemporary strands of systems and management thinking leads not to the reduction of domination, but to a new form of integral domination. Janosch Schobin and Philipp Staab close the section by presenting a thoughtful analysis of the technological foundations of digitalized working environments through the lens of gamification. By arguing that gamification has been a central element in most, if not all, digital interfaces, they focus our attention on the ways in which attempts at controlling work are deeply woven into the genealogy of our material technologies and how emancipation depends on the ability of users to adapt, master, and subvert these.

The second part of the book is concerned with the promises of emancipation that have always accompanied the history of *automation and digital fabrication*, complementing fears of deskilling, mass unemployment, or domination by the machine. Resisting the binary logic of such narratives, these articles offer deep empirical insight into concrete cases linking digital fabrication to hopes of emancipation. In doing so, they shed light on their inbuilt biases, ironies, and contradictions.

Philipp Frey and Christoph Schneider use the concept of *concrete utopias* to compare and criticize the *post work* and the *maker movements*, two cases in which digital fabrication technologies have been hailed as the harbinger of liberation. Demonstrating that the post-work movement focuses only on emancipation from work, while the maker movement limits itself to emancipation in work, they argue that both movements operate on a limited notion of emancipation. Klara-Aylin Wenten is also concerned with the maker movement. However, in her case study, promises of emancipation through grassroots practices of innovation are being recuperated by corporate actors. While the maker movement thus partly succeeds in changing prevalent routines, its practices are also being robbed of their critical edge and become part of the industrial apparatus of production. In the article concluding this section, ginger coons shows how the promises of "reshoring" industrial production to countries of the Global North through advances in automation amount to a rhetorical diminution of workers in other parts of the world. Through analyzing the discourse around the *reshoring* of a high-tech water heater to the USA, she shows how automation can become an opportunity to devalue the labor of workers in the Global South, while celebrating the imagined "return of jobs back home."

The final section of the book is concerned with the question of *how digitalization reconfigures the relationship between industries and the users* they are supposed to serve. This last set of texts approaches this issue by pointing out that the same digitalization processes can trigger contradictory dynamics of emancipation *and* domination, which are often much harder to disentangle than popular corporate or governmental storytelling would suggest. Starting off this part of the book, Attila Bruni and Fabio Esposito show how digital platforms such as Airbnb actively enroll their users as part of their own infrastructures of production and maintenance. Taking a performative approach to this relationship, they point out that platform organizations produce and depend on the very subjects they dominate. Gunhild Tøndel and David Seibt offer an empirically grounded critique of the Norwegian technocare policy of welfare technology and its promises of guaranteeing the independence of senior citizens through technology. Using the concepts of *inscription* and *description*, they show how the purportedly emancipatory welfare-gadgets occasioned a reorganization of the world of care which benefitted the rise of a new industry, but ended up discriminating against some of the elderly as well as the people caring for them.

In the concluding contribution to this volume, Andreas Möllenkamp offers an account of the effects the digitalization in the musical instruments industry has had on its users. Rooting his account in a detailed examination of the development of digital instruments he argues for a differentiated view. According to his analysis, digitalization opens up new artistic possibilities for musicians and at the same time is the source of a growing precarization in the profession.

What we would like our readers to take away from the multifaceted contributions assembled in this book, is the idea that digitalization in industry has lost none of its importance as a key component of contemporary societies and that it does, therefore, continue to constitute a relevant subject for the social sciences. However, this relevance does not stem from the fact that we are currently living through a new industrial revolution. Rather, the analysis of digitalization will remain an ongoing task as society and technology continue to shape each other, spawning ever new—and sometimes old—dynamics between the poles of emancipation and domination. It is precisely in times in which the narrative of revolutionary technological changes and clear-cut societal consequences resurfaces in public and scholarly discourse that we are most in need of such rigorous critical analysis. We hope that this volume will be considered a worthwhile contribution to this task.

Notes

1. See, for example, the discussion on the topic in Norbert Wiener's early book on cybernetics (Wiener, 1950).
2. Our readers may disagree with this selection, wondering, perhaps, why we have not organized the volume along classical axes of domination, such as those relating to gender, race, class, disability, sexual orientation, and national origin. Or, alternatively, as suggested by Weber, along the sources of legitimacy on which domination is founded. Our answer to such objections would be that we have focused on the dynamics of emancipation and domination which are to some degree specific to the issue of digitalization in industry with which we are concerned. However, insofar as some axes of domination pervade contemporary Western societies as a whole, they do also become relevant in industries and the contributors to this volume have tried to tackle some of the ways in which they are re-negotiated in these contexts.
3. It should be noted that some forms of the internalization of norms, especially those that take the form of discipline, have also been understood as

an effect of power (Foucault, 1995) and indeed as a basis of domination (Weber, 1968, p. 53).

4. This deviates from Weber's definition according to which domination "is the probability that a command with a given specific content will be obeyed by a given group of persons" (Weber, 1968, p. 53). Thus, for Weber, power is socially amorphous, whereas domination takes the specific form of command and obedience. In our definition, the emphasis is on the structural asymmetry in a power relation, regardless of its form.
5. Note that, even though the two terms were used to signify the same phenomenon, they occurred with different frequencies in different regions of the world. A Google Trend search suggests that the term "digitization" used to be more popular in English-speaking countries, including the USA, Canada, UK, and Australia, while "digitalization" has been more frequently searched for in continental Europe. The search also indicates that, while digitization used to be more common overall, the two terms are now on par in terms of search volume.
6. For example, Wikipedia forwards from digitalization to digitization, while the Oxford dictionary offers the same definition for both terms. The Encyclopedia Britannica covers neither digitization, nor digitalization and the same is true of more specifically sociological dictionaries (Abercrombie et al., 2006; Bruce & Yearley, 2006; Marshall, 2003; Turner, 2006).
7. https://www.gartner.com/it-glossary/digitalization/, accessed 17.06.2018.
8. https://www.plattform-i40.de/I40/Navigation/EN/Industrie40/WhatIsIndustrie40/what-is-industrie40.html, accessed 17.06.2018.
9. https://www.arbeitenviernull.de/experimentierraeume/start.html, accessed 17.06.2018.

References

Abercrombie, N., Hill, S., & Turner, B. S. (2006). *The Penguin Dictionary of Sociology* (5th ed.). New York, NY: Penguin Books (Penguin reference).

Berger, P. L. (1967). *The Sacred Canopy; Elements of a Sociological Theory of Religion*. Garden City and New York: Doubleday.

Bell, D. (1976). *The Coming of Post-Industrial Society*. New York: Basic Books.

Benkler, Y. (2006). *Wealth of Networks: How Social Production Transforms Markets and Freedom*. New Haven and London: Yale University Press.

Benkler, Y. (2016). Peer Production and Cooperation. In B. Johannes & M. Latzer (Eds.), *Handbook on the Economics of the Internet* (pp. 91–119). Cheltenham: Edward Elgar.

Bijker, W. E., Hughes, T. P., Pinch, T. (Eds.). (2012 [1987]). *The Social Construction of Technological Systems: New Directions in the Sociology and History of Technology*. Cambridge, MA: MIT Press.

Bijker, W. E., & Law, J. (Eds.). (1992). *Shaping Technology/Building Society: Studies in Sociotechnical Change*. Cambridge, MA: MIT Press.

Blau, P. M., McHugh Falbe, C., McKinley, W., & Phelps, T. K. (1976). Technology and Organization in Manufacturing. *Administrative Science Quarterly, 21*(1), 20–40. https://doi.org/10.2307/2391876.

Blauner, R. (1964). *Alienation and Freedom: The Factory Worker and His Industry*. Oxford: Chicago University Press.

Boltanski, L. (2011). *On Critique: A Sociology of Emancipation*. Hoboken: Wiley.

Bourdieu, P. (1984). *Distinction: A Social Critique of the Judgement of Taste*. Cambridge, MA: Harvard University Press.

Braverman, H. (1998 [1974]). *Labor and Monopoly Capitalism: The Degradation of Work in the Twentieth Century* (25th Anniversary ed.). New York and London: Monthly Review.

Braybrooke, K., & Smith, A. (2018). Liberatory Technologies for Whom? Exploring a New Generation of Makerspaces Defined by Institutional Encounters. *Journal of Peer Production* (12), 1–13.

Brennen, J. S., & Kreiss, D. (2016). Digitalization. In K. B. Jensen, R. T. Craig, J. D. Pooley, & E. W. Rothenbuhler (Eds.), *The International Encyclopedia of Communication Theory and Philosophy* (pp. 556–566). Chichester: Wiley Blackwell.

Briken, K., Chillas, S., Krzywdzinski, M., & Marks, A. (Eds.). (2017). *The New Digital Workplace: How New Technologies Revolutionise Work*. Critical Perspectives on Work and Employment. London: Palgrave.

Bruce, S., & Yearley, S. (2006). *The Sage Dictionary of Sociology*. Repr. Los Angeles: Sage.

Burawoy, M. (1985). *The Politics of Production: Factory Regimes Under Capitalism and Socialism*. London and New York: Verso.

Collins, H. M. (1983). An Empirical Relativist Programme in the Sociology of Scientific Knowledge. In K. D. Knorr-Cetina & M. Mulkay (Eds.), *Science Observed: Perspectives on the Social Study of Science* (pp. 85–113). London: Sage.

Cooley, M. (1980). Computerization—Taylor's Latest Disguise. *Economic and Industrial Democracy, 1*, 523–539.

coons, g. (2016). *Something for Everyone: Using Digital Methods to Make Physical Goods*. Available online https://tspace.library.utoronto.ca/handle/1807/72952.

Dahlander, L., & Magnusson, M. G. (2008). How Do Firms Make Use of Open Source Communities? *Long Range Planning, 41*(6), 629–649. https://doi.org/10.1016/j.lrp.2008.09.003.

Dahrendorf, R. (1964). Amba und Amerikaner. Bemerkungen zur These der Universalität von Herrschaft. *European Journal of Sociology, 5*(1), 83–98.

Dahrendorf, R. (1967). *Pfade aus Utopia. Arbeiten zur Theorie und Methode der Soziologie*. München: Piper.

DiMaggio, P. J., & Powell, W. W. (1983). The Iron Cage Revisited: Institutional Isomorphism and Collective Rationality in Organizational Fields. *American Sociological Review, 48*(2), 147–160.

Dosi, G., Teece, D. J., & Chytry, J. (Eds.). (1998). *Technology, Organization, and Competitiveness: Perspectives on Industrial and Corporate Change*. Oxford and New York: Oxford University Press.

Drewlani, T., & Seibt, D. (2018). Configuring the Independent Developer. *Journal of Peer Production, 12,* 96–114.

Drucker, P. F. (1993). *Post-Capital Society*. Oxford: Butterworth-Heinemann.

Durkheim, E. (1982). *Rules of Sociological Method*. New York: Free Press.

Featherstone, M. (2007). *Consumer Culture and Postmodernism*. Theory, Culture & Society (2nd ed.). London: Sage.

Ferdinand, J.-P., & Meyer, U. (2017). The Social Dynamics of Heterogeneous Innovation Ecosystems. *International Journal of Engineering Business Management, 9,* 184797901772161. https://doi.org/10.1177/1847979017721617.

Ferdinand, J., Petschow, U., & Dickel, S. (Eds.). (2016). *Decentralized and Networked Future of Value Creation* (1st ed.). Cham: Springer.

Foucault, M. (1995). *Discipline and Punish: The Birth of the Prison*. New York: Random House.

Fourastié, J. (1989 [1949]). Le grand espoir du XXe siècle. Ed. définitive. Paris: Gallimard.

Frey, C. B., & Osborne, M. A. (2017). The Future of Employment: How Susceptible Are Jobs to Computerisation? *Technological Forecasting and Social Change, 114,* 254–280. https://doi.org/10.1016/j.techfore.2016.08.019.

Fuchs, C. (2016). Henryk Grossmann 2.0: A Critique of Paul Mason's Book "Postcapitalism: A Guide to Our Future". *Triple C, 14*(1), 232–243.

Gershenfeld, N. (2005). *FAB: The Coming Revolution on Your Desktop—From Personal Computers to Personal Fabrication*. New York: Basic Books.

Giddens, A. (1984). *The Constitution of Society: Outline of the Theory of Structuration*. Cambridge: Polity Press.

Hancock, A. (2016). *Intersectionality. An Intellectual History*. New York: Oxford University Press.

Haude, R., & Wagner, T. (1999). *Herrschaftsfreie Institutionen. Studien zur Logik ihrer Symbolisierungen und zur Logik ihrer theoretischen Leugnung*. Baden-Baden: Nomos.

Hippel, E.v. (2005). *Democratizing Innovation*. Cambridge, MA: MIT Press.

Hippel, E.v., & Katz, R. (2002). Shifting Innovation to Users via Toolkits. *Management Science, 48*(7), 821–833. https://doi.org/10.1287/mnsc.48.7.821.2817.

Hyysalo, S., Jensen, T. E., & Oudshoorn, N. (2016): Introduction to the New Production of Users. In H. Sampsa, E. J. Torben, & O. Nelly (Eds.), *The New Production of Users: Changing Innovation Collectives and Involvement Strategies* (pp. 1–42). New York: Routledge.

Jasanoff, S. (Ed.). (2004). *States of Knowledge: The Co-production of Science and the Social Order*. New York: Routledge.

Jasanoff, S., & Kim, S. (2009). Containing the Atom: Sociotechnical Imaginaries and Nuclear Power in the United States and South Korea. *Minerva, 47*(2), 119–146. https://doi.org/10.1007/s11024-009-9124-4.

Jensen, T. E., & Krogh Petersen, M. (2016). Straddling, Betting and Passing: The Configuration of User Involvement in Cross-Sectorial Innovation Projects. In H. Sampsa, E. J. Torben, & O. Nelly (Eds.), *The New Production of Users: Changing Innovation Collectives and Involvement Strategies* (pp. 136–159). New York: Routledge.

Johnson, M., Mozaffar, H., Campagnolo, G. M., Hyysalo, S., Pollock, N., & Williams, R. (2014). The Managed Prosumer: Evolving Knowledge Strategies in the Design of Information Infrastructures. *Information, Communication & Society, 17*(7), 795–813. https://doi.org/10.1080/1369118x.2013.830635.

Kagermann, H., Lukas, W.-D., & Wahlster, W. (2011). Industrie 4.0: Mit dem Internet der Dinge auf dem Weg zur 4. industriellen Revolution. *VDI Nachrichten, 13*, 2.

Knorr-Cetina, K. (1999). *Epistemic Cultures: How the Sciences Make Knowledge*. Cambridge, MA and London: Harvard University Press.

Latour, B. (1987). *Science in Action*. Cambridge, MA: Harvard University Press.

Latour, B., & Woolgar, S. (1986). *Laboratory Life: The Construction of Scientific Facts*. Princeton, NJ: Princeton University Press.

MacKenzie, D. A., & Wajcman, J. (Eds.). (1985). *The Social Shaping of Technology: How the Refrigerator Got Its Hum*. Milton Keynes: Open University Press.

Marcuse, H. (1964). *One-Dimensional Man*. London: Routledge.

Marshall, G. (Ed.). (2003). *A Dictionary of Sociology*. Oxford and New York: Oxford University Press.

Marx, K. (1976): *Capital: A Critique of Political Economy* (Vol. 1). London: Penguin Books in Association with New Left Review.

Mason, P. (2015). *Postcapitalism: A Guide to Our Future*. London: Penguin Books.

McAfee, A., & Brynjolfsson, E. (2014). *The Second Machine Age*. New York: W.W. Norton.

Meyer, J. W., & Rowan, B. (1977). Institutionalized Organizations: Formal Structure as Myth and Ceremony. *American Journal of Sociology, 83*(2), 340–363.

Meyer, J. W., Scott, W. R., & Deal, T. E. (1983). Institutional and Technical Sources of Organizational Structure: Explaining the Structure of Educational Organizations. In W. M. John, B. Rowan, & W. R. Scott (Eds.), *Organizational Environments: Ritual and Rationality* (pp. 45–67). Beverly Hills: Sage.

Meyer, U. (2018): Digitalisierung ohne Technik? Das Beispiel eines Praxislabors zu Arbeit 4.0. *AIS-Studien, 11*(2), 229–246.

Meyer, U. (2019). The Emergence of an Envisioned Future: Sensemaking in the Case of "Industrie 4.0" in Germany. *Futures, 109,* 130–141.
Meyer, U. (in publication). Industrie 4.0 als sozio-technische Zukunftsvorstellung. Zur Bedeutung von organisationaler Sinnerzeugung und -stiftung. Industrie 4.0 als sozio-technische Zukunftsvorstellung. In: Soziale Welt.
Miller, D. (1987). *Material Culture and Mass Consumption.* Social Archaeology. Oxford: Blackwell.
Moulier-Boutang, Y. (2011). *Cognitive Capitalism.* Cambridge: Polity Press.
Narr, W. (2015): *Niemands-Herrschaft: Eine Einführung in die Schwierigkeiten, Herrschaft zu begreifen* (Uta von Winterfeld, Ed.). Hamburg: VSA.
Nelson, R. R., & Winter, S. G. (1982). *An Evolutionary Theory of Economic Change.* Cambridge, MA: The Belknap Press of Harvard University Press.
Noble, D. F. (2011 [1984]). *Forces of Production: A Social History of Industrial Automation.* New Brunswick and London: Transaction.
Orlikowski, W. J. (2002). Knowing in Practice: Enacting a Collective Capability in Distributed Organizing. *Organization Science, 13*(3), 249–273. https://doi.org/10.1287/orsc.13.3.249.2776.
Oudshoorn, N., & Pinch, T. (Eds.). (2003). *How Users Matter: The Co-construction of Users and Technologies.* Cambridge, MA: MIT Press.
Perrow, C. (1986). *Complex Organizations: A Critical Essay.* New York: Random House.
Pfeiffer, S. (2017). The Vision of "Industrie 4.0" in the Making—A Case of Future Told, Tamed, and Traded. *Nanoethics, 11* (1), 107–121. https://doi.org/10.1007/s11569-016-0280-3.
Piller, F. T. (2004). Mass Customization: Reflections on the State of the Concept. *International Journal of Flexible Manufacturing Systems, 16*(4), 313–334.
Pine, B. J. II. (1993). *Mass Customization. The New Frontier in Business Competition.* Boston, MA: Harvard Business Press.
Raymond, E. S. (2001). *The Cathedral and the Bazaar: Musings on Linux and Open Source by an Accidental Revolutionary* (Rev. ed.). Beijing and Cambridge, MA: O'Reilly.
Rifkin, J. (2011). *The Third Industrial Revolution: How Lateral Power Is Inspiring a Generation and Transforming the World.* Basingstoke: Palgrave Macmillan.
Ritzer, G., & Jurgenson, N. (2010). Production, Consumption, Prosumption. The Nature of Capitalism in the Age of the Digital 'Prosumer'. *Journal of Consumer Culture, 10*(1), 13–36.
Sattelberger, T., Welpe, I., & Boes, A. (Eds.). (2015). *Das demokratische Unternehmen. Neue Arbeits- und Führungskulturen im Zeitalter digitaler Wirtschaft.* Freiburg: Haufe-Lexware GmbH & Co. KG.

Schaupp, S. (2017). Digital Self-Evaluation and the Cybernetic Regime: A Sketch for a Materialist Apparatus Analysis. *tripleC: Communication, Capitalism & Critique, 15*(2), 872–886. https://doi.org/10.31269/triplec.v15i2.912.

Sennett, R. (2008). *The Craftsman*. New Haven: Yale University Press.

Srnicek, N., & Williams, A. (2015). *Inventing the Future: Post Capitalism and a World Without Work*. London: Verso.

Staab, P., & Nachtwey, O. (2016). Market and Labour Control in Digital Capitalism. *tripleC: Communication, Capitalism & Critique. Open Access Journal for a Global Sustainable Information Society, 14*(2). https://doi.org/10.31269/triplec.v14i2.755.

Star, S. L. (Ed.). (1995). *Ecologies of Knowledge: Work and Politics in Science and Technology*. New York: State University of New York Press.

Thompson, P., & Briken, K. (2017). Actually Existing Capitalism: Some Digital Delusions. In K. Briken, S. Chillas, M. Krzywdzinski, & A. Marks (Eds.), *The New Digital Workplace: How New Technologies Revolutionise Work*. Critical Perspectives on Work and Employment (pp. 241–263). London: Palgrave.

Tönnies, F. (1957). *Community and Society* [Gemeinschaft und Gesellschaft]. East Lansing: Michigan State University Press.

Touraine, A. (1971). *The Post-Industrial Society: Tomorrow's Social History: Classes, Conflicts and Culture in the Programmed Society*. New York: Random House.

Turner, B. S. (2006). *The Cambridge Dictionary of Sociology*. Cambridge, England and New York: Cambridge University Press.

Weber, M. (1968). *Economy and Society*. Berkeley, CA: University of California Press.

Wexler, M. N. (2011). Reconfiguring the Sociology of the Crowd: Exploring Crowdsourcing. *International Journal of Sociology & Social Policy, 31*(1/2), 6–20. https://doi.org/10.1108/01443331111104779.

Wiener, N. (1950). *The Human Use of Human Beings: Cybernetics and Society*. Boston: Houghton Mifflin.

Woodward, J. (1980 [1965]). *Industrial Organization: Theory and Practice* (2nd ed.). Oxford: Oxford University Press.

Woodward, J. (Ed.). (1970). *Industrial Organization: Behaviour and Control*. London: Oxford University Press.

Wooten, M., & Hoffman, A. J. (2016). Organizational Fields Past, Present and Future (Ross School of Business, Working Paper No. 1311).

Zuboff, S. (1988). *In the Age of the Smart Machine: The Future of Work and Power*. New York: Basic Books.

Zuboff, S. (2019). *The Age of Surveillance Capitalism: The Fight for the Human Future at the New Frontier of Power*. London: Profile Books.

PART I

Emancipation and Domination in the Workplace

CHAPTER 2

Labor Democracy in Digitalizing Industries: Emancipating or "Sandboxing" Participation in Discourses on Technology and New Forms of Work?

Yannick Kalff

Digitalization and Democratization

The ongoing digitalization of society, the economy, organizations, and labor create two distinct narratives. Either popular opinions on digital technologies anticipate the emancipatory potential of controllable and shapeable technology, or they see threats to the social fabric through the technological determinisms. While the first group overstates the social construction of technology, the latter underestimates its malleability (Boyd & Holton, 2018, p. 333). Above that, social transformation is projected onto technological change. Digitalization appears as the salvation or as the downfall of humanity. The positivity of technological change is undisputed and marks a "technological *fetishism*" (Hand & Sandywell, 2002, p. 198) with determined development paths.

Y. Kalff (✉)
University of Osnabrück, Osnabrück, Germany
e-mail: yannick.kalff@uni-osnabrueck.de

U. Meyer et al. (eds.), *Digitalization in Industry*,
https://doi.org/10.1007/978-3-030-28258-5_2

This "fetishism" grasps optimistic as well as pessimistic trajectories, which I (for brevity) consider *utopian* or *dystopian* narratives.

Utopian positions see radical change that will emancipate humanity from toils such as hard manual labor, scarcity, capitalism, or autocracy (Brynjolfsson & McAfee, 2014; Srnicek & Williams, 2015). Digital technologies promise new levels of automation and redistribute labor in society. Immaterial, non-rivalry goods change the logic of contemporary (capitalist) economies' value and pricing mechanisms (Mason, 2015, p. 175). Algorithms offer planning and distribution efficiency that reinvigorate the "cybernetics of liberation" (Schaupp, 2017, pp. 60–68). Digital technology heralds the vanguard of post-capitalism—the overcoming of capitalism on its own structural terms.

Dystopian designs of digitalized societies predict growing precariousness and immiseration, job substitution, new modes of capital accumulation that valorize knowledge, symbol interpretation, communication and affects, or intensified regimes of control and surveillance (Bauman et al., 2014; Lazzarato, 2014; Sewell, 2009). The negative impact of digitalization is multilayered and opaque. It influences individuals on different levels like deskilling, uncertainty, control, or the valorization of privacy data and creativity.

Obviously, I arranged both extremes to highlight the continuum in between; the empirical reality is more complex, ambiguous, and uncertain. Interest groups shape technology, its application, and its scope—and thus its impact. Additionally, the positive or negative implications of technology are neither solely determined by technological trajectories nor do they result from sovereign power. Digital technologies change social relations in the production process in ambivalent ways that consist of emancipatory potential as well as new forms of "computer control" (Elliott & Long, 2016, p. 137). Industrial and economic digitalization brings forth contradictory and complementary potentials and pitfalls. Programmatic concepts like German "Industrie 4.0" are discursively shaped and group interests contest their implementation. They are not a concrete deterministic reality. In discourses, actors attribute social meaning to digitalization according to hegemonic power relations. These relations influence how technology directly or indirectly transforms industries by coining programs like "Industrie 4.0," which evoke specific expectations (Meyer, 2019). Discursive actors downplay the negative and emphasize positive side effects of technology to match political strategies and promises.

The debate on democratic participation is a good example to illuminate the complex reality of digitalization processes in contemporary industries. In this contribution, I will analyze *democratic participation*[1] as a contested opportunity of digital technologies. Digitalization offers new ways to implement democratic principles, form opinions, and provide referenda to reinvigorate democracy and its political subjects. Digitalization provides new channels of participation and decision making that are sought to substantially strengthen democratic processes in organizations (Blum & Zuber, 2016; Schoemann, 2018). However, the concepts of democratic participation are ambiguous: They differ in concept, scope, and political entitlement. Democratization is defined discursively and contains varying and contradicting notions that are brought forth by strategic actors. Opposing strategies, goals, conceptions of industry and industrial production, as well as its organization shape diverging understandings of democratic participation.

This raises one question: *how does a hegemonic perspective envision 'democratic participation' within* Industrie 4.0 *discourse?* The topic of labor democracy connects to emancipatory projects of the labor movement and re-emerges in contemporary participation models. However, since the 1990s, democratic participation has been an integral part of rationalization strategies built on *lean production* that fully integrated employees into valorization processes (Gorz, 1999, pp. 36–39). This raises another question: *how is democratization emancipatory (if at all) when discourse hegemony defines its scope and core?* Democratic participation is subject to interests and its realization diverges according to the strategies and goals of different actors.

The empirical case that grounds my argumentation is the consultation process "*Work 4.0*," initiated by the *Federal Ministry of Labour and Social Affairs*. It took place in Germany from April 2015 until November 2016. This consultation is a segment of the discourse on *Industrie 4.0*, which I use to scrutinize hegemonic positions on democratic participation. The process consisted of an opening conference, which produced a *Green Paper* on development trends, anticipated scenarios, and questions about the ongoing transformation. A multitude of societal, institutional, and individual actors engaged in a dialogue process that ended with a closing conference and a *White Paper*, released in 2017. This publication aggregated the results of the dialogue and answered questions from the *Green Paper*. The condensed *White Paper* is itself a product of hegemonic power relations with a clear proposition on democratic participation in *Industrie 4.0* to secure the future development of German industry. Its results describe the dominant take on the digitalization of industrial democracy and its challenges.

This contribution proceeds as follows: I will briefly outline the methodological framework ("Approach: 'Industrie 4.0' and the 'Work 4.0' Consultation as Hegemonic Materializations"). Digitalization and democratization are of interest, thus I will reconstruct labor democracy, participation, and alternative cooperatives ("Workplace Democracy, Participation, and Democratic Organizations"), as well as the discursive emergence of *Industrie 4.0* ("*Industrie 4.0* as a Discursive Construct: Origins and Logic"). Then, I will analyze the consultation process "*Work 4.0*" with a focus on participation ("Contexts of New Forms of Participation in Industrie 4.0"). Finally, the results will be contextualized to show how democratic participation is co-opted in the *Industrie 4.0* discourse's *Green* and *White Papers*, which emphasize flexibility and financialization strategies and target growth politics ("'Sandboxed' Participation and Naturalized Technological Impact").

Approach: "Industrie 4.0" and the "Work 4.0" Consultation as Hegemonic Materializations

In the 1960s, the "linguistic turn" highlighted (critical) inquiries in language as the structural foundation of knowledge and cognition. Post-structuralism extended this program to a "discursive turn" that understands social meaning and social structures not as preexistent, but as a "product of social practices" (Angermüller, Maingueneau, & Wodak, 2014, p. 3). Accordingly, societal institutions are the result of discursive formations that generate and fixate social meaning, structures, and modalities by acts of contributing to a discourse. Philipps and Hardy (2011, p. 3) "define a discourse as an interrelated set of texts and the practices of their production, dissemination, and reception, that brings an object into being." Discourses are a medium and place of social ordering, which is precarious and contested:

> [...] social relations shape and are shaped by discursive practices. Indeed, society and its actors, social inequality and its agents, symbolic and cultural orders and their subjects are no givens; they are made and unmade in discursive practices. (Angermüller et al., 2014, p. 6)

Discourse analysis scrutinizes different logics of "speaking in" a discourse, as well as practices and contexts in which these contributions are embedded. Research literature distinguishes manifold approaches and schools of discourse theory and analysis, from linguistic approaches that focus on language and how it constructs the social world to critical discourse analysis that scrutinizes how power relations shape discourses and the social (Angermüller et al., 2014; Fairclough, 2008; Marttila, 2015). The object *Industrie 4.0* is a discursive construct with strategies, tactics, and motives of engaged actors that have individual political scopes and aims. *Industrie 4.0* is inherently ambivalent and torn between strategic positions and power relations. Laclau and Mouffe (1985/2014) theorize discourse together with *hegemony*: hegemonic power relations temporarily stabilize the contingent social order. In discourses, antagonistic actors struggle for the hegemonic fixation of social meaning and institutions. This approach has been labeled *post-foundational discourse analysis* to indicate that social meaning has no "common ground" but is negotiated and struggled for (Marttila, 2015; Townshend, 2004).

The advantage of this approach is its focus on political antagonism. It helps me to conceptualize *Industrie 4.0* as the result of hegemonic struggles for definition, technological adaptation, and implementation, and as their consequences for organizational principles that assign social meaning to concepts of democratic participation. "It is the general openness of the social to the infinitude of possible and equally valid (and invalid) conceptualizations of the social that constitutes hegemonic practices' ontological condition of possibility" (Marttila, 2015, p. 52). Hegemonic practices temporarily close the openness to stabilize an interpretation frame. The discourse has been closed, "sedimented in the form of objectivated sets of meaning, subject roles and associated identities" (Marttila, 2015, p. 61).

Concerning the empirical case, this theoretical frame uncovers the dominant position in the consultation process. Thus, the *White Paper* as well as the consultation contributions are materialized representations of already structured, hegemonic ideas and definitions of democratic participation in the digitalization processes. The hegemonic essence lies in separating the discourse from its authors: "social and cultural orders become more self-evidential and immune to critique the more their presence has been decoupled from subjects instigating them" (Marttila, 2015, p. 58). Democratic participation in the *White Paper* is decoupled from its origin that was an emancipatory struggle for workers' rights and for the socialization of the means of production. From this goal, participation shifted to a functionalist approach of labor process subjugation that plays on the ambiguity of freedom in self-organization and control by the factual constraints of the post-Fordist organization.

Democratic Participation and Digitalization: Brief Accounts

The following section reconstructs the narratives of workplace democracy and of *Industrie 4.0*. The democratization of the workplace has been a political project since industrialization. I argue that capital co-opted participation in decision-making and workplace democracy and provided a new means of labor organization. Participation is ambivalent, and hegemonic appropriation strips it of its political intentions. The *Industrie 4.0* program bundles economic strategies to propel innovation cycles (Pfeiffer, 2017a, 2017b). Participation is embedded in this hegemonic discourse, and consequently, it is shaped by it.

Workplace Democracy, Participation, and Democratic Organizations

Democracy in industry, organizations, and in the workplace has different scopes. On a macro-level, one can distinguish direct and indirect participation. Workers participate directly or via elected delegates. Further, the ability to participate can be limited to an exclusive group like unions or worker councils (Gospel, 2011, pp. 60–61). Especially in Germany, these indirect forms are referred to as co-determination, which is a basic pillar of the democratic system (Müller-Jentsch, 2016).[2] Direct democracy on the organizational levels has a lower historical profile. It co-developed alongside direct and indirect concepts of industrial democracy since industrialization. The micro-level refers to workplace democracy that ranges from self-determination to indirect participation in the labor process.

Concepts of democratic participation have different degrees of entitlement. The right to worker's self-management increases and forms an "escalator of participation" (Marchington & Wilkinson, 2005, p. 401). Accordingly, the bottom line is to inform employees about decisions. Subsequent are communicating and, further, consulting workers. The fourth step, co-determination, stands for institutionalized participation in decision processes. The highest level is (workers') control where workers actively make decisions for themselves. Additionally, range, scope, or places of participation vary: From task to departmental or corporate level, decisions can have "trivial" to strategic consequences indicating different degrees of potentiality: Participation can include questions on property, budgeting, or distribution of profits. Participation can be more or less emancipatory.

Direct workplace democracy and institutionalized labor organization, unions, or representative workers' councils share a complicated relationship. Democratic labor and organization are core concepts of anarchist self-organization strategies of the nineteenth century that developed "little utopias" (Ackers, 2016, p. 542) in contrast to alienated, immiserated capitalist labor relations. Pierre-Joseph Proudhon emphasized that industrial democracy, with the democratic organization of the workplace as its constituting nucleus, is the key to equality, liberty, and responsibility (Ansart, 1967). This core reflects equality in the cooperative effort of production, socialized liberty in opposition to despotism of property or community, and responsibility to self-organize production. Its sporadic opposition to representative labor organization and capitalistic workplace organization was founded in the ideological rejection of the capitalist economy. Until today, workplace democracy has lost some of its radicalism. Democratic principles proposed by several authors concern the ownership of goods produced, self-determination, or self-organization, but not necessarily as part of a left agenda. Ross (1964) in particular classifies democratic firms as an undogmatic third way alternative to capitalism and socialism. This third way of democratic firms is understood as more "common sense" in liberal, democratic societies (Schwartz, 2012).

Ross, and later Ellerman, construct democratic firms on legal arguments, which grant workers "natural and inalienable rights to the fruit of their labor" (Ellerman, 1999, p. 112) as well as to "democratic self-determination" (Ellerman, 1990, p. 9). Workers are de facto responsible for production and the resulting goods. Thus, they should also be *de jure* responsible (Ellerman, 1999, p. 116). This "responsibility principle is the old idea that property should be founded on people getting the (positive or negative) fruits of their labor" (Ellerman, 2016, p. 319; 2017, pp. 179–183). In addition to property, the employment relationship is a key to understanding how private owners claim property rights (Ellerman, 1990, pp. 208–209). As private owners and investors, they provide capital (means of production) and are employers as well, which grants direct control over the labor process and installs them as "residual claimants" of profit and surplus value (Ellerman, 1990, pp. 74–76; 2017, p. 177).

Jossa argues that labor democracy updates Marxist economic theory. Labor-managed firms critically engage the theory of value, alienation, and subject-object relations in capitalism (Jossa, 2012, 2015). He argues that "a system of self-managed firms is the most readily acceptable and credible alternative to capitalism" (Jossa, 2012, p. 823). Thus, a democratic firm has to be considered a "merit good" that is valued "by its direct users and by the community at large" (Jossa, 2017, p. 15). The democratic cooperative firm provides a new economic base for the social superstructure and establishes a new production mode. It emancipates by democratizing the means of production and stabilizes the economy (Jossa, 2015, pp. 645–646). For Jossa, the introduction and expanse of labor-managed firms constitutes historical materialism "as [a] theory of production modes" where "social revolution is assumed to be the introduction of democratic worker control of firms" (Jossa, 2015, p. 662). However, concerning transition paths, his work lacks specific approaches and remains on an abstract theoretical level.

Webb and Cheney analyze worker cooperatives that can outperform public or private investor-owned companies, making them more resilient and economically sustainable. These advantages consist of "comparatively less pressure to maximize profit, democratic and dynamic decision-making structures, the marriage of labor and capital with social purpose, and connections to member and community need" (Webb & Cheney, 2014, p. 64). Co-operations are to date one of the most sophisticated approaches to democratic enterprises that combine economic with cultural and social goals (The Lavaca Collective, 2007). Their structure is value-driven and consists of basic principles for organization and for individuals: "equality, equity, mutual self-help, democracy and solidarity. These are reinforced by the personal values expected of co-operators of honesty, openness, social responsibility and caring for others" (Webb & Cheney, 2014, p. 71). Cooperatives significantly integrate and support attempts to expand the bottom-up democratization of economies and societies, for example in organizing urban resource systems (Sauer, Elsen, & Garzillo, 2016).

In contrast to the three preceding paragraphs, a recent treatment of democratic firms highlights their benefits in competitive markets. Labor and workplace democracy are not essentially disempowering for management and economic logic anymore. They activate remaining resources and previously undiscovered reservoirs of subjective labor force, innovation capabilities, and problem-solving competences (Sattelberger, 2015; Sattelberger & Wagner, 2015). Democratic structures ensure competitive advantages in a global challenge of new modes of production. Enterprise democracy facilitates innovation processes that might allow Germany's economy to compete with Silicon Valley innovations. Frontier industries and technology start-ups in digital economies rely on flat hierarchies and increasingly democratic decision making to ensure competitive innovativeness. According to Sattelberger, subjects should not be patronized by workers' representative institutions like unions or factory councils, or by managerial hierarchies. Instead, emancipated, responsible employees represent themselves in direct democratic participation without protective rights (Sattelberger & Wagner, 2015, p. 13). However, Sattelberger's workplace democracy reminds one of Ayn Rand's libertarian philosophy in which egoistic entrepreneurial self-orientation expresses the highest virtue.

Since the 1990s, a more pragmatic approach emerged and consolidated participation rights in work organizations. With the introduction of semi-autonomous group work, employees are granted participation and increased worker autonomy (Benders, Huijgen, & Pekruhl, 2002). This core concept of, for example, the German automobile industry targets rationalization reserves that cannot be activated by further standardizing the production process (Pearson, 1992). Participation in workplace organization (not in company politics) granted rights to elect group representatives, as well as deciding job rotation and work shifts. Participatory group work increased workers' content while the overall commitment remained nearly unaffected (Procter & Mueller, 2000, pp. 17–19). Group work provided conditional autonomy with "new contradictions" that "produce an 'economizing logic'" which would turn itself against group autonomy (Carnall, 1982, p. 291). This became obvious in the aftermath of the New Economy bust in 2001. Progressive participation systems were scaled back and standardization and determination re-institutionalized. Dörre (2002, p. 22) speaks of the "back swing of the pendulum"[3] toward hierarchical and determinate labor relations. Economic imperatives and the erroneous implementation of semi-autonomous group work led to a return to heteronomy—although group work has been considered a key of contemporary *lean production* trends (Gorz, 1999, p. 39; Moldaschl & Weber, 1998, pp. 373–376).

Kühl (2001, p. 199) ironizes the "successful failing of group work projects" that suffered from recentralized and reestablished hierarchies.

Workplace democracy faces criticism as well. For Kerr, democratic participation is exploitative and its success factors rely on its utility for economic performance and competitive advantages. "Because it more fully engages and exploits the individual, democratic process will be most valuable where the organization's workforce possesses unique capabilities and attributes" (Kerr, 2004, p. 91). It is obvious that any democratic enterprise that still operates under capitalist premises adheres to capitalist structural logic. Organizational governance limits democratic structures: Accountability to the governed, equal rights of participation, free information exchange, and representation of the governed are hardly realized in managerial organizations (Kerr, 2004, p. 84). Additionally, Stohl and Cheney (2001) stress that participation suffers from paradoxes—i.e., the implementation of democratic participation produces undemocratic situations. They name four basic types of paradoxes: structure, agency, identity, and power, which counteract democratic intentions. Examples would include "imposing" participation from the top or coercive team structures that diminish individual freedom (Barker, 1993; Stohl & Cheney, 2001, pp. 359–390). Nonetheless, the authors suggest that each paradox can result in a synthesis to overcome contradictions "to leverage new forms of participation" (Stohl & Cheney, 2001, p. 396). Participation in this conception is never "finished" and has to be reassessed to continuously create a "modified working consensus" (Stohl & Cheney, 2001, p. 396). Heller (1998, pp. 144–187) provides a detailed discussion of theoretical shortcomings and empirical evidence "against" democratic participation. The theoretical objections include qualification issues to inauthentic or voluntary non-participation, which means that individuals refuse to take part in self-organizing or participatory processes. Empirically, participation is stressful for workers: Taking part in decision processes and coping with autonomy might have a severe influence on workers' mental health. However, Kalleberg, Nesheim, and Olsen (2009, pp. 105–112) conclude that there are no unidirectional results that support this assertion. While increased autonomy and integration in decision processes reduce stress, work environments having self-directed *and* supervised teamwork have an impact on stress.

These five directions of economic or organizational participation are exemplary for diverse interpretations of democratic principles in the economy. Their reconstruction highlights the contingency of either logic of organizing and managing social relations or different modes of economic activity. The visibility of alternatives sharpens discussions about democratizing labor in the digital transformation. They propose a space of possibility—a range for structural or normative arguments of how labor relations react to technological changes. Above that, the historical threads of workplace and firm democracy reflect emancipatory potential without necessarily being radical. Juridical arguments sharpen wits for contingencies in capitalistic ways of organizing production and property distribution, while cooperatives propose alternatives to volatile market and labor relations. After all, these discussions show that capitalistic, hierarchical, profit-oriented organizations are not a historical inevitability; they are the result of a specific development path of economic and social institutions (Schwartz, 2012).

To conclude, two dimensions are visible: direct versus indirect participation and global versus local levels. The latter dimension describes the scope of democratic organization that (in its extreme) includes and organizes an entire company. The dimension's other pole describes a limited range of participation that empowers workers to self-organize the labor process and the workplace within a generally heteronomous organization. Historically, democratization changed its orientation. As radical or as a third way, labor democracy struggled for direct participation and raised issues about property rights. Later, pragmatic approaches in the context of *lean* transformation advanced self-organization. Self-organization, however, lags behind initial claims of workplace democracy. Self-organization and participation are elements of new rationalization strategies that benefit from workers' knowledge of the production process and valorize their experience and skills. Above that, democratic participation can create paradoxical effects when economic interests come into play. Democratic firms that engage in capitalistic market economies depend on (at least self-sustaining) profits. Majority opinions might not be emancipatory at all, especially since in democratic organizations, corporate strategies adhere to the very same factual constraints that govern heteronomous decision making.

Industrie 4.0 *as a Discursive Construct: Origins and Logic*

The topic of digitalization as a technological, political, and economic program of *Industrie 4.0* emerged in 2011 at the *Hanover Fair*. The suffix "4.0" anticipates a fourth revolution that disruptively transforms industry and society. In theory, *cyber-physical systems* link digital data with material production to realize new synergies. Networked data collection and interpretation allow integrated manufacturing with *smart* machines, big data, and digital interfaces in production work. In short: The goal is to close the digital divide on the shop floor; production becomes “intelligent” and flexible. Henning Kagermann, Wolf-Dieter Lukas, and Wolfgang Wahlster, who allegedly coined the term “Industrie 4.0,” are the “inventors” of a digitalization strategy that leads to the report paper *Recommendations for implementing the strategic initiative Industrie 4.0* (Acatech, 2013). One suggestion concerned the formation of a cooperation agreement, the *Plattform Industrie 4.0* chaired by the German *Federal Ministry for Economic Affairs and Energy*. Over 140 economic, scientific, and societal institutions and individuals are actively engaged in the platform. Further, in 2015 the *Federal Ministry of Labour and Social Affairs* initiated the dialogue process “*Work 4.0*” to grasp *Industrie 4.0*’s impact on labor and work organization. This consultation provides my empirical case. The following paragraphs describe the discursive emergence of *Industrie 4.0* to show how hegemonic power relations shaped the occurring narrative.

It seems—and parts of the origin discourse relentlessly stress this—that *Industrie 4.0* is the result of German engineering ingenuity. However, Pfeiffer shows its different roots: “Industrie 4.0 got its discursive wings not primarily from the rise of new technical possibilities but rather from economic ‘exigencies’ as identified by economic elites” (Pfeiffer, 2017b, p. 113). *Industrie 4.0* is concerned with economic growth paths (Pfeiffer, 2017a, p. 23). Pfeiffer points out that the rediscovery of industry after the financial crisis in 2007 facilitated *Industrie 4.0*. “Between 2009 and 2010, a number of widely noticed studies were published, mainly by business consultants. Written in the shadow of the international financial crisis, they fueled a rediscovery of the significance of the industrial sector despite previous long-term trends of deindustrialization” (Pfeiffer, 2017b, p. 112). These studies critically assessed the leading industrial nations’ future economic development. They anticipated substantial challenges in international competition, especially for Germany. Several initiatives launched, for example, by the *World Economic Forum*, established the “Future of Manufacturing,” which consisted of narratives on digital data in manufacturing. They ultimately led to the *Industrie 4.0* terminology. Complementing the veiled economic origin of *Industrie 4.0*, one major goal is new potential for economic growth (Pfeiffer, 2017a, pp. 26–28). By 2025, Germany's core branches promise economic growth of 78 billion euros while the amount for all branches exceeds 267 billion euros (Pfeiffer, 2017b, p. 114). Thus, Pfeiffer speaks of *Industrie 4.0* as "professionally managed agenda setting" that initiates a technological project, yet hides its origins behind an innovation narrative and questionable growth promises (Pfeiffer, 2017b, p. 112).

Pfeiffer concludes with an interpretation following Michael Burawoy's *Politics of Production* (Pfeiffer, 2017a, pp. 33–37). A substantially new form of "digital despotism" is sensible in production that tears down Burawoy's differentiation between "brutal coercion" in peripheral industries and "silent submission" in industrialized countries. In digitalizing industries, both forms are becoming dominant and are "supplemented by increasingly important ***digitalized*** silent coercion" (Pfeiffer, 2017a, p. 35). In combination with new forms of micro-task management and dissolving industrial relations, digitalization combines technology-based forms of control and surveillance with a new despotic disciplining of the workforce in an increasingly deregulated policy field of labor and global markets. New forms of technology do not demarcate a "new phase of capitalist development" but indicate "an evolution of Burawoy's hegemonic despotism in a new geopolitical situation" (Pfeiffer, 2017a, p. 37). Fuchs interprets *Industrie 4.0* as a mismatch between ideas and reality, constituting a "digital German Ideology" (Fuchs, 2018, p. 280). *Industrie 4.0* mirrors existing class relations and modes of production. Thus, it is not a neutral technological discourse, but "an ideological phantom formed in the contemporary bourgeoisie's collective brain. It aims at advancing new forms of accumulation, control and class struggle from above" (Fuchs, 2018, p. 287). On an economic level, the German digitalization project is a strategy to decrease costs for a highly productive yet comparatively expensive labor force, which exceeds the costs of buying and maintaining digitalized production lines (Fuchs, 2018, p. 283).

In my view, *Industrie 4.0* is an economic project, which is not a "neutral", value-free technological discourse. Its origin as Pfeiffer shows derives from economy-driven agenda building to tackle locational advantages, as well as new growth paths for ailing economies after the financial crisis. It is not surprising that in this aftermath, the interest in industrial production was reinvigorated. Moreover, Fuchs contextualizes *Industrie 4.0* in societal dominion relations that brands technology an authoritarian project aiming to intensify accumulation: "In digital capitalism, capital aims to appropriate digital machines as instruments for political control, economic accumulation, and ideological manipulation. Social struggle in digital capitalism is one over the control and shaping of digital machines" (Fuchs, 2018, p. 287). Thus, the appropriation and possibilities of technology, as I have pointed out in the introduction, are discursively contested. In this case, workplace democratization and participation are entwined in diverging strategies and factual constraints like market requirements. These, possibly contradictory, positions realize the emancipating or dominating effects of digital technologies for employee participation.

Fuchs and Pfeiffer point out the capital-driven origin of *Industrie 4.0* and deconstruct the superficial false front of German engineering ingenuity. Technological proofs of concept alone are not a sufficient reason for technological development and implementation. This "agenda setting" (Pfeiffer, 2017b) is a strategy to "pool heterogeneous developments and make them enforceable" (Dörre, 2015, p. 270). Any structural, technological, or social change that can be subsumed under the label *digital* or *Industrie 4.0* becomes "innovative" and thus desirable. Digital technology is not value-neutral. It is developed and applied with strategic interests and is a technology of sovereignty, with dominating and disciplining effects on the labor process organization.

Interim Conclusion: A Working Definition of Democratic Participation

The *Industrie 4.0* discourse follows a growth strategy. The sociological tenor suggests that the discourse creates deterministic technological development paths and emphasizes necessary innovation drivers. Connected with this structural goal of technological change are forms of labor and work organization that sustain these envisioned transitions. Any strategy for democratic participation finds itself in this conflict of diverging interests of capital and labor. Thus, dominant discursive strategies influence democratic participation in practice as well as in its distinct discursive images. The same structural effects that shape *Industrie 4.0* affect the consultation process "*Work 4.0*" and thus, how future labor is perceived. This justifies a detailed analysis to make the hegemonic discursive strategies and narratives visible.

Heller sorts participation strategies for involving workers in decision making into three threads: a "humanistic" approach to "enhance human dignity" (Heller, 1998, p. 8); "power-sharing" as a critique of "autocratic relationships [that] are inherently unjust and inconsistent with the values of a democratic society" (Heller, 1998, pp. 8–9); and "organizational efficiency" (Heller, 1998, p. 9). The first two groups are normative concepts while the third is a functionalist understanding of participation. It is obvious that these baseline values unequally qualify for emancipatory changes in work organization. The aforementioned "little utopias" (Ackers, 2016) of labor democracy fit into the first two strategies. So do Ellerman's and Jossa's conceptualizations of democratic firms. The participation debate since the 1990s primarily serves the third strategy to increase labor efficiency. Interestingly enough, the current topic of democratic firms initiated by Sattelberger et al. superficially targets humanistic ideals to free workers from managerial or collective determination; the subtle libertarian strategy targets efficiency topics of innovation and flexibility.

Concerning emancipatory potential, I see democratic participation as an ambivalent concept. Heller's distinction shows that humanistic and power-sharing motives are emancipatory in their normative scope. Both seek equality and human dignity by re-appropriating labor process control and—on larger scale—property relations of the means of production. The smallest and least emancipating scope uses participation as an efficiency strategy. In this case, work relations remain capitalistically determined and participation is reduced to self-management in organizational heteronomy. Democratization stops at a specific organizational level and limits the possibility to partake. Firms remain capitalistic, which stalls emancipation. "[T]ranscending capitalism," Hahnel and Wright (2016, p. 18) argue, "is a necessary condition for the fullest possible realization of democratic-egalitarian values." The factual constraints of capitalism narrow the emancipating content of democratic participation. Pragmatic approaches might circumvent these issues; however, they are vulnerable to co-optation and lose their egalitarian side by reinforcing social hierarchies and structures *beyond* democratic decision making.

Contexts of New Forms of Participation in *Industrie 4.0*

The consultation process of the *Federal Ministry of Labour and Social Affairs* collected statements on digitalized labor. The products of this process are discursive materializations; they summaries specific hegemonic positions on *Industrie 4.0* and their influence on labor and work organization. The collection is itself the product of an actor within the discourse with a political agenda. To refine the hegemonic position that is conveyed in the consultation, I will also analyze strategy papers from *acatech*. Its head of personnel shaped the programmatic discussion. In contrast to a discourse analysis that accounts for the entire complexity of the field and systematically includes material from different media, my approach concentrates on the consultation process and describes hegemonic mediations on participations. Thus, the complexity and power relations are neglected to some extent; yet, I show that hegemonic logics persist and shape democratic organization.

Transforming Co-determination and Participation for Flexibility

The federal ministry's *White Paper* emphasizes employees' rights to participate in decision making on technological implementations that control workers' performance or behavior. This trait of German industry and social market economy provides an advantage for technological implementation: "Wherever workers' co-determination and participation is ensured on an equal footing, solutions at the company-level can be used to tailor statutory requirements" (Federal Ministry of Labour and Social Affairs, 2017, p. 98). Nonetheless, these participatory rights constrain technological implementations.

> The fault lines are particularly clear when it comes to works councils' participatory rights in relation to the introduction of technical devices (Section 87 (1) no. 6 of the Works Constitution Act). On this point, companies and employers' associations would like to see "modernisation", in the sense of "limiting" the right of co-determination "to those cases in which monitoring is actually intended". In all other cases – i.e. even if technical devices generate data which could potentially be used for monitoring, but the employer does not intend to make use of this possibility – the works council's right of co-determination could be replaced, it is suggested, by a right for the works council to be informed of significant changes to technical devices. (Federal Ministry of Labour and Social Affairs, 2017, p. 147)

The proposition is to constrain the co-determination of workers' councils that is granted by the Work Constitution Act. The *White Paper* suggests in terms of employers' associations that participation could be limited. In a reflection of the "escalator of participation" (Marchington & Wilkinson, 2005, p. 401), this means stepping back the degree of participation from institutionalized partnership levels to a simple right to get informed without the possibility of interference. While the respective § 87 (1), no. 6[4] is a "relic" of Taylorist rationalization processes to balance workplace automation and technical monitoring, its scope again becomes relevant in digitalization:

> In practice, however, Section 87 (1) no. 6 of the Works Constitution Act gives the works council a right of co-determination in relation to many processes in the digital working world. Originally, this provision had a relatively narrow scope of application, but due to the wider use of IT in the digital working world, in practice it now covers a large proportion of hardware and software use. This not only includes the use of cameras, biometric access controls, smart glasses and mobile phones, for example, but also software which processes user data (including data collected by non-technical means). The introduction and use of such devices, or even a mere software update, cannot go ahead without the works council's consent. (Federal Ministry of Labour and Social Affairs, 2017, p. 149)

Strategies that see technological modernization as a factual constraint contest co-determination and participation in technological implementation processes, especially in cases that generate process data on individuals and individual behavior or performance, which is true for big data and digital technologies. Institutionalized legal frames of co-determination challenge these implementations. This line of argumentation is representative for tensions between technology (and its adoption) and participatory rights where the latter appear as decelerative forces that hinder the advancement of innovative and sustainable (i.e., fit for the future) production technologies. Trade unions and workers' councils thus are under pressure to adapt to these new factual constraints—at least according to employers' associations or business representatives. Flexibility and speed are central challenges for new modes of negotiation processes and decision making to match market dynamics:

> These changes [constant change, increased information density, acceleration of processes, individualization of products and services; Y.K.] substantially challenge the traditional German system of co-determination. On the one hand, formal processes of co-determination have to be significantly accelerated – for instance if new business units or new IT systems are implemented. On the other hand, employees' and employers' representatives have to cover a greater spectrum of individual interests and requirements. (Eller, 2016, p. 100)

Further:

> Both parties must come to quicker and more agile forms of negotiation. In the future, they have to orient themselves more towards the spirit of the matter. Because one thing is sure: without moderate flexibilization, Germany will face considerable losses in its competitiveness in a digitalized and globalized economy. (Eller, 2016, p. 101)

Eller, president of the *Federal Association of Human Resource Managers*, plays institutionalized participation against competitiveness. For her, it is obvious that co-determination has to elaborate new forms of dynamic participation that guarantee accelerated decision making and pave the way toward "co-determination 4.0" (Eller, 2016, p. 101). The *Industrie 4.0* initiators see the necessity to "[d]evelop a modern understanding of co-determination" that "provides safeguards and thus fosters flexibility in people's minds as well as in the relevant procedures" (Jacobs, Kagermann, & Spath, 2017, p. 11). Given the fact that the consultation process focalized "a new flexibility compromise" (Federal Ministry of Labour and Social Affairs, 2017, p. 79) the dangers of "one-way flexibility from workers" (Federal Ministry of Labour and Social Affairs, 2017, p. 170) is imminent. The federal ministry points out increased requirements for agile processes:

> Given that new ways of organising work are placing growing emphasis on horizontal concentration of knowledge, possibilities for participation by individual workers and self-organisation in teams, it is also in the organisation's best interest to *strengthen participatory elements at workplace level.* Agile markets need agile corporate decision-making processes to allow rapid responses to changes in customer preferences or other market requirements. In the long term, this is only possible with the optimal involvement of all talents, perspectives and skills in the company. (Federal Ministry of Labour and Social Affairs, 2017, pp. 153–154, emphasis in the original)

While the pooling of individual knowledge on the shop floor requires horizontal participation in decision making, the statement stresses that flexible and agile methods of responding to accelerated market requirements are imperative. Neither technological possibilities nor social innovation but market demands drive new modes of co-determination. In its essence, this argument reflects the discourse's origins that Pfeiffer and Fuchs laid out: Financialization and capital-orientation exert influence through technological debates.

Nonetheless, the German Trade Union Confederation (DGB) points out that co-determination needs further development to cope with ongoing changes (Federal Ministry of Labour and Social Affairs, 2017, p. 149). The Rail and Transport Union (EVG) argues in the same direction: "'new' problem arenas" initiated by digital technologies require "strengthened and internationalised" co-determination (Federal Ministry of Labour and Social Affairs, 2017, p. 152). The union-oriented Hans Böckler Foundation stresses that "[...] digitalization and Work 4.0 implicitly relate to participation and co-determination; at the same time, attempts to deregulate industrial relations are sensible" (Hans Böckler Foundation, 2015, p. 31). This is important because the consultation process targeted the temporal and local flexibility of employees, which erode co-determination. Thus, the United Service Trade Union (ver.di) demands an "amendment of the Works Constitution Act and the Staff Representation Act" (ver.di, 2015, p. 8). Systematically, the requirements of employers miss those of employee representation: While the first seek a reformed co-determination model that does not obstruct flexibility, the latter emphasize the need to adapt co-determination to new boundaryless working realities. Following the comments on the *Green Paper*, several unions and the Union Confederation underline the importance of expanding co-determination. However, the *White Paper* sees almost no such claims. Most likely, they have been truncated for the "new flexibility compromise" as phrased by the DGB (Federal Ministry of Labour and Social Affairs, 2017, p. 79).

The discourse clarifies that digital technologies and their influence on organizational participation are based on technological necessities. One line of discourse indicates agility and flexibility as key challenges for economy and enterprises. Thus, models of co-determination have to reflect them, since traditional channels of participation are considered as decelerating processes. In light of the agile processes, I conclude that decision making has to adhere to the core value of flexibility.

How democratic participation can ultimately achieve these goals remains unclear. It would not be surprising if democratic processes "underperform" in such scenarios, since democratic opinion formation and decisions are complex and time-consuming. Especially, the anticipated deregulation of institutionalized industrial relations is an important result if the effects of digitalization on participation have to be assessed.

Democratization and Participation: New Influences on Leadership

Collective labor organization, participation, and co-determination represent the relationship between two interest groups on the industry or company level. Actors in the consultation processes put forth another aspect: changing relationships in leadership and between management and workers. The federal ministry's *Green Paper* raised among others the following central question: "What working conditions create an innovation-friendly atmosphere in companies?" (Federal Ministry of Labour and Social Affairs, 2015, p. 71). The publication suggests an extension beyond the institutionalized modes of co-determination. It points out "a culture of participation" that a multitude of concepts reflect, which "can help to balance the interests of companies and workers in a new flexibility compromise" (Federal Ministry of Labour and Social Affairs, 2015, p. 70, without emphasis). Overall, "co-determination and economic success" correlate and indicate an important location factor (Federal Ministry of Labour and Social Affairs, 2015, p. 68; cf. ver.di, 2015). Josephine Hofmann, head of *Competence Center Business Performance Management* at the *Fraunhofer Institute for Industrial Engineering IAO*, argues that since new generations with new needs take over the working world, new social and organizational relations are needed as well:

> The Generation of Digital Natives increasingly questions traditional patterns of authority and demands participation and involvement. Is classic leadership still necessary in this context? What does this leadership work consist of? Who appoints, dismisses or promotes executives to what positions? Are there dates of expiry for executives, and if so, would it not be necessary to reassign management tasks again and again? (Hofmann, 2016, p. 65)

It is striking that new forms of labor and workplace organization are associated with stereotypical "generations" like *Digital Natives* or the frequently invoked *Generation Y*. Albeit these typifications only bear minimal analytical rigor, they can tell a lot about the anticipated impact of *Industrie 4.0*. One point is the rising necessity for the democratic sharing of leadership positions and self-electing respective positions, which will increase opportunities to participate in democratic processes.

> What is vital in this context is, primarily, a ***willingness and ability to reach a consensus through negotiation***. This requires structural conditions and forums for such negotiations, as well as an ability to compromise and a willingness to learn from past developments. Looking at individual forms of democratic participation and institutional co-determination together can benefit both, and can increase workers' opportunities for participation as a whole. (Federal Ministry of Labour and Social Affairs, 2017, p. 153, emphasis in original)

Participation and co-determination are part of emerging new designs of work organization. With its novelty, new requirements for individuals arise as well. The "willingness and ability" refers to rudimentary political subjectivities that can and will engage in political consensus formation. This claim is obvious since in the past, industrial production and wage labor were usually organized in heteronomy without any possibility to democratically elect or decide on organizational or working issues. *Industrie 4.0* is itself seen as a propellant that will create significant transformations (or ruptures) in the social fabric. The initiators of *Industrie 4.0* point out that "[in] smart factories, the role of employees will change significantly" and will focus on individual responsibility and development, which require "participative work design and lifelong learning measures" (Acatech, 2013, p. 6). Ensuring job quality is a local responsibility: "the specifics [...] can best be negotiated and designed by social partners and at the workplace level" (Federal Ministry of Labour and Social Affairs, 2017, p. 95). Nonetheless, new emancipatory initiatives open spaces in the labor process, which foremost serve flexibility in production and require new regulations. "Flexibility needs discipline: an accordance of self-fulfillment and responsibilization of employees" (Hofmann, 2016, p. 66). This does not mention disciplined flexibility, but disciplined subjects for flexibility.

Changing organizational structures hollows out institutionalized co-determination. Its grip on social relations in production processes runs short (Hans Böckler Foundation, 2016, p. 123). Alternatives like workplace democracy, however, cannot prevail without collective bargaining: "on the contrary, the latter [collective bargaining; Y.K.] creates the preconditions and the freedom of action for individual participation and the seizing of individual rights" (Hans Böckler Foundation, 2016, p. 124). When new modes of participation appear, they are embedded in traditional forms of co-determination as well as in self-responsibility and self-organization, which gained influence in the 1990s group work debates. Nonetheless, especially the *Green* and *White Papers* suggest that *Industrie 4.0*'s success relies essentially on the well-tested German system of co-determination. The strengthening of relations between social partners and collective bargaining processes, "not as contradictory, but as complementary hallmarks of innovative and democratic businesses," constitutes a sustainable project of new participation that is a cornerstone of democratic social market economy (Buhr, 2015, pp. 12–13; Federal Ministry of Labour and Social Affairs, 2017, p. 9).

Concerning new models of leadership, collaboration, and work organization, democratic participation is entangled with the *Industrie 4.0* discourse. If flexibility potential is the true goal of new participation strategies, then the work attitude of an entire generation dictates substantial change in hierarchical organizations. The Hans Böckler Foundation fears an erosion of social relations in the workplace due to digitalization and claims that targeted models of democratic participation cannot survive (or even be bargained for) if strong collective representation is not guaranteed.

> Even participation and individual involvement in the workplace are used instead of joint co-determination: Direct participation through more autonomy and more personal responsibility for employees can be found in many concepts of personnel leadership. This means more self-directed performance provisions. (Hans Böckler Foundation, 2015, p. 31)

Their warning is a single voice where other positions stress the necessary co-dependency of co-determination and new participatory ideas. I see these advocates of co-dependency as an attempt to downplay and to make invisible the dangers for institutionalized employee representation. Yet, their hegemonic position is ambivalent: On the one hand, it decreases institutionalized co-determination and labor organization for a comprehensive engagement of the individual in democratic processes. On the other hand, this development threatens the individual by undermining their bargaining power, which it draws from collective action.

Individuals' capability to self-organize is the foundation of direct democratic participation, but they are the source of a new valorization of the labor force in new digitalized and democratized work forms. As long as valorization is dominant, it misuses individuals' impulse to democratic self-organizing.

New Workers' and Employees' Roles

The previous two subsections also contrasted a change in organizational roles. On the discursive level, the role and responsibility of workers and employees in digitalizing industries becomes an active one. The discourse avoids putting workers into a passive role of enduring technological change and highlights their role in sustaining the ongoing transition. This argument legitimizes the technological transformation of industries that does not exclude labor interests. Digitalization is impossible without the consent and support of empowered shop floor personnel. "Involvement of workers in this process of change is important at all levels. Workplace innovation is necessary to implement technological innovation successfully at company level" (IndustriAll, 2015, p. 5). Even in the case for agile and flexible responses to market demands, the suggestions from the consultation process of the *Green* and *White Papers* speak of *new* forms of co-determination or participation—whatever they include and whatever counterbalance they can be.

In the initial recommendation for the implementation of a unified program for *Industrie 4.0*, *acatech* follows the German unions' strategy "better, not cheaper" and argues that a "labour-oriented organisational design with enhanced participation rights, co-determination and training opportunities" (Acatech, 2013, p. 54) ensures a successful digital transformation. Digitalization requires training opportunities and skill development to integrate the existing workforce and to run more complex production systems efficiently. As for democratic participation, no concrete upskilling is implied. This underlines the point that democratic participation in the discourse is reductionist. For taking a democratic approach to decision making, the role of workers has to be extended—and especially, the responsibilities of employees have to be clarified when it comes to voting. On the one hand, Sattelberger suggests the necessity for a *citoyen* model of a "sovereign entrepreneurial citizen" (Sattelberger & Wagner, 2015, pp. 14–15). Yet, he does not exemplify how informing, discussion, or negotiation processes can take place. In the logic of entrepreneurial action, decision making is a simple cost–benefit analysis rather than being democratic or consensual. On the other hand, the federal ministry—as I have discussed above—points out the willingness of individuals that relies on a coherent and thorough democratic subjectivity and motivation that are not necessarily given. Democracy in the firm or the workplace requires adaptation and coherent political subjectivities that are not only capable but also willing to take decisions.

At this point, democratic participation's or workplace democracy's ambivalence becomes tangible. While the discourse stresses the importance and potential of new forms of decision making, different proposals have diverging interests and concepts in mind. Democracy in this hegemonic proposition is an alternative to co-determination and indirect representation. Either participation's purpose is to increase flexibility and innovation potential, or to weaken the traditional means of co-determination that erode in digitalized and automated production processes anyway due to massive substitution of living labor. Nonetheless, both threads point out that digitalization—and especially *Industrie 4.0*—is a revolutionary process. A contradicting interpretation from social sciences argues that the development is anything but disruptive but rather evolutionary and path-dependent. The argument links digitalization to prerequisites like *lean production*, which is also sensible in goals like flexibility and agility. These are indicators for a new paradigm of rationalization, embedded in digital processes and an extension of *lean production* (Butollo, Jürgens, & Krzywdzinski, 2018). For workers, this means two things: First, their role in the production process is currently determined not only by digitalization and by new modes of participation. Moreover, persisting requirements for agility and flexibility in production and a tighter value stream orientation dominate—as has been the case with group work since the 1990s. Second, democracy provides liberties in production processes but is restricted to the workplace and limited in scope. Heteronomy and factual constraints reduce the range of democratic self-organization severely.

In this environment, participation and democratic workplace organization are—in my interpretation—ambivalent. The explanation that democratic, agile processes sustain flexible market requirements is reasonable at first—however, information collection and distribution, negotiating and decision making are time-consuming processes as examples from *liquid democracy* show (Blum & Zuber, 2016, pp. 171–172).

The orientation toward value streams in the tradition of *lean thinking* does not include decision processes and participation—unless they are directly focusing on value creation, which is highly doubtful.

"Sandboxed" Participation and Naturalized Technological Impact

The analysis of participation in the "*Work 4.0*" consultation reveals a mismatch. The emancipatory ideal behind workplace democracy and participation is levered out when market flexibility and innovation potential are key drivers of new forms of social organization. This reduces democratic participation to utilitarian value to provide market advantages and organizational efficiency benefits. The technological discourse urges new forms of organization that connect social and technological innovation. For workers as well as capital, this can create new advantages. On the one hand, employees contribute immaterial skills that become increasingly relevant for advanced industries as well as for complex and innovative products. On the other hand, capital valorizes these new subjectivities and integrates labor as well as social organization entirely. However, the role of technology in these discussions, as I proved, is fixed: The consultation process reveals digital technologies' deterministic effects on social organization, participation, or co-determination. Whether digitalization will occur or not is out of the question. The single relevant issue is how the cooperation of different interest groups in the production process must adapt to emerging necessities and the factual constraints of international markets. Discursive positions are noncontroversial, which indicates that hegemonic consolidation installed a powerful interpretation of *Industrie 4.0* and its effects on participation and cooperation.

My analysis shows that hegemonic positions on employee participation in digitalization hollow out institutionalized representative structures, which they deem inefficient and time-consuming. Thus, collective representation erodes while individual representation as voting rights is advanced. The effects on bargaining power might be fundamental but remain to be seen. Emancipatory participation emphasizes dignity and power redistribution (Heller, 1998), while the hegemonic "consent" favors individuation. The endpoints of these positions diverge from egalitarian cooperation in democratic firms and economies (i.e., socialized production process): Individuals participate in accelerated, highly flexible production economies. Decision making is limited to short- or mid-range issues and has no influence on production politics, economic, and organizational strategies, or the social fabric of the firm. Participation is, in my interpretation, "*sandboxed*"—to borrow a concept from IT security, where untrusted programs run in a secure container (i.e., sandbox)—to prevent harm to the (organizational) environment. This stresses the ongoing stratification of organizational hierarchies in decision competences. When combined with rigidized flexibility imperatives that use living labor as flexibility potential, this form of participation ultimately fails the litmus test of emancipation in my outlined understanding. In Heller's terms, participation serves efficiency gains and neglects the collective goals of cooperation, which are central in practical examples of worker cooperatives, democratic firms, or democratic participation.

The conflict becomes obvious when the technological implementation reacts to factual constraints. Yet, this implies that the struggle has to be problematized—and the factual constraints have to be demystified. The emancipating potential of technology is only includable in digitalization discourses when factual constraints of technology adaptation are lifted. In my opinion, this leaves two options: Either denaturalize the technological inevitability that digitalization brings into economies and conceptual programs like *Industrie 4.0*—or demystify the market centeredness of economic action and organization. In both cases, counter-hegemonic positions are necessary for a public debate on digital technologies and industrial development, which realize the malleability of technology and its liberating or emancipating potential—as well as its downsides, uncalculated side effects or dominating impact. However, emancipatory and dominating technological effects occur on different levels and—for *Industrie 4.0*—they are not mutually exclusive. As long as the impact of technology remains naturalized, intervening strategies on technology and workplace organization are limited. This affects the struggle against authoritarian uses of technology like increased surveillance or an ideologically misguided form of democratic participation as well. The usage strategies and potential of technology must be re-opened to design, discussion, and appropriation.

As for the *Industrie 4.0* discourse, I conclude that hegemony monopolizes democratic participation as "progressive" politics for growth strategies, labor process legitimacy, and individual responsibilization to enrich the workforce potential. A first emancipatory step has to reclaim the concept and reactivate its normative frame against functionalist reductionism.

Acknowledgements I would like to thank Elena Arnold, who aided in the preparation of this contribution, and the editors for their comments, which improved my paper and argument.

Notes

1. I use labor-managed firm, democratic enterprise, democratic participation, and other forms of direct representation synonymously.
2. The German case of industrial democracy and industrial citizenship is special. In Germany, the right to organize, strike, and autonomously represent workers' interests are legal institutions that have existed since the 1920s and reach back to the German Empire (1871–1918). In the 1950s, the Works Constitution Act granted co-determination and made possible the implementation of factory councils. Co-determination at the factory level is separate from collective bargaining at the societal level. The term "dual structure of interest representation" reflects this and distinguishes local from global "arenas" for labor politics Müller-Jentsch (2016, p. 51). For example, work councils struggle for working conditions at the factory level, while unions bargain for quantitative working hours or payment. In contrast to other European countries, German labor struggles are highly embedded in institutional frameworks, laws, and citizen rights, which as a result have led to the pacification of labor conflicts by, for example, prohibiting wildcat strikes. This model sees industrial relations as *social partnerships*—the idea that antagonistic interest groups cooperate but also fight conflicts in institutionalized settings.
3. The author carefully translated all of the following German sources into English.
4. The respective paragraph regulates co-determination and explicitly covers "the introduction and use of technical devices designed to monitor the behavior or performance of the employees" (§87 (1) 6 Works Constitution Act).

References

Acatech. (2013). *Recommendations for Implementing the Strategic Initiative INDUSTRIE 4.0: Securing the Future of German Manufacturing Industry*. Munich. Retrieved from http://www.acatech.de/fileadmin/user_upload/Baumstruktur_nach_Website/Acatech/root/de/Material_fuer_Sonderseiten/Industrie_4.0/Final_report__Industrie_4.0_accessible.pdf.

Ackers, P. (2016). Experiments in Industrial Democracy: An Historical Assessment of the Leicestershire Boot and Shoe Co-operative Co-partnership Movement. *Labor History, 57*(4), 526–548. https://doi.org/10.1080/0023656X.2016.1239876.

Angermüller, J., Maingueneau, D., & Wodak, R. (2014). The Discourse Studies Reader: An Introduction. In J. Angermüller, D. Maingueneau, & R. Wodak (Eds.), *The Discourse Studies Reader: Main Currents in Theory and Analysis* (pp. 1–14). Amsterdam: Benjamins.

Ansart, P. (1967). *Sociologie de Proudhon*. Paris: PUF.

Barker, J. R. (1993). Tightening the Iron Cage: Concertive Control in Self-Managing Teams. *Administrative Science Quarterly, 38*(3), 408–437. https://doi.org/10.2307/2393374.

Bauman, Z., Bigo, D., Esteves, P., Guild, E., Jabri, V., Lyon, D., … Walker, R. (2014). After Snowden: Rethinking the Impact of Surveillance. *International Political Sociology, 8*(2), 121–144. https://doi.org/10.1111/ips.12048.

Benders, J., Huijgen, F., & Pekruhl, U. (2002). What Do We Know About the Incidence of Group Work (if Anything)? *Personnel Review, 31*(3), 371–385. https://doi.org/10.1108/00483480210422769.

Blum, C., & Zuber, C. I. (2016). Liquid Democracy: Potentials, Problems, and Perspectives. *The Journal of Political Philosophy, 24*(2), 162–182.

Boyd, R., & Holton, R. J. (2018). Technology, Innovation, Employment and Power: Does Robotics and Artificial Intelligence Really Mean Social Transformation? *Journal of Sociology, 54*(3), 331–345. https://doi.org/10.1177/1440783317726591.

Brynjolfsson, E., & McAfee, A. (2014). *The Second Machine Age: Work, Progress, and Prosperity in a Time of Brilliant Technologies*. New York: Norton.

Buhr, D. (2015). *Social Innovation Policy for Industry 4.0*. Bonn. Retrieved from https://library.fes.de/pdf-files/wiso/11479.pdf.

Butollo, F., Jürgens, U., & Krzywdzinski, M. (2018). *From Lean Production to Industrie 4.0: More Autonomy for Employees?* (Discussion Paper No. SP III 2018-303). Berlin. Retrieved from https://bibliothek.wzb.eu/pdf/2018/iii18-303.pdf.

Carnall, C. A. (1982). Semi-Autonomous Work Groups and the Social Structure of the Organization. *Journal of Management Studies, 19*(3), 277–294. https://doi.org/10.1111/j.1467-6486.1982.tb00109.x.

Dörre, K. (2002). *Kampf um Beteiligung: Arbeit, Partizipation und industrielle Beziehungen im flexiblen Kapitalismus*. Wiesbaden: Westdeutscher Verlag.

Dörre, K. (2015). Digitalisierung—neue Prosperität oder Vertiefung gesellschaftlicher Spaltungen? In H. Hirsch-Kreinsen, P. Ittermann, & J. Niehaus (Eds.), *Digitalisierung industrieller Arbeit: Die Vision Industrie 4.0 und ihre sozialen Herausforderungen* (pp. 269–284). Baden-Baden: Edition Sigma.

Eller, E. (2016). Von formalisierter Mitbestimmung zu Chancen neuer Partizipation. In Federal Ministry of Labour and Social Affairs (Ed.), *Wie wir arbeiten (wollen)* (Werkheft No. 02, pp. 100–101). Berlin. Retrieved from http://www.arbeiten-viernull.de/fileadmin/Downloads/BMAS_Werkheft-2.pdf.

Ellerman, D. P. (1990). *A Democratic Worker-Owned Firm: A New Model for the East and West*. Boston, London, Sydney, and Wellington: Unwin Hyman.
Ellerman, D. P. (1999). The Democratic Firm: An Argument Based on Ordinary Jurisprudence. *Journal of Business Ethics, 21*(2/3), 111–124.
Ellerman, D. P. (2016). Rethinking Common Versus Private Property. *American Journal of Economics and Sociology, 75*(2), 319–345. https://doi.org/10.1111/ajes.12142.
Ellerman, D. P. (2017). On the Labor Theory of Property: Is the Problem Distribution or Predistribution? *Challenge, 60*(2), 171–188. https://doi.org/10.1080/05775132.2017.1279906.
Elliott, C. S., & Long, G. (2016). Manufacturing Rate Busters: Computer Control and Social Relations in the Labour Process. *Work, Employment & Society, 30*(1), 135–151. https://doi.org/10.1177/0950017014564601.
Fairclough, N. (2008). *Critical Discourse Analysis: The Critical Study of Language*. Harlow: Longman.
Federal Ministry of Labour and Social Affairs. (2015). *Green Paper Work 4.0: Re-imagining Work*. Berlin. Retrieved from Federal Ministry of Labour and Social Affairs Website http://www.bmas.de/SharedDocs/Downloads/DE/PDF-Publikationen/arbeiten-4-0-green-paper.pdf?__blob=publicationFile&v=2.
Federal Ministry of Labour and Social Affairs. (2017). *White Paper Work 4.0: Re-imagining Work*. Berlin. Retrieved from Federal Ministry of Labour and Social Affairs Website http://www.bmas.de/SharedDocs/Downloads/EN/PDF-Publikationen/a883-white-paper.pdf?__blob=publicationFile&v=3.
Fuchs, C. (2018). Industry 4.0: The Digital German Ideology. *Triple C Communication, Capitalism & Critique, 16*(1), 280–289.
Gorz, A. (1999). *Reclaiming Work: Beyond the Wage-Based Society*. Cambridge and Malden: Polity Press.
Gospel, H. (2011). Employee Representation and the Sustainable Company. In S. Vitols & N. Kluge (Eds.), *The Sustainable Company: A New Approach to Corporate Governance* (pp. 59–74). Brussels: European Trade Union Institute.
Hahnel, R., & Wright, E. O. (2016). *Alternatives to Capitalism: Proposals for a Democratic Economy*. London and New York: Verso.
Hand, M., & Sandywell, B. (2002). E-topia as Cosmopolis or Citadel: On the Democratizing and De-democratizing Logics of the Internet, or, Toward a Critique of the New Technological Fetishism. *Theory, Culture & Society, 19*(1–2), 197–225.
Hans Böckler Foundation. (2015). *Arbeiten 4.0 – Diskurs und Praxis in Betriebsvereinbarungen* (Diskurs und Praxis in Betriebsvereinbarungen No. 14). Düsseldorf. Retrieved from http://www.arbeitenviernull.de/fileadmin/Futurale/Statements/PDFs/Hans-Boeckler-Stiftung.pdf.

Hans Böckler Foundation. (2016). Mitbestimmung. In Federal Ministry of Labour and Social Affairs (Ed.), *Wie wir arbeiten (wollen)* (Werkheft No. 02, pp. 123–124). Berlin. Retrieved from http://www.arbeitenviernull.de/fileadmin/Downloads/BMAS_Werkheft-2.pdf.

Heller, F. A. (1998). *Organizational Participation: Myth and Reality*. Oxford and New York: Oxford University Press.

Hofmann, J. (2016). Schaffen neue Arbeitsformen neue Beziehungsformen? In Federal Ministry of Labour and Social Affairs (Ed.), *Wie wir arbeiten (wollen)* (Werkheft No. 02, pp. 62–67). Berlin. Retrieved from http://www.arbeitenviernull.de/fileadmin/Downloads/BMAS_Werkheft-2.pdf.

IndustriAll. (2015). *Digitalisation for Equality, Participation and Cooperation in Industry: More and Better Industrial Jobs in the Digital Age* (No. 66/2015). Brussels. Retrieved from http://www.industriall-europe.eu/committees/IP/PolPaper/PositionPaper_2015-02_DigitalisationOfIndustry_EN.pdf.

Jacobs, J. C., Kagermann, H., & Spath, D. (Eds.). (2017). *Acatech Discussion. The Future of Work in the Digital Transformation: Agility, Lifelong Learning and the Role of Employers and Works Councils in Changing Times*. Munich: Herbert Utz Verlag. Retrieved from http://www.acatech.de/fileadmin/user_upload/Baumstruktur_nach_Website/Acatech/root/de/Publikationen/acatech_diskutiert/acatech_DISKUSSION_HR-Kreis_engl_01.pdf.

Jossa, B. (2012). A System of Self-Managed Firms as a New Perspective on Marxism. *Cambridge Journal of Economics, 36*(4), 821–841.

Jossa, B. (2015). Historical Materialism and Democratic Firm Management. *Review of Political Economy, 27*(4), 645–665. https://doi.org/10.1080/09538259.2015.1072314.

Jossa, B. (2017). On the Advantages of a System of Labour-Managed Firms. *Journal of Entrepreneurial and Organizational Diversity, 5*(1), 1–19. https://doi.org/10.5947/jeod.2016.002.

Kalleberg, A. L., Nesheim, T., & Olsen, K. M. (2009). Is Participation Good or Bad for Workers? Effects of Autonomy, Consultation and Teamwork on Stress Among Workers in Norway. *Acta Sociologica, 52*(2), 99–116.

Kerr, J. L. (2004). The Limits of Organizational Democracy. *Academy of Management Executive, 18*(3), 81–97.

Kühl, S. (2001). Über das erfolgreiche Scheitern von Gruppenarbeitsprojekten: Rezentralisierung und Rehierarchisierung in Vorreiterunternehmen der Dezentralisierung. *Zeitschrift Für Soziologie, 30*(3), 199–222.

Laclau, E., & Mouffe, C. (2014). *Hegemony and Socialist Strategy: Towards a Radical Democratic Politics* (2nd ed.). London and New York: Verso (Original work published 1985).

Lazzarato, M. (2014). *Signs and Machines: Capitalism and the Production of Subjectivity*. Los Angeles: Semiotext(e).

Marchington, M., & Wilkinson, A. (2005). Direct Participation and Involvement. In S. Bach (Ed.), *Managing Human Resources: Personnel Management in Transition* (4th ed., pp. 398–423). Malden and Oxford: Blackwell.

Marttila, T. (2015). *Post-Foundational Discourse Analysis: From Political Difference to Empirical Research*. Basingstoke: Palgrave Macmillan.

Mason, P. (2015). *Postcapitalism: A Guide to Our Future*. London: Lane.

Meyer, U. (2019). The Emergence of an Envisioned Future: Sensemaking in the Case of "Industrie 4.0" in Germany. *Futures*. Advance online publication. https://doi.org/10.1016/j.futures.2019.03.001.

Moldaschl, M., & Weber, W. G. (1998). The "Three Waves" of Industrial Group Work: Historical Reflections on Current Research on Group Work. *Human Relations, 51*(3), 347–388.

Müller-Jentsch, W. (2016). Formation, Development and Current State of Industrial Democracy in Germany. *Transfer: European Review of Labour and Research, 22*(1), 45–62. https://doi.org/10.1177/1024258915619294.

Pearson, C. A. L. (1992). Autonomous Workgroups: An Evaluation at an Industrial Site. *Human Relations, 45*(9), 905–936. https://doi.org/10.1177/001872679204500903.

Pfeiffer, S. (2017a). Industrie 4.0 in the Making—Discourse Patterns and the Rise of Digital Despotism. In K. Briken, S. Chillas, M. Krzywdzinski, & A. Marks (Eds.), *The New Digital Workplace: How New Technologies Revolutionise Work* (pp. 21–41). London: Palgrave Macmillan.

Pfeiffer, S. (2017b). The Vision of "Industrie 4.0" in the Making—A Case of Future Told, Tamed, and Traded. *Nanoethics, 11*(1), 107–121. https://doi.org/10.1007/s11569-016-0280-3.

Phillips, N., & Hardy, C. (2011). *Discourse Analysis: Investigating Processes of Social Construction*. Thousand Oaks, London, and New Delhi: Sage.

Procter, S., & Mueller, F. (2000). Teamworking: Strategy, Structure, Systems and Culture. In S. Procter & F. Mueller (Eds.), *Teamworking* (pp. 3–24). London: Macmillan.

Ross, N. (1964). *The Democratic Firm*. London: Fabian Society.

Sattelberger, T. (2015). Abhängiger oder souveräner Unternehmensbürger – der Mensch in der Aera der Digitalisierung. In T. Sattelberger, I. Welpe, & A. Boes (Eds.), *Das demokratische Unternehmen: Neue Arbeits- und Führungskulturen im Zeitalter digitaler Wirtschaft* (pp. 33–53). Freiburg and Munich: Haufe.

Sattelberger, T., & Wagner, S. (2015). Zur Einführung – ein Gespräch mit Thomas Sattelberger. In T. Sattelberger, I. Welpe, & A. Boes (Eds.), *Das demokratische Unternehmen: Neue Arbeits- und Führungskulturen im Zeitalter digitaler Wirtschaft* (pp. 11–18). Freiburg and Munich: Haufe.

Sauer, T., Elsen, S., & Garzillo, C. (2016). *Cities in Transition: Social Innovation for Europe's Urban Sustainability*. London and New York: Routledge.

Schaupp, S. (2017). Vergessene Horizonte: Der kybernetische Kapitalismus und seine Alternativen. In P. Buckermann, A. Koppenburger, & S. Schaupp (Eds.), *Kybernetik, Kapitalismus, Revolutionen: Emanzipatorische Perspektiven im technologischen Wandel* (pp. 51–73). Münster: Unrast-Verlag.

Schoemann, K. (2018). Digital Technology to Support the Trade Union Movement. *Open Journal of Social Sciences, 6*(1), 67–82. https://doi.org/10.4236/jss.2018.61005.

Schwartz, J. (2012). Where Did Mill Go Wrong? Why the Capital-Managed Firm Rather Than the Labor-Managed Enterprise Is the Predominant Organizational Form in Market Economies. *Ohio State Law Journal, 73*(2), 219–285.

Sewell, G. (2009). The Labor Process, Surveillance, and the Person in the Sight of the Organization. In S. R. Clegg & C. L. Cooper (Eds.), *The Sage Handbook of Organizational Behavior: Volume 2: Macro Approaches* (pp. 267–286). Los Angeles, London, New Delhi, Singapore, and Washington: Sage.

Srnicek, N., & Williams, A. (2015). *Inventing the Future: Postcapitalism and a World Without Work*. London and New York: Verso.

Stohl, C., & Cheney, G. (2001). Participatory Processes/Paradoxical Practices: Communication and the Dilemmas of Organizational Democracy. *Management Communication Quarterly, 14*(3), 349–407. https://doi.org/10.1177/0893318901143001.

The Lavaca Collective (Ed.). (2007). *Sin patrón: Stories from Argentina's Worker-Run Factories*. Chicago: Haymarket Books.

Townshend, J. (2004). Laclau and Mouffe's Hegemonic Project: The Story so Far. *Political Studies, 52*(2), 269–288.

Ver.di. (2015). *ver.di-Stellungnahme zum Grünbuch "Arbeiten 4.0."*. Berlin. Retrieved from ver.di website: https://www.arbeitenviernull.de/fileadmin/Futurale/Statements/PDFs/Verdi.pdf.

Webb, T., & Cheney, G. (2014). Worker-Owned-and-Governed Co-operatives and the Wider Co-operative Movement: Challenges and Opportunities Within and Beyond the Global Economic Crisis. In M. Parker, G. Cheney, V. Fournier, & C. Land (Eds.), *The Routledge Companion to Alternative Organization* (pp. 64–88). London and New York: Routledge.

CHAPTER 3

From Lean Production to Industrie 4.0: More Autonomy for Employees?

Florian Butollo, Ulrich Jürgens and Martin Krzywdzinski

Introduction

Accounts of *Industrie 4.0* often refer to the new technologies' potential to improve working conditions. In addition to ergonomic improvements, particular emphasis is placed on aspects of autonomy. The "Implementation Recommendations" of Acatech and Forschungsunion, one of the founding documents of *Industrie 4.0*, are one such example (cf. also Reinhart et al., 2017, p. 63):

> It is highly likely that work in *Industrie 4.0* will place significantly higher demands on all employees in terms of complexity, abstraction, and problem solving. In addition, employees will be required to have very high levels of self-direction, communicative skills, and self-organization abilities.

F. Butollo (✉) · U. Jürgens · M. Krzywdzinski
WZB Berlin Social Science Center/Weizenbaum Institute
for the Networked Society, Berlin, Germany
e-mail: florian.butollo@wzb.eu

U. Jürgens
e-mail: ulrich.juergens@wzb.eu

M. Krzywdzinski
e-mail: martin.krzywdzinski@wzb.eu

U. Meyer et al. (eds.), *Digitalization in Industry*,
https://doi.org/10.1007/978-3-030-28258-5_3

> In short: Employees' subjective skills and potential will face even greater challenges. This offers opportunities for qualitative enrichment, interesting work contexts, increasing individual responsibility, and self-development. (Acatech & Forschungsunion, 2013, p. 57)

However, the question arises as to whether these technological promises are justified, especially since initial research findings contradict the expectations of improved work quality and increasing autonomy, instead finding that since the introduction of *Industrie 4.0* technologies, structurally conservative developments have tended to dominate (see Hirsch-Kreinsen, 2018) and innovative approaches to work organization are still lacking.

In the following, we seek to discuss the issue of autonomy of work in an *Industrie 4.0* environment by scrutinizing this concept itself and asking about continuities and discontinuities with the lean production system, which is still dominant in Germany and globally. We therefore do not take the technical possibilities themselves as our point of departure and derive the (possible) effects on work from them, but concentrate on the use of technology in existing production systems and the changes—technology-related and otherwise—in them. In our view, this approach is in line with the prevailing incremental way in which the new digital technologies have been introduced. Instead of assuming that the emergence of new technologies automatically leads to a new *stage* of industrial production or a new production model, we see *Industrie 4.0* rather as a *bundle of technologies* that are integrated selectively into existing production systems depending on the respective contexts, i.e., the sector, products, and processes affected. Significant changes in processes and work organization that affect the extent of worker autonomy may emerge as a result of these technologies. However, the changes should be interpreted with regard to their path dependencies on previous practices.

We will illustrate our arguments using empirical cases drawn from literature as well as from our current research projects. Our aim is to present meaningful examples of companies which practice lean production systems and are now engaged in implementing *Industrie 4.0* technologies. We do not claim to provide a representative sample of companies by sector, size, or other characteristics, and we neither conduct a systematic comparison of the conditions which might influence work organization and working conditions, like for instance the production process and the skill composition of the workforce, the company-specific understanding of lean production, the role and strength of the works council and others. The conclusions developed in this analysis are, therefore, not to be understood as results of a systematic empirical analysis, but rather as hypotheses about what *Industrie 4.0* is and how it might impact work—hypotheses to be analyzed in a systematic way in further research.

In the following, we first summarize the discussion on process organization and the autonomy of work within the context of lean production ("Standardization and Participation in Lean Production"). We then go on to discuss three technology-related developments that we regard as significant innovations ("*Industrie 4.0* and Autonomy: Continuity or Breach with Lean Production?"): the use of digital assistance systems, new control systems in automated manufacturing areas and maintenance, and (currently still experimental) new concepts of modular assembly. The empirical findings call into question the technological promise of greater autonomy in work processes. The use of digital technology can be clearly located within a continuous trend toward the greater standardization of workflows. Yet the complementary element of an integration of the shop floor into improvement processes, which was at least conceptually a cornerstone of work organization in lean production, has hardly been taken into account in recent *Industrie 4.0* approaches. In an examination of prospects for the future ("Conclusions"), we reflect on this finding with reference to Adler's theses (2007), which criticize the critical labor sociology's fixation on the concept of autonomy. We also raise the question of whether, in addition to autonomy and participation, other criteria should also be taken into account when assessing *Industrie 4.0* applications, for example, the potential of these concepts to aid the integration of new groups of employees or help meet changing needs with regard to working hours and flexibility.

Standardization and Participation in Lean Production

Since at least the 1990s, lean production has been the internationally dominant reference model for designing industrial production systems. Lean production was systematically developed and implemented over a long period, from the mid-1940s to the 1970s at Toyota (Fujimoto, 1999; Holweg, 2007; Jürgens, 2017; Shimokawa & Fujimoto, 2009).

The original core of this system is the just-in-time principle (Krafcik, 1988, p. 43), which is essentially just another way of describing the flow principle, which Henry Ford brought to prominence with his production system for the Model T (Williams, Haslam, & Williams, 1992). Yet just-in-time is only seemingly a simple system, and the more complex the process chains become and the more organizationally differentiated they are, the more difficult the system is to implement. It requires producing the precise quantity of each elementary component needed for the next manufacturing step at every point in the value chain. This in turn implies a high degree of interdependence between all actors and processes and makes precise timing and matter-of-fact coordination necessary. In this respect, lean production is an extremely interdependent, failure-prone, and "nervous" system (Krafcik, 1988).

Part of lean production's self-image and recipe for success is that robust organizational routines are necessary to cope with this extreme interdependence: flat hierarchies, the immediate rectification of errors, a strengthening of local problem-solving competences, and above all the so-called Kanban system, by means of which the supply of materials is regulated according to needs (cf. on the significance of the Kanban system Shimokawa & Fujimoto, 2009, p. 16).

The just-in-time principle has also resulted in both restraint and caution with regard to automation measures, as these—according to the assumption—almost inevitably lead to waste in the form of overproduction and thus interim storage in the production process due to fluctuating demand and the need to fully utilize existing facilities for cost reasons. Nevertheless, digital technologies were quickly implemented in lean production systems, in particular enterprise resource planning (ERP) and manufacturing execution systems (MES) (cf. Mormann, 2016; Pfeiffer, 2003).

The characteristics of lean production have had mixed consequences for work on the shop floor. Lean production requires a strict adherence to prescribed operation standards and is thus in the tradition of Taylorism (cf. Dohse, Jürgens, & Malsch, 1984). Only a strict adherence to standards can enable a synchronization of the various processes. Standardized work is also a prerequisite for the optimization of work processes and troubleshooting. Only in standardized processes can the causes of errors be identified, which is why optimized solutions must always be set as new standards (Liker & Hoseus, 2008; Springer, 1999).

Yet the system's high interdependence and sensitivity to disruptions requires ongoing optimization and problem-solving processes involving the knowledge and experience of all shop floor actors. Participation in continuous improvement activities is thus a functional requirement and not a concession to labor (Jürgens & Krzywdzinski, 2016; Liker & Hoseus, 2008). Here, lean production goes beyond classical Taylorism and tempers the separation of planning and execution that is characteristic for the latter. Adler (2007) has emphasized this point in order to question the fixation of criticism of lean production on the concept of autonomy. He has argued that in view of the high interdependence of actors in value chains in modern industry, individual autonomy in the work process is hardly feasible. The more relevant criterion for assessing the quality of work is thus the extent to which employees can participate, including questions of control and governance of the entire company.

Now, it should be noted that the reality of lean production systems—even in Japan and Toyota—only partially reflects the model. In particular, the opportunities for employees to participate are often limited (Fucini & Fucini, 1990; Graham, 1995; Ihara, 2007; Jürgens & Krzywdzinski, 2016; Stewart et al., 2009). In many companies, continuous improvement processes (CIP) are often ritualistically ossified and little attention is paid to the contribution of workers. Nevertheless, the tension between the standardization of work and the participation of employees in standard setting remains a crucial point in the design of work within lean production. To what extent is this balance changing with the evolution of production systems due to the use of *Industrie 4.0* technologies?

Industrie 4.0 and Autonomy: Continuity or Breach with Lean Production?

Whether it is labeled a "revolution" or not, the distinctive feature of socio-technical changes subsumed under the term *Industrie 4.0* is the introduction and diffusion of the Internet of things, which promotes the networking of assembly parts, transport carriers, machines, and measurement instruments. This enables new forms of digital process analysis, control, and optimization based on real-time information exchange, big data, and machine learning (Artificial Intelligence), along with the use of assistance systems that provide information in the work process in a situation-specific and real-time manner (Kagermann, 2014).

As already mentioned, these technologies are used selectively and incrementally, with a number of factors playing a role—from the actors' perception and framing of changes, to the resources and objectives of the companies in question to the forms of process and work organization practiced in each case, which accordingly offer different starting points for digitally mediated optimization (cf. Hirsch-Kreinsen, 2018). Hence, *Industrie 4.0* is rather to be conceived as a bundle of technologies with context-specific applications than as a comprehensive new stage of production.

This perception is echoed by academic contributions from the engineering sciences that emphasize that there is no rupture between lean production and *Industrie 4.0*, thus contradicting the metaphor of a 'revolution' widely invoked in the media. In fact, most articles emphasize the compatibility of both approaches, and lean production is even seen as a prerequisite for the successful introduction of *Industrie 4.0* (cf. Buer, Strandhagen, & Chan, 2018; Dombrowski, Richter, & Krenkel, 2017; Meier, 2017; Rüttimann & Stöckli, 2016; Schlick, Stephan, Loskyll, & Lappe, 2014). In their comparison of lean production and *Industrie 4.0*, Schlick et al. (2014, p. 76) state "that neither the goal of optimization nor the areas to be optimized will change in the context of *Industrie 4.0*." Rüttimann and Stöckli (2016, p. 499) recommend that production managers implement lean production instead of waiting for the "promised land" of *Industrie 4.0*. The latter, they state, is "the topping on that cake. It makes Lean Production more flexible; whether it makes it faster, smoother, and more stable and more accurate has to be proven" (ibid., p. 500).

However, the relationship between lean production and *Industrie 4.0* can also be defined differently as it pertains to work. In this vein, the advocates of *Industrie 4.0* claim that data-based analysis and optimization are the key to managing increasing demands regarding quality, time-to-market, and interdependencies in the supply chains. Here, a shift appears to be occurring away from lean production's emphasis on shop-floor-based experiential knowledge, which is treated as secondary to data-based optimization. At the same time, the expansion of digital knowledge management and assistance systems is expected to support the integration of different groups of employees and especially of semiskilled workers into the work processes by way of instant instruction on standardized working routines on the job. In the following, we will discuss these points based on three application areas in which *Industrie 4.0* technologies are used: the application of digital assistance systems in logistics and assembly, data-optimized control and assistance in the area of automated equipment operators and maintenance work, and changes in assembly line work as part of new modular production concepts.

The Use of Assistance Systems in Logistics and Assembly

Digital assistance systems are a central element of the *Industrie 4.0* technology bundle. In the following, we will discuss their use, especially in the areas of logistics and assembly work that are usually characterized by low- or semiskilled work. Due to increasing requirements in terms of quality and speed in increasingly complex value chains, logistics and assembly are under increasing pressure to prevent errors in order-picking and component assembly. Whereas originally lean production concepts emphasized the necessity to mobilize the informal experiential knowledge of employees, digital assistance systems are increasingly applied to meet these requirements with the effect of supplementing or even substituting the active involvement of workers.

A central area of application is internal logistics operations in industrial enterprises. So-called pick-by-light and pick-by-voice assistance systems have been used in this field for some time. They show picking staff the articles to be selected via light signals or computer-generated voices. Examples of technologies that further develop such approaches are pick-by-vision systems supported by data glasses (cf. Evers, Krzywdzinski, & Pfeiffer, 2018). In addition to identifying picking errors, the main goal of introducing these pick-by-vision techniques according to the engineering literature is to reduce picking times (Baumann, 2013; Günthner, Blomeyer, Reif, & Schedlbauer, 2009).

The data glasses are connected (mostly via WiFi) to the order management system. This provides information about what products are needed, where they are in the warehouse, and in what order they have to be picked. All details and instructions are displayed step by step on the data glasses. The camera built into the data glasses or the RFID chips[1] worn on the body confirm that the correct products have been picked. It is also (at least theoretically) possible to pinpoint the exact location of employees. Reports on the use of data glasses at Tesco and Amazon show that employees' productivity data, movements, and interactions are recorded, evaluated, and used to monitor performance (Moore & Robinson, 2016; Nachtwey & Staab, 2016; Rawlinson, 2013; Wilson, 2013), although comparative surveillance techniques do not appear to be common in the automotive industry to date.

The use of assistance systems in assembly of industrial products can be illustrated by a pilot project conducted on a multiproduct assembly line at an automotive supplier.[2] The company strongly emphasizes the importance of lean production and understands *Industrie 4.0* technologies as a way to optimize its production system. In the visited plant, assistance systems were introduced and tested in a U-shaped production line comprising nine workstations. At the first one, the workpiece is inserted into a workpiece carrier equipped with an RFID chip, thus ensuring reliable position data. Gripping of the parts is controlled by light signals. If the incorrect part is gripped, the subsequent processes are also blocked at the next workstations. Employees log on to the workstation via a Bluetooth device, which stores information about their height, physical characteristics, and their specific previous knowledge. This information is used to adapt the workstations to the employees' individual requirements. Employees' hand movements are followed by cameras, which display whether these have been carried out correctly on a projection screen. The target times for the individual activities are supplied by the industrial engineering department. The system aims to ensure that the activities are carried out in accordance with predefined standards down to the smallest detail (e.g., how built-in parts are gripped and installed).

Of course, these few examples do not offer a sufficient basis from which to generalize. However, it becomes clear that the introduction of assistance systems does not necessarily increase autonomy, personal responsibility, and self-development as claimed by the statement quoted in the introduction of this chapter. Of course, assistance systems can also be designed to adapt flexibly to the level of knowledge and support required by employees, for example, when information is transmitted according to their level of experience. Whether they are used in this way depends, however, on the orientation of human resources policies in the respective company (cf. Kuhlmann, Splett, & Wiegrefe, 2018). Even in a positive scenario, in which assistance systems adapt flexibly to the needs of employees and focus on the provision of process-related information, their impact on learning might by problematic. This can be illustrated with cases from Krzywdzinski and Evers' project on the use of assistance systems running on wearable devices in production and logistics (cf. Evers et al., 2018). Their case studies show that learning effects in work settings where digital assistance systems were used for training might be weaker than expected because employees just let themselves be guided by the technology without actively processing the individual work steps—a phenomenon that is comparable to the "satnav effect" in geographical navigation.[3] In addition, the use of assistance systems raises the question of how the application of such technologies shapes the content of experiences and ideas employees can contribute to improvement processes. It seems likely that employees will then focus on the functioning of the assistance systems themselves, thus directing problem-solving activities toward secondary problems rather than toward the production processes as such.

Although the current motivation for the use of assistance systems is to ensure a greater standardization and control of work, some studies show relatively high employee acceptance of the systems (cf. Evers et al., 2018; Kuhlmann et al., 2018). There may be problems regarding poor wearing comfort (e.g., glasses that are too heavy), limited field of vision, limited battery life, etc., yet employees rarely criticize the external control by the technical systems themselves. An important reason is that the systems also offer advantages such as reductions in workplace stress arising due to growing pressures to avoid errors in an increasingly complex work environment. These stressors seem to us under-researched in the field of sociology of work. Increasing individual autonomy in a highly interdependent and standardized work process might not be a feasible strategy for improving work quality. A more promising approach might focus on enriching work in the sense of including more problem-solving and optimization activities (which also provide learning opportunities) and providing more time autonomy, i.e., more freedoms to switch between production work and other activities.

Data-Based Process Management and Skilled Work

A major element of *Industrie 4.0* is the integration of different layers of the company-internal information systems (see Gronau, 2014, p. 7), from machine control systems and MES to ERP systems, which is intended to create comprehensive process transparency. Nyhuis, Hübner, Quirico, Schäfers, and Schmidt (2017; see also Meyer, Zander, Knapper, & Setzer, 2018; Schlick et al., 2014) show in their work on the transformation of production planning that new optimization potential may arise, for example, in (a) production program planning, through the use of big data analyses to forecast future demand, (b) order management, through real-time information on the status of order processing, and (c) production control, due to more and more precise data on machine utilization, order status, and faults.

This might also have an impact on areas of work that have traditionally required high skills and work experience.

It can be expected, for instance, that the work of automated equipment operators will change. Our argument can be illustrated using the case of an automotive electronics supplier.[4] The company's production system relies on lean production principles. The company is now under high pressure from Asian competitors and is introducing *Industrie 4.0* technologies with the goal of increasing efficiency and quality. Here, a core element of *Industrie 4.0* is a new order management and production control concept which is going hand in hand with changes of the work organization. Prior to the changes, each production line in the factory was operated by a highly skilled equipment operator who was responsible for monitoring, maintenance, and also material supply for his or her line. Under the new system, specialized teams now take care of monitoring/problem-solving, maintenance, and material supply. Every worker is equipped with a tablet computer and the order management and production control system informs the teams (ideally: in real time) if a problem occurs in the production process or in the supply chain. The system should automatically recognize which employees are available and qualified for the task. While each team is responsible for a specific task (e.g., process monitoring or maintenance), all workers in a team should be able to take care of each production line. The aim is to achieve greater flexibility and better utilization of working hours of equipment operators. The impact on skill requirements is ambiguous. We can observe a polarization of skill requirements between the teams, because material supply tasks can now, for example, also be allocated to semiskilled workers, while in the area of problem-solving and maintenance at least some of the skilled workers must be familiar with multiple pieces of equipment, which goes hand in hand with increasing skill requirements.

Far-reaching changes are already visible in the area of maintenance as well. Such tasks are currently undertaken by highly qualified and experienced groups of employees whose work is hard to standardize as it affords instant reactions to very specific problems that so far could barely be predicted in advance. It is reasonable to expect that new data-based process optimization techniques will lead to a decrease in repair and maintenance activities. Self-diagnostic systems in machines and plants are already highly developed and so-called IoT gateways (Internet of things interfaces) are gaining in importance, i.e., software systems that bring together and display sensor data from plants in real time. In this way, immediate action can be taken or preventive measures can be planned. Within comprehensive process management and support systems, data from many production lines are combined and can serve as a base for new process optimization strategies (e.g., through data mining).

The "smart maintenance" approaches discussed in the context of *Industrie 4.0* take this development one step further (Acatech, 2015; Günther, Benisch, Dankl, & Isopp, 2015). Günther et al. (2015, p. 20) emphasize that the maintenance profession is moving away from the image of the "machine whisperer," i.e., a profession that needs to rely on extensive working experience with machines, toward a focus on data analytics. The concept of "smart maintenance" formulated by Acatech emphasizes the possibility of centralizing equipment monitoring and problem-solving processes resulting from the new quality of data availability and the opportunities offered by real-time data analysis. In such maintenance centers, university-trained engineers could work together with data analysts. Maintenance personnel themselves follow the instructions from the maintenance center and would therefore require less experience and technical knowledge:

> From this maintenance center, the operational workers who have completed a basic qualification as generalists or generalists in maintenance would be individually guided in their work. In conjunction with the use of suitable assistance systems, this approach compensates for workers' lack of experience or qualifications and enables them to be deployed throughout the field. (Acatech, 2015, p. 24)

Although these approaches are still in their infancy, there are signs that such a standardization of activities is underway. Replacing mechanical safety systems in the elevator industry with electronic solutions means, for example, that elevator monitoring and planning can be handled by central monitoring centers. Malfunctions are largely avoided by predictive maintenance. Today's elevator mechanics are increasingly acting as "parts exchangers."

The current rationalization of maintenance and automated equipment operators' work is following a path which has been developed by lean production concepts. Systematic process monitoring and statistical process control concepts were among the core ideas that were taken up by Japanese companies and further developed into so-called total productive maintenance (TPM). In line with this, predictive maintenance systems have been established in many companies since the 1990s in which forecasts on possible failures are made based on data on material loads and wear durations. This allows maintenance work to be planned in such a way that affected parts and components are replaced before the system fails (Wireman, 1991), even though the existing systems and data are still far from perfection. The need to get rid of fixed equipment control stations and to flexibly use equipment operators have also already been highlighted in earlier papers as an important element of Toyota's approaches to automation (Sugimori, Kusunoki, Cho, & Uchikawa, 1977, p. 558).

However, there is an important difference between the TPM concepts and "smart maintenance." The TPM literature emphasizes the need for crossfunctional and crosshierarchical improvement processes, in which the shop floor teams should also be included (Japan Institute of Plant Maintenance, 1996; Shirose, 1996). Under the heading "autonomous maintenance," the shop floor teams take on tasks such as equipment monitoring, registration of faults and problems, problem analysis, and simple maintenance activities. To ensure that these tasks are completed, the team activity boards list the daily TPM duties (Japan Institute of Plant Maintenance, 1996). The team activities are part of the comprehensive optimization activities, which also include the maintenance department and supervisors and managers from several hierarchy levels.

While the tradition of lean production emphasizes the combination of data-based analysis with competence development and shop floor experience, such an emphasis is absent in the discussion about *Industrie 4.0* applications. The concept of "smart maintenance" rather suggests making such investments in shop floor knowledge superfluous through technology.

However, it is doubtful whether this technology-fixated approach will actually work. At the very least, experience with previous automation processes suggests that the elimination of experience and learning opportunities through data-based process control, monitoring, and optimization can lead to a lack of human problem-solving competences in the event of unexpected system failures (Bainbridge, 1983; Weyer, 1997, 2007). For this reason, too, works councils and researchers should underscore the importance of experiential knowledge on the shop floor against concept-heavy IT expertise and defend the importance of skilled workers when testing and adapting *Industrie 4.0* solutions to meet changing circumstances and requirements.

New Approaches to the Design of Assembly Line Work

Companies from different industries are working on approaches to modularized production using cyber-physical systems in assembly and logistics.[5] It is emphasized that such approaches would grant leeway for a more innovative work design, since they supposedly represent a departure from the corset of tight coupling of processes in assembly line work. The scope and limits of these approaches can be illustrated by an experimental concept developed by Audi (2018), which we discuss here based on the company presentations and publications available. According to this concept—which is so far implemented in a laboratory only—the vehicles are to be placed on autonomous transport systems and provided with information on the possible sequence of the assembly steps. On the basis of this information, the vehicles themselves then decide which assembly station they will go to next, taking into account the capacity utilization of the station, the "traffic situation," and other relevant factors. This will potentially create a self-regulating system.

Efficiency gains are expected from the fact that each vehicle seeks its optimum path through production, which means unnecessary steps can be skipped, for example, when a part is not needed for a particular model. The assembly stations can thus be optimally utilized. Disruptions at individual stations due to malfunctions also do not necessarily have to affect the entire production flow.[6] Such systems may overcome the limitations of present-day lean production systems related to the rigidity of the assembly line.

One of the goals of the project, according to Audi, is to increase the autonomy of employees in assembly. The intention is that each of the future assembly stations will be responsible for a complete work step (e.g., the assembly of the cockpit). To enable this, uniform cycle times will be abandoned. The duration of the work steps will instead depend on the quantity and content of the tasks and range between one and four minutes. Compared to the highly rationalized assembly line work following a uniform cycle time, this should offer the possibility of increasing the quality of work. At the same time, the intention is to create scope for managing stressors and for improving the working conditions for older or disabled employees. The flexibility of the system should also reduce stress potential, for example, if employees are missing and work at individual stations thus takes longer or if an error has to be rectified. The desired flexibility of the cycle time of the individual assembly stations to up to four minutes goes only slightly beyond the scope offered by today's assembly lines, but potentially even greater deviations from the principle of uniform cycle time could be feasible. Such concepts recall Swedish approaches to the reorganization of work in the 1980s and 1990s (Sandberg, 1995).

To sum up, the new assembly approaches could theoretically lead to an expansion of the work content and an enrichment of the work tasks at the stations with indirect activities related to team organization, problem-solving, and other tasks. Nevertheless, since this model is also subject to high profitability pressures, it is at least unclear to what extent the promises of autonomy offered by this socio-technical path can actually be realized. It is true that in the case of modular production described here, the rigidity of the processes on the assembly line is loosened up, but it is misleading to interpret this as a departure from flow production. The reorganization of the assembly line could even open up scope for an intensification of work. After all, the processes could be timed much more flexibly and the activities at the individual stations could bundled in such a way that the "idle times," in which employees wait for the next task, are reduced and work is thus condensed.

Conclusions

Our discussion of *Industrie 4.0* projects casts doubt on the assertion that these developments will be accompanied by greater autonomy for workers. Although the empirical findings to date do not allow us to paint a precise nor a conclusive picture, they suggest that the use of digital technologies intensifies the tendencies toward standardization and control of work inherent in lean production. In fact, the applications of new digital assistance systems even go beyond traditional lean production techniques, in that they enable real-time control of work processes and individualized guidance for employees.

Although the presented cases thus cast doubt on the claim of increased "autonomy" for workers, it would be mistaken to take this tendency as the single yardstick for the evaluation of working conditions in emergent production systems. Looking back at the debates about lean production in labor sociology, Adler (2007) criticized the fixation on the ideal of workers' autonomy as backward-looking, because it is based on the model of an isolated craftsman, which is no longer compatible with the conditions of modern production. Using Marx's argument about the dialectic between productive forces and relations of production, Adler emphasized that an increasing use of technology inevitably strengthens interdependence at various levels in the long term. More complex technologies also require a stronger integration of different functions, such as development, planning, production, etc. All this reinforces interdependence in the work process.

The decisive question is not, therefore, whether the organization of work enables individual autonomy, but whether the rules of interdependence and cooperation are defined in a participatory and cooperative process instead of top-down. The reference point for emancipatory demands on work should be a participatory interdependence (Adler speaks of "collaborative interdependence") rather than individual autonomy.

The way in which *Industrie 4.0* technologies are currently implemented does not suggest a progress toward collaborative interdependence. While in lean production concepts, the team-based involvement of the shop floor employees in improvement processes and problem-solving has always been emphasized, this aspect is largely absent in the *Industrie 4.0* discussion. Debates on the implementation of such technologies are rather dominated by approaches that focus on data-based process control whereas they neglect the importance of practical knowledge and shop floor competences. An important challenge for the organization of work is therefore to design new forms of employee participation, especially as the approaches taken so far have been inadequate. Although employees in the automotive companies, we studied are informed and consulted on the introduction of digital assistance systems, these are typically one-off events that are mostly limited to questions of ergonomics and handling (cf. Evers et al., 2018). So far there are no studies on how the use of digital assistance systems affects teamwork and problem-solving activities on the shop floor. The first studies in the logistics sector conclude that, especially with regard to simple tasks, digitalization leads to a reduction of the "need for independent problem solving" on the shop floor (Mättig, Jost, & Kirks, 2018, p. 70).

There might, however, be a better ways of implementing *Industrie 4.0* technologies that can serve to strengthen the autonomy of workers to determine working times and working schedules according to their needs. We can observe an increased demand for flexible and shorter working hours, as well as for the scope to shift between part-time and full-time work, leave periods for child-rearing, and time spent taking care of relatives. This results in difficulties to coordinate processes and ensure a supply of adequately skilled workers as employees need to shift from workstation to workstation more frequently. Digital systems to guide work processes and assign tasks can help manage these challenges and reconcile employee-oriented working time policies with productivity requirements. The new technologies can also have positive effects in terms of supporting greater task rotation and integrating new groups with little industrial experience into production. In general, *Industrie 4.0* technologies are being used in a context of demographic changes, which are reflected in growing recruitment problems and high employee turnover rates. In many companies in manufacturing industries, a generational rupture is imminent, and the younger employees might be less willing to accept rigid working time schedules and task allocations.

The extent to which *Industrie 4.0* applications can be used to influence working time and work organization does not, however, depend on technology as such, but on the outcome of bargaining around such issues. The technology-fixated discussion about *Industrie 4.0* can be used as a chance to address the conditions of employment at a time of demographic change comprehensively—and thus to make corresponding demands related to working conditions and work schedules.

Yet it is important to acknowledge that the ability of workers to act in such a way is impacted by the way in which digital process control and assistance systems are currently implemented as this affects power relations in the workplace. Since these technologies often reduce the importance of the employees' practical knowledge and make their inputs more exchangeable, they could undermine their bargaining power. Under these circumstances, institutionalized resources of labor power, such as co-determination in Germany, as well as associational power through organizing efforts might become all the more important.

Notes

1. Radio Frequency Identification (RFID) is a central technological element that facilitates the coordination of logistics. RFID enables the contactless and unique identification of objects and is thus a fundamental element of the industrial application of the internet of things.
2. The case study was conducted by Ulrich Jürgens and is based on a factory visit and interviews with the production manager and works council.
3. This refers to the effect that occurs when using satnav devices in road traffic. Such devices guide users relatively reliably to their chosen destination

and thus technically enhance their navigation skills. However, trust in the technology can lead to a loss of independent navigation ability if individuals blindly follow satnav directions without making individual efforts to orient themselves or contextualize the information.

4. The case was analyzed in the research project "Wearable computing in manufacturing and logistics," conducted by Martin Krzywdzinski and Maren Evers at the WZB and funded by Hans Böckler Foundation.
5. Cyber-physical systems are networks of machines, storage systems, and equipment in which the components "exchange information independently, trigger actions, and control each other independently" (Acatech & Research Union, 2013, p. 5). Together with a number of partners such as the Fraunhofer Society, the University of Stuttgart, and other organizers, Daimler operates the Arena2036 research factory, in which new modular assembly concepts based on cyber-physical systems are being tested (Daimler, 2018; Steegmüller & Zürn, 2017). Audi has already switched over to transporting vehicles between individual assembly stations at the R8 assembly plant in Neckersulm using driverless transport systems, which means that the assembly layout can now be changed much more flexibly, but otherwise the assembly at the R8 still seems to follow traditional flow and pull concepts (Plattform Industrie 4.0, 2018).
6. At the same time, however, the complexity of the assembly system and the difficulties in synchronizing the material flow increase. To give just one example: If the assembly stations can be started up again and again in a new sequence, how are the logistics processes organized and the JIT parts supply ensured? The superiority of the experiments in modular production must therefore still be demonstrated in practice.

Literature

Acatech. (2015). *Smart Maintenance für Smart Factories*. Munich/Berlin.

Acatech & Forschungsunion. (2013). *Umsetzungsempfehlungen für das Zukunftsprojekt Industrie 4.0*. Berlin: Forschungsunion.

Adler, P. S. (2007). The Future of Critical Management Studies: A Paleo-Marxist Critique of Labour Process Theory. *Organization Studies, 28*(9), 1313–1345.

Audi. (2018). *Fertigungsinseln statt Fließband*. Retrieved from https://blog.audi.de/modulare-montage-bei-audi/. Accessed last 5 July 2018.

Bainbridge, L. (1983). "Ironies of Automation." Analysis, Design and Evaluation of Man–Machine Systems. *Automatica, 19*(6), 775–779.

Baumann, H. (2013). *Order Picking Supported by Mobile Computing*. Dissertation. Bremen.

Buer, S. V., Strandhagen, J. O., & Chan, F. T. (2018). The Link Between Industrie 4.0 and Lean Manufacturing: Mapping Current Research and

Establishing a Research Agenda. *International Journal of Production Research, 56*(8), 1–17.
Daimler. (2018). Arena2036. Retrieved from https://www.arena2036.de/de/. Last accessed 5 June 2018.
Dohse, K., Jürgens, U., & Malsch, T. (1984). Vom „Fordismus" zum „Toyotismus"? Die Organisation der industriellen Arbeit in der japanischen Automobilindustrie. *Leviathan, 12*(4), 448–477.
Dombrowski, U., Richter, T., & Krenkel, P. (2017). Interdependencies of Industrie 4.0 & Lean Production Systems: A Use Cases Analysis. *Procedia Manufacturing, 11,* 1061–1068.
Evers, M., Krzywdzinski, M., & Pfeiffer, S. (2018). *Designing Wearables for Use in the Workplace: The Role of Solution Developers.* WZB Discussion Paper SP III 2018-301. Berlin.
Fucini, J., & Fucini, S. (1990). *Working for the Japanese: Inside Mazda's American Auto Plant.* New York: Free Press.
Fujimoto, T. (1999). *The Evolution of a Manufacturing System at Toyota.* New York: Oxford University Press.
Graham, L. (1995). Subaru-Isuzu: Worker Response in a Nonunion Japanese Transplant. In B. Steve (Pub.), *Lean Work: Empowerment and Exploitation in the Global Auto Industry* (pp. 199–206). Detroit: Wayne State University Press.
Gronau, N. (2014). *Enterprise Resource Planning.* München: Oldenbourg.
Günther, G., Benisch, M., Dankl, A., & Isopp, J. (2015). *Roadmap der Instandhaltung 4.0.* Salzburg.
Günthner, W., Blomeyer, N., Reif, R., & Schedlbauer, M. (2009). *Pick-by-vision: Augmented Reality unterstützte Kommissionierung.* Garching.
Hirsch-Kreinsen, H. (2018). *Arbeit 4.0: Pfadabhängigkeit statt Disruption.* Soziologisches Arbeitspapier 52/2018. Dortmund.
Holweg, M. (2007). The Genealogy of Lean Production. *Journal of Operations Management, 25,* 420–437.
Ihara, R. (2007). *Toyota's Assembly Line: A View from the Factory Floor.* Melbourne: Trans Pacific Press.
Japan Institute of Plant Maintenance. (1996). *Autonomous Maintenance for Operators.* Portland.
Jürgens, U. (2017). Lean Production/Toyotismus. In H. Hirsch-Kreinsen & H. Minssen (Eds.), *Lexikon der Arbeits- und Industriesoziologie* (pp. 204–207). Baden-Baden: Nomos.
Jürgens, U., & Krzywdzinski, M. (2016). *New Worlds of Work: Varieties of Work in Car Factories in the BRIC Countries.* Oxford: Oxford University Press.
Kagermann, H. (2014). Chancen von Industrie 4.0 nutzen. In T. Bauernhansl, M. Hompel, & B. Vogel-Heuser (Eds.), *Industrie 4.0 in Produktion, Automatisierung und Logistik* (pp. 603–614). Wiesbaden: Springer Fachmedien Wiesbaden.

Krafcik, J. (1988). Triumph of the Lean Production System. *Sloan Management Review, 30*(1), 41–52.

Kuhlmann, M., Splett, B., & Wiegrefe, S. (2018). Montagearbeit 4.0? Eine Fallstudie zu Arbeitswirkungen und Gestaltungsperspektiven digitaler Werkerführung. *WSI-Mitteilungen, 71*(3), 182–188.

Liker, J. K., & Hoseus, M. (2008). *Toyota Culture: The Heart and Soul of the Toyota Way*. New York: McGraw-Hill.

Mättig, B., Jost, J., & Kirks, T. (2018). Erweiterte Horizonte – Ein technischer Blick in die Zukunft der Arbeit. In S. Wischmann & E. A. Hartmann (Eds.), *Zukunft der Arbeit – Eine praxisnahe Betrachtung* (pp. 63–72). Berlin: Springer Vieweg.

Meier, K. J. (2017). Lean QRM 4.0 – Das Beste aus Lean Production, QRM und Industrie 4.0 vereint in einem gemeinsamen Managementansatz. In R. Koether & K. J. Meier (Eds.), *Lean Production für die variantenreiche Einzelfertigung* (pp. 119–135). Wiesbaden: Springer Gabler.

Meyer, A., Zander, S., Knapper, R., & Setzer, T. (2018). Decision Support Pipelines – Durchgängige Datenverarbeitungsinfrastrukturen für die Entscheidungen von morgen. In S. Wischmann & E. A. Hartmann (Eds.), *Zukunft der Arbeit – Eine praxisnahe Betrachtung* (pp. 207–209). Berlin: Springer Vieweg.

Moore, P., & Robinson, A. (2016). The Quantified Self: What Counts in the Neoliberal Workplace. *New Media & Society, 18*(11), 774–792.

Mormann, H. (2016). *Das Projekt SAP: Zur Organisationssoziologie betriebswirtschaftlicher Standardsoftware*. Bielefeld: Transcript.

Nachtwey, O., & Staab, P. (2016). Die Avantgarde des digitalen Kapitalismus. *Mittelweg 36, 24*(6), 59–84.

Nyhuis, P., Hübner, M., Quirico, M., Schäfers, P., & Schmidt, M. (2017). Veränderung in der Produktionsplanung und -steuerung. In G. Reinhart (Ed.), *Handbuch Industrie 4.0* (pp. 31–50). Munich: Carl Hanser.

Pfeiffer, S. (2003). SAP R/3 & Co. Integrierte Betriebswirtschaftliche Systeme als stille Helferlein des Lego-Kapitalismus. *FIfF-Kommunikation, Mitteilungsblatt des Forum InformatikerInnen für Frieden und gesellschaftliche Verantwortung (FIfF) e.V., 20*(3), 9–13.

Plattform Industrie 4.0. (2018). *Flexible Montage in der Fahrzeugproduktion*. Retrieved from https://www.plattform-i40.de/I40/Redaktion/DE/Anwendungsbeispiele/137-wandelbare-r8-manufaktur/beitrag-wandelbare-r8-manufaktur.html. Last accessed 5 June 2018.

Rawlinson, K. (2013, February 13). Tesco Accused of Using Electronic Armbands to Monitor Its Staff. *The Independent*. Retrieved from http://www.independent.co.uk/news/business/news/tesco-accused-of-using-electronic-armbands-to-monitor-its-staff-8493952.html. Last accessed 12 July 2018.

Reinhart, G., Bengler, K., Dollinger, C., Intra, C., Lock, C., Popova-Dlogosch, S., … Vernim, S. (2017). Der Mensch in der Produktion von Morgen. In G. Reinhart (Ed.), *Handbuch Industrie 4.0* (pp. 51–88). Munich: Carl Hanser.

Rüttimann, B. G., & Stöckli, M. T. (2016). Lean and Industry 4.0—Twins, Partners, or Contenders? A Due Clarification Regarding the Supposed Clash of Two Production Systems. *Journal of Service Science and Management, 9*, 485–500.

Sandberg, A. (Publ.). (1995). *Enriching Production: Perspectives on Volvo's Uddevalla Plant as an Alternative to Lean Production*. Aldershot: Avebury.

Schlick, J., Stephan, P., Loskyll, M., & Lappe, D. (2014). Industrie 4.0 in der praktischen Anwendung. In T. Bauernhansl, M. Hompel, & B. Vogel-Heuser (Eds.), *Industrie 4.0 in Produktion, Automatisierung und Logistik* (pp. 57–84). Wiesbaden: Springer Fachmedien Wiesbaden.

Shimokawa, K., & Fujimoto, T. (2009). *The Birth of Lean: Conversations with Taiichi Ohno, Eiji Toyoda, and Other Figures Who Shaped Toyota Management*. Cambridge: Lean Enterprise Institute.

Shirose, K. (1996). *TPM—Total Productive Maintenance: New Implementation Program in Fabrication and Assembly Industries*. Tokyo: Japan Institute of Plant Maintenance.

Springer, R. (1999). *Rückkehr zum Taylorismus? Arbeitspolitik in der Automobilindustrie am Scheideweg*. Frankfurt/Main: Campus Verlag.

Steegmüller, D., & Zürn, M. (2017). Wandlungsfähige Produktionssysteme für den Automobilbau der Zukunft. In G. Reinhart (Ed.), *Handbuch Industrie 4.0* (pp. 27–44). Munich: Carl Hanser.

Stewart, P., Richardson, M., Danford, A., Murphy, K., Richardson, T., & Wass, V. (2009). *We Sell Our Time No More: Workers' Struggles Against Lean Production in the British Car Industry*. London: Pluto Press.

Sugimori, Y., Kusunoki, K., Cho, F., & Uchikawa, P. (1977). Toyota Production System and Kanban System, Materialisation of Just-in-Time and Respect-for-Human System. *International Journal of Production Research, 15*, 553–564.

Weyer, J. (1997). Die Risiken der Automationsarbeit. *Zeitschrift Für Soziologie, 26*(4), 239–257.

Weyer, J. (2007). Autonomie und Kontrolle. Arbeit in hybriden Systemen am Beispiel der Luftfahrt. *Technikfolgenabschätzung– Theorie und Praxis, 16*(2), 35–42.

Williams, K., Haslam, C., & Williams, J. (1992). Ford Versus 'Fordism': The Beginning of Mass Production. *Work, Employment & Society, 6*(4), 517–555.

Wilson, H. J. (2013, September). Wearables in the Workplace. *Harvard Business Review*. Retrieved from https://hbr.org/2013/09/wearables-in-the-workplace. Last accessed 12 July 2018.

Wireman, T. (1991). *Total Productive Maintenance—An American Approach*. New York: Industrial Press.

CHAPTER 4

"Designing Freedom": On (Post)Industrial Governmentality and Its Cybernetic Fundaments

Felix Maschewski and Anna-Verena Nosthoff

Various sociological studies (Bröckling, 2016, 2017; Mau, 2017; Meißner, 2015; Moore, 2017; Schaupp, 2016a, 2016b; Traue, 2010) have recently examined (post)industrial forms of subjectivation and organization against the background of an extensive process of digital "quantification." When outlining key factors that determine this dynamic, these analyses often refer to concepts such as participatory feedback, self-tracking, rating, monitoring, and resilience—terms that, as has rightly been examined (cf. Bröckling, 2017; Schaupp, 2016a, 2016b), relate to first- and second-order cybernetics. In line with this, the following article aims to substantiate that cybernetic concepts, as articulated throughout the second half of the twentieth century, are currently undergoing a renaissance and, furthermore, an *actualization* on the basis of the feedback-based technical devices now available

F. Maschewski
Humboldt University, Berlin, Germany
e-mail: maschewf@hu-berlin.de

A.-V. Nosthoff (✉)
Albert-Ludwigs-University, Freiburg, Germany
e-mail: anna.verena.nosthoff@posteo.net

U. Meyer et al. (eds.), *Digitalization in Industry*,
https://doi.org/10.1007/978-3-030-28258-5_4

to actively implement them (see, specifically, Hörl & Hagner, 2008 in this context). We specify in the following article that this holds not only for the context of political governance (as we have examined elsewhere, see Maschewski & Nosthoff, 2019a) but also for organizational structures in general and current industrial contexts in particular.

While various different definitions of cybernetics exist, we understand the science of "control and communication in the animal and the machine" (Wiener, 1948) with Claus Pias (2004, p. 325, transl. by the authors) as both a politics and a "technology of perpetual, small interventions [...] and subtle corrections." To put it very broadly, cybernetics aims at regulating behavior via permanent feedback, guaranteeing a frictionless functioning of organizations by reducing disruptions and adjusting irregularities through self-learning. Against this background, the article particularly investigates the following key concepts of cybernetics that, as we argue, can still be considered influential: steering, self-regulation/control, adaptive/autocorrective behavior, and the systemic focus on organizations as autopoietic mechanisms. By tracing these notions back to cybernetics, our aim is to understand the cybernetic roots of current forms of (post)industrial governmentality and to analyze these foundations critically. To provide an adequate frame for the digital industrial context, we specifically focus on recent developments in neocybernetic management thought with a view to its origins in organizational cybernetics. More practically, we also look at how some of these developments are echoed in current trends in the digital service industry.

Furthermore, to subsequently examine the relation between domination and emancipation in current (post)industrial contexts, we consider it particularly helpful to focus on an aporetic interdependence that has accompanied cybernetic systems thinking since its very beginning: the interplay between freedom and control. Indeed, cybernetics posits these concepts not as opposed but as intertwined. As we try to show in the second part of this paper, the counterintuitive combination of freedom and control is still relevant for an understanding of contemporary streams of systems and management thinking and, relatedly, of the forms of governmentality implied and induced by them. Against this background, our aim is to eventually highlight that current forms of neocybernetic regulation tend less toward a reduction in domination than to its transformation into a new form of what we term, along with Günther Anders, *integral* domination. Such a form of domination operates precisely on the very basis of a participatory and collaborative environment;

it is less exerted by a centralized power and more inscribed into the very processes shaping the overall organizational field.

From Drucker to Beer: Early Models of Organizational "Self-Control"

To provide a short overview of the most fundamental principles of cybernetic systems thought that we consider crucial for an understanding of its current neocybernetic actualizations, we discuss three early thinkers of management systems and organizational and group behavior: Peter F. Drucker, Stafford Beer, and Kurt Lewin. We focus on these theorists in particular, as they still exert a crucial influence on contemporary management theory: Lewin's model of behavioral change is still a major reference in various streams of so-called change management, whereas Beer's concept of self-regulation and Drucker's systemic approach are often read together in the contemporary literature on organizations (i.e., specifically in what management theorist Fredmund Malik terms "systemic management" [cf. Malik, 2004b]). In addition, we discuss Lewin's models of self-regulation and self-learning, Beer's idea of liberty as a "programmable function," and Drucker's concept of "self-control." As we argue, these concepts are of crucial importance with a view to neocybernetic organizations thought, particularly Pentland's idea of "social physics" as well as Thaler's and Sunstein's concept of a "nudge," which we will subsequently examine. In this vein, it can eventually be argued that not only Lewin and Beer but also Drucker have articulated implicit notions of steering that rely on a rather reductive notion of freedom as well as a restrictive model of participation and emancipation. Specifically, Drucker's concept of "Management by Objectives and Self-Control" (short: "MbO" (2012 [1954]), Beer's "viable system model" (1959), and Lewin's "Three-Phase-Model" of systematic change (cf. 1947a) are paradigmatic in this context.[1]

i. *Peter Drucker's systemic vision: Managing oneself, controlling oneself*

Starting with Peter F. Drucker, it might seem surprising to align him with the history of cybernetics. To be sure, in contrast to Lewin and Beer, Drucker was neither related to the inner circle of cyberneticists nor was he a participant in the Macy conferences on cybernetics, let alone an explicit cyberneticist. However, as we argue, Drucker can be considered to have foreseen at least some tendencies that later became relevant in management cybernetics, specifically the work of Stafford Beer.

Drucker, who was one of the most influential management consultants of the twentieth century, can be seen as an early advocate of reducing hierarchical domination and replacing it with self-control enabled through performance measurement. Promoting a form of integrative thinking grounded in a broader ecological vision, he poignantly describes his early *The Practice of Management* as the first attempt to introduce concepts such as "objectives" and "key result areas" with the purpose of "direct[ing] and steer[ing] a business" (2006, p. 6). According to Drucker, the set objectives were in need of continuous monitoring and quantification and therefore had to rely on key management information systems. To be able to measure and judge the "provable performance" of a business unit—Drucker considered quantified work outcome the most objective indicator—he suggested implementing not only external evaluations of individual or collective results but also a way of permanently controlling one's own achievements while providing workers with the freedom to take part in the goal-setting process. This, according to Drucker, enhances the overall performance in the long run, as it increases the workers' sense of identification with, and responsibility for, the tasks defined.

Drucker thereby promotes a way of understanding the organization as embedded in and responsive to a broader environment, while conceiving of the enterprise "as a whole" (2006, p. viii)—the closeness to cybernetic terminology and systems thinking is, indeed, quite notable. Furthermore, he conceives of the firm as a "system" comprising a set of subsystems that operate quasi-autonomously—a thought that will reoccur in detail and in a radicalized form in Stafford Beer's later *Brain of the Firm*. In addition, Drucker describes his work as having introduced a form of "governance," a term that derives from the Latin "gubernator." It has the same etymological origin as the Greek *kybernētēs*—a literal translation would be "steersman" or "navigator"—from which "cybernetics" is derived (cf. Wiener, 1948). In this context, it is notable that as one of the best approaches to management thinking, Drucker cites Xenophon's *Kyropaidaia,* which can be read as an early affirmation of a model of governance that relies on a good shepherd who governs by educating the herd that he takes care of. As such, it can be viewed as an early version of what Foucault would later term "pastoral power" (which, as we will expand on later, is today partly revitalized under the rubric of "nudging").

Drucker was thus an early advocate of understanding management as governance. He was also convinced that, in a rather pedagogical fashion, to be able to govern and self-govern, management needed to create a "desire to improve" (2006, p. 219). However, although Drucker's approach to management still defines a particular leadership style that partly includes top-down relations, it is primarily based on "creating relationships of (...) responsibility" (2006, p. 7). As such, it already envisions the worker as highly self-reflexive, autonomous, and engaged. Indeed, Drucker's early concept of self-steering was particularly developed against Taylor's idea of management by domination, which considered hierarchy and unidirectionality as preconditions for efficiency. In contrast, similar to cybernetic systems thought, Drucker thought of control as compatible with self-organization and autonomy (cf. Seibel 2016, p. 218). In fact, Drucker was, as early as 1959, convinced that a major epistemic-organizational shift had taken place in the 1930s, 1940s, and 1950s: The relevance of cause and effect had been supplemented by the increasing importance of understanding and analyzing patterns and processes to comprehend systems. Against this background, Drucker foresaw the rise of the "knowledge worker." As he claimed, the latter is ideally capable of self-management, continuous learning, continuous teaching, and continuous innovation (cf. Drucker, 1993, p. 198) while usually aiming at effective problem-solving. Drucker's description of the "knowledge worker" indeed tacitly anticipated what Gilles Deleuze (1992, p. 5) would, decades later, in a critical fashion, term the "dividual," the electronically divisable individual emerging from "the societies of control." As Drucker describes it in his *Management*: "It demands that we impose the responsibility for their productivity on the knowledge workers themselves. Knowledge workers have to manage themselves. They have to have autonomy" (1993, p. 197).

Given his focus on continuous improvement, it comes as no surprise that in his essay "Managing Oneself," Drucker explicitly refers to the importance of individual "feedback analysis," especially with regard to the emerging "knowledge worker": "Whenever one makes a key decision and whenever one takes a key action, one writes down what one expects will happen. And nine months or twelve months later, one then feeds back from results to expectations" (1993, p. 481f.). Interestingly, Drucker here does not explicitly refer to cybernetics but traces the concept of feedback back to John Calvin and Ignatius of Loyola. According to Drucker, the "routine feedback (...) enabled them" as early as the sixteenth century "to focus on performance and results, and with it, on achievement and satisfaction." In a similar vein, in the context of management, Drucker finds feedback to be particularly useful: It can "tell people, first, where their strengths are—and this is probably the most important thing to know about oneself. It will also show them what they do or fail to do that deprives them of the full yield from their strengths" (p. 482). Although feedback as defined in this sense works neither automatically nor immediately as, for instance, Wiener's antiaircraft predictor (AAP) was designed to function (cf. Galison, 1994), Drucker's definition of feedback is nevertheless implicitly at least partly analogous to cybernetics. For him, as for Wiener, feedback is in the first place a circular tool of control and adaptation. In fact, Drucker was aware of Wiener's antiaircraft predictor and its underlying feedback technology enabling control through adjustment, which he explicitly and affirmatively refers to when discussing automation and its impact on the firm (cf. Drucker, 2006, p. 20). For Drucker, thus, negative feedback serves as a source of information to direct the process of self-learning and correct expectations—an aim that is close to Wiener's flexible calculation of expected flight paths. It thus mirrors an intent that was also articulated in cybernetics: the assumption that the mechanisms underlying the AAP could be applied to any type of behavior—including human behavior (cf. Bigelow, Rosenblueth, & Wiener, 1943).

Additionally, in Drucker's case, feedback is a means for controlling one's own performance in various fields and to then direct one's effort to the field that proves the most effective. It is a measure to increase performance where one is capable of being productive and to let others perform where one proves rather unable to do so. Thus, this measure is based on self-observation and is in line with the imperative "Place yourself where your strengths can produce performance and results" (p. 482). For Drucker, information and advances in technology were more generally effective tools to ensure such mutual evaluation.

Thus, for Drucker, control is partly delegated to the individual to internalize and exert it in a creative and the most effective manner. At the same time, where possible, strengths should be improved and "updated": "The feedback analysis adequately shows where a person needs to improve skills or has to acquire new knowledge" (ibid.). Another key factor is what Drucker calls "relationship responsibility," i.e., one worker ought to be aware of the values of another worker while organizations should be built on mutual adaptiveness. Indeed, no longer is the manager conceived of as being in the ultimate superior position to subordinates. Rather, individuals in a corporation form flexible sub-centers. Therefore, coordination is established through mutual feedback and a constant exchange of information. It is thus relevant not only to know oneself but also to know others as well. Against this background, it is no coincidence that Drucker's concept of "Management by Objectives" ("MbO"), developed as early as 1954 and primarily for the "manager," currently reads like a manual for what sociologist Ulrich Bröckling (2016) terms the "entrepreneurial self": "What the business enterprise needs is a principle of management that will give full scope to individual strength and responsibility, and at the same time give common direction of vision and effort, establish team work, and harmonize the goals of the individual with the commonweal. (...) management by objectives and self-control (...) substitutes for control from outside the stricter, more exacting and more effective control from the inside. It motivates the manager to action not because somebody tells him to do something or talks him into doing it, but because the objective needs of his task demand it. He acts not because somebody wants him to but because he himself decides that he has to—he acts, in other words, as a free man" (Drucker, 2001, p. 126).

Drucker can be seen as a representative of an early form of systems thinking. His model of organization is based on a comprehensive approach that pictures management as an "organ" (2006, p. x) that keeps the enterprise alive. Thereby, Drucker sought to put both responsibility and autonomy in the hands of the worker for the sake of increasing overall efficiency. Being already quite explicit about the role of feedback and overall self-regulation for the sake of controlling a system, the terms were furthermore implied in some of his most influential and earliest concepts, such as the continuous set-actual-comparison as part of his "Management by Objectives." In fact, only a few years later, some of Drucker's insights would be echoed in the works of Stafford Beer, whom Norbert Wiener referred to as the "father of management cybernetics" and whose thinking one of Drucker's intellectual followers, the Swiss management expert Fredmund Malik, would later (cf. Malik, 2004a, 2004b) align with Beer's, and coin one of the most influential concepts of and practical approaches to contemporary systemic management.

ii. *Stafford Beer: On self-regulation and liberty as a "programmable function of effectiveness"*

While Drucker emphasized the importance of long-term corporate values and norms, Beer focused instead on aligning firms and industries with flexible biological models to optimize their outcome in the long run. He thus conceived of the firm as a brain and the workers as part of a larger nervous system, with their daily operations ideally processing as unconsciously as the regulatory metabolism, or the immune system, of the human body. One of Beer's prior aims was to enhance organizational robustness vis-a-vis exceeding complexity: The demand to constantly adapt to the environment to guarantee the system's long-term survival replaces, according to his radical cybernetic account, Drucker's commitment to the quasi-sovereign individual that is at least—albeit influenced by external feedback—capable of sticking to fundamental and ahistorical commitments that are independent from systemic demands. The shift from a partial reliance on normativity to a rather value-free form of effectiveness could also be witnessed in their conceptions of freedom: For Drucker, "genuine freedom (…) under the law" had to do in the first place with ensuring "performance by converting objective needs into personal goals" (1993, p. 126). Beer considered liberty as the outcome of a defined process, a "programmable function of effectiveness" (1973, p. 6) as he put it regarding "Project Cybersyn," his politico-economic approach to steer Allende's socialist Chile on the basis of feedback technologies. Beer's vision for the management context was not far from his cybernetic model of governance. Indeed, for Beer, norms seemed rather antiquated and inflexible. In his view, an enterprise was to be steered not so much on the basis of individual values influencing concrete decisions as through self-regulating, adapting, and learning, in short, by partly steering itself through reducing complexity via feedback. His idiosyncratic slogan for this processual logic was: "POSIWID"—short for "The purpose of a system is what it does" (1990, p. 128). Beer's focus was, thus, much more explicit on a dynamic system than on the individual, i.e., on "points connected by a network of relationships" (Beer, 1959, p. 7).

His systemic view of the firm as an organism also led him to conceive the mutual dependency of its various parts as the decisive factor in a firm's long-term survival, culminating in what he termed a "viable system model" (VSM). In this model, Beer radicalized Drucker's concept of "management by self-control," applying it to any element of the firm. Indeed, management was not a task exerted by the few but a common operative framework that anyone could and should participate in for the sake of what Beer defined as the new ultima ratio of the organization: self-learning aimed at ultrastability. Therefore, the prior aim of a system is to constantly produce itself. As Beer puts it autopoietically in his classic *Brain of the Firm*: "the firm really runs itself and the manager intervenes 'by exception'" (1981, p. 104). This mechanism goes hand in hand with its very own focus on the management of the organization, as exemplified by the VSM. As Beer claims, if viable systems "are to be regulated at all, they must be regulated from within" (1966, p. 263). In line with this, Beer's VSM pictured the enterprise as consisting of quasi-autonomous yet codependent subsystems. These operated in a nonlinear manner, whereby centralization and decentralization were, according to Beer, by no means contradictory but mutually complementary. Indeed, in Beer's thought, the dichotomy is eventually entirely deconstructed (cf. Beer, 1994a), with the VSM requiring "a complicated blend of central and peripheral regulatory information" (Beer, 1994a, p. 83).

Beer's aforementioned early insight that freedom in complex systems (i.e., particularly in an organization) can only be realized in a prestructured, controllable frame corresponds to this logic. While he was aware that unforeseeable events escaping the anticipation of any systems designer might occur, it was imperative for a system to adapt in such a case. Indeed, if anything escaped control, it had to be integrated for any possible future occasion. To be fair, Beer did not think in terms of power asymmetries but in terms of self-producing, flexible, and dynamic structures. However, even though discussing domination and emancipation might have escaped Beer's own conceptual scheme, they appear to be somehow entwined from the very beginning, as paradoxical as it may seem and despite the cybernetic intention to reduce classical hierarchies. Indeed, in his model, they are inscribed into the organizational structures themselves. As we will see particularly drastically regarding contemporary neocybernetic organizational models and technologies, it is only through the aporetic interplay between them that a comprehensive steering aimed at efficiency and self-stabilization can be guaranteed in the long run. Similar to Beer's model, control is here not to be exerted in a top-down fashion but by productively shaping an entire field of relations, particularly *human* relations.

Before we explicitly turn to contemporary neocybernetic theories, it is thus helpful to discuss several key concepts of an earlier theorist who specifically focused on human relations, that is, more precisely, regulatory behavior and group dynamics: Kurt Lewin.

iii. *Kurt Lewin: social regulation through feedback analysis and adaptation*

Lewin was more of a "group-dynamic social engineer" (Bröckling 2017, 201, transl. by the authors) than an explicit management theorist. However, he can be considered among the first thinkers to experiment with models of self-regulation and self-learning to enhance efficiency in a social organization and cooperation between groups. As Bröckling claims (2017, p. 202), in Lewin's—similar to Beer's—cybernetic thinking[2] the regulation of behavior was not based on the exertion or application of external norms. Rather, it followed a data-based approach of external supervision, mutual responsiveness, and permanent mediation between potentiality and actuality on the basis of an open and experimental process. In this vein, Lewin considered "social life" as a whole to be "circular in character": "Organized life is full of such circular channels. Some of these circular processes correspond to what the physical engineer calls feedback systems, that is, systems which show some kind of self-regulation" (Lewin as cited in Richardson, 1991, p. 99).

One of Lewin's central aims was to model social relations mathematically, whereby his "topological psychology" conceived of any individual as situated in an environment that could be understood as a dynamic field constantly shaping the self. Individual behavior was thus perceived as representable by a mathematical formula consisting of the variables the "self" and the "environment" (cf. Seibel, 2016, p. 136). Moreover, Lewin did not only develop the so-called three-phases-model, a still highly influential approach (for a contemporary interpretation and the extent of his influence on change management approaches, see Cummings, Bridgman, and Brown [2016]) to adjusting behavior by irritating and subsequently altering habitual patterns (the three phases being: unfreezing/changing/refreezing; see Lewin, 1947a, p. 34ff.), which was very much in line with what cyberneticists later on termed "adaptive behavior" (cf. Ashby, 1966). He can also be seen as the pioneer of an implicit proposal for 360° feedback established for a group's self-control, i.e., a form of "circular process" leading to the constitution of "a group via observing its own constitution" (Bröckling, 2017, p. 205, transl. by the authors). Participation in the group was thus not only a way of articulating demands and making one's voice heard. Even more so, it was equal to valuable information to be considered and acted upon by the rest. Any given piece of information enhanced the effectiveness and depth of self-knowledge and subsequently the chances of succeeding in self-regulation. With Drucker and Beer, Lewin thus shared a focus on measurable performance established through radical transparency and based on new "sociometric techniques" and "reliable data" (1947a, p. 8). Thereby, he considered it impossible to "predict group behavior without taking into account group goals, group standards, group values and the way a group 'sees' its own situation and that of other groups." Thus, for Lewin, experimentation with group dynamics and human interrelations was in the first place "a form of social management" (p. 9). According to him, however, it did not suffice to mainly consider only the individual or the group. Rather, to effectively change behavior and organize communication productively, it was necessary to take into account the totality of circumstances leading to decisions and particular actions: that which is currently called a "choice architecture," particularly by nudging theorists—to be considered in greater detail in the second part of this paper: "The constellation of the social field as a whole has to be studied and so reorganized that social events flow differently" (Lewin, 1947a, p. 32). Lewin's model of social regulation used feedback as a mechanism to replace centralized domination with the integrative power of mutual assessments. Such mutual evaluation should at best more or less automatically result in a willed, i.e., an individually as well as collectively desired, correction of behavior for the sake of a greater good. Objective standards, however, were equally relevant to achieve this:

> An efficient steering of social action presupposes that fact-finding methods have to be developed which permit a sufficiently realistic determination of the nature and position of the social goal and of the direction and the amount of locomotion resulting from a given action. To be effective, this fact-finding has to be linked with the action organization itself: it has to be part of a feedback system which links a reconnaissance branch of the organization with the branches which do the action. The feedback has to be done so that a discrepancy between the desired and the actual direction leads "automatically" to a correction of actions or to a change of planning. (Lewin, 1947b, p. 150)

Lewin here already anticipates a radical form of autopoiesis: The adjustment of behavior functions automatically at best, i.e., the mechanism of correction and harmonization between ought and is works immediately. Adjustment is nothing but a reaction to a registered signal and is habitualized to such an extent that it is no longer even recognizable as a major change. Thus, in contrast to the Enlightenment tradition that thought of emancipatory action as premised on the reasoned insight of the individual, here inwardness—i.e., the reasons for acting differently—plays next to no role. It is no longer relevant to know *how* and on *what grounds* change works, what merely matters is *that* change occurs as intended. Self-learning, as defined in this manner, should proceed permanently and subtly. As will be illustrated in the next section, this intention has currently become realizable to an extent rather unimaginable to Lewin—through feedback-based real-time technologies reinforcing extreme forms of adaptive, mutually adjusting and self-corrective behavior. Thus, we will now turn to new developments in neocybernetic thought, particularly Pentland's idea of social physics and Thaler's/Sunstein's idea of "nudging." As we shall argue, several of the ideas discussed by Drucker, and particularly by Beer and Lewin, are currently being radicalized and developed further—sometimes even to an extent that some of the early authors would probably not approve of.

Neocybernetic Approaches: From Systemic Management to Nudging in the Digital Service Industry

Lewin's, Beer's, and Drucker's early approaches prove significant at a time when concepts of steering, self-regulation, and homeostasis have reached entirely new practical dimensions in industrial contexts not only through the applications of smart devices and intelligent sensor systems but also through the emergence of big data-related instruments such as HR analytics, "people operations," "people analytics,"[3] "business intelligence," or "Social Media Analytics."[4] Although Beer, for example, had always been ahead of his time—as the motto of his *Brain of the Firm* (1981) put it, "If it works it's out of date"—the contemporary usage of big data in large organizations finally marks the actual condition of possibility to implement his cybernetic vision within the framework of digital capitalism (cf. Morozov, 2014; Schaupp, 2017; Vehlken, 2004). Thus, cybernetic concepts such as feedback, self-organization, and real-time control are not only implemented by start-ups or in enterprises, firms, or the headquarters of the much-discussed digital giants (e.g., Facebook, Google, Amazon). Most significantly, they have given rise to a new digital proletariat. Its most radical examples are Amazon workers and Uber drivers that are being monitored 24/7 and in real time always facing the threat of potentially falling below a specific rating (cf. Dyer-Witheford, 2017). Taking this into account, it should come as no surprise that contemporary forms of what can be termed "neocybernetic" organizational thinking both theoretically and practically exert a significant impact. Indeed, as has already been hinted at in the previous sections, Fredmund Malik's so-called systemic management, one of the most influential organizational concepts worldwide, that intends to navigate "the complexity of the new world" (2013) with cybernetic systems, is highly influenced by both Drucker and Beer and the fathers of cybernetics in general (particularly Wiener). In fact, the Malik Management Zentrum St. Gallen, which focuses on Malik's systemic approach, has even physically reconstructed Beer's Chilean Opsroom as a systemic prototype for enterprises and corporations (cf. Vehlken, 2004, p. 111ff.). Lewin, particularly his 3-phase model, proved influential in what is currently termed "change management," a broader approach at changing behavior in organizations through so-called change agents (for the most recent developments in this context, see Krüger [the 5-steps-model, 2015] and Kotter [the 8-phases-model, 1996]). Further examples are the head of the MIT media lab Alex Pentland's neocybernetic concept of "social physics" (2015a) as well as the popular method of "nudging" (Thaler and Sunstein).

i. *Nudging: Altering choice architectures, changing behavior in real time*

To start with the latter approach, which has been the focus of numerous studies and public debates in recent years, especially in the context of political governance and public policy, "nudge" is a term coined by the behavioral economist Richard Thaler and legal theorist Cass Sunstein.[5] Although significant, its impact on the digital industries has been little discussed. While nudging techniques were not specifically or exclusively developed for the management context, they are equally relevant for understanding current organizational thinking. Indeed, they have had a lasting impact on recent developments in management thought and praxis (see Braun, Cornelissen, & von Hehn, 2015; as well as Pentland, 2015b; Rothman, 2014). To name only a few prominent examples, Google offers external as well as internal nudge research on its own platform "re:work." Furthermore, Deliveroo refers explicitly to the concept in a job description for the position of a data scientist: "How can we most effectively and automatically nudge riders to maximize their earnings while providing a delightful service to our customers?" (cf. Maschewski & Nosthoff, 2018). Uber, in a similar vein, uses insights from behavioral economics to nudge its drivers into picking up more fares, often to their own disadvantage. As Scheiber (2017) points out in a *New York Times* piece,

> Employing hundreds of social scientists and data scientists, Uber has experimented with video game techniques, graphics and noncash rewards of little value that can prod drivers into working longer and harder—and sometimes at hours and locations that are less lucrative for them. To keep drivers on the road, the company has exploited some people's tendency to set earnings goals—alerting them that they are ever so close to hitting a precious target when they try to log off. It has even concocted an algorithm similar to a Netflix feature that automatically loads the next program, which many experts believe encourages binge-watching. In Uber's case, this means sending drivers their next fare opportunity before their current ride is even over. And most of this happens without giving off a whiff of coercion.

Another example is Amazon, which recently patented wristbands relying on a haptic feedback system that vibrates if a worker touches a wrong package, thus rather forcefully "nudging" him or her in the right direction (cf. Solon, 2018). Thus, as Felin (2014) claims, nudges are being used productively in various organizational areas, such as in the context of hiring, training, and developing "human capital," as well as strategy and innovation. Often, this—alongside the developments in and implementation of wearable technologies—goes hand in hand with an increase in worker surveillance and a decrease in worker privacy (cf. Ajunwa, Crawford, & Schultz, 2017). In the case of Amazon in particular, the extent of cybernetic control implemented through wearables has even been interpreted as new "digital Taylorism" (cf. Nachtwey & Staab, 2016)—a radicalization that, to be fair, Beer and Drucker would certainly not have approved of, even if Beer was an advocate of the idea of "real time control."

Similar to Pentland, whose concept of "social physics" we will subsequently discuss, nudging originally focused on implementing "initiatives that maintain freedom of choice while also steering people's decisions in the right direction (as judged by the people themselves)" (Sunstein, 2014, p. 17). The aim here is not to directly influence the individual but to alter and design the environment within which a specific choice is made. Fundamental to this is a praxis of "libertarian" or "soft paternalism," a subtle form of influence that is so tacit that it is hardly recognized by the deciding self. Thus, the individual still maintains a sense of sovereignty, although the choices surrounding him or her are externally posited in such a way as to improve the probability of a specific, desired behavior to occur.

Nudging is a prototypical example of behavioral economics that is indeed focused on opposing the ideal type figure of homo economicus and aimed at establishing a more realistic version of economic theory. One consequence of this is that behavioral economics is much more praxis-related. Similar to the sense in which Tiqqun (2001) defined the "cybernetic hypothesis",[6] the so-called choice architects are seeking not only to understand the decision-making process of individuals but also to rationalize it with the help of feedback mechanisms. That is, the aim is to set incentives that adjust behavior—in the author's own words, to "steer people's choices in directions that will improve their lives" (Sunstein & Thaler, 2008, p. 14). To install a "more correct" behavior, liberal paternalism's form of intervention is characterized by maintaining a rather paradoxical balance between self-regulation and external control (cf. Bröckling, 2017, p. 189). One prior intention is, as Sunstein (2014, p. 3) puts it poignantly, to "protect them [the deciding individuals] from themselves." The freedom to choose is thereby, as is repeatedly emphasized by the authors, not suspended but merely redefined on the basis of "micro dispositifs"[7]—i.e., practices, environments and gestures that are minimally modulated (Poljanšek, 2017, p. 23; cf. Schaupp, 2016a, pp. 26–42). A better, less euphemistic example than the often-quoted, reasonably understandable and indeed harmless cafeteria design that puts the organic apple in front of the unhealthy chocolate bar is the rather all-encompassing way in which workplaces are created to foster a productive climate. Such a climate puts collaboration, communication, and knowledge transfer first to enhance creativity, innovation, and efficiency—the abovementioned exploitative techniques of driver services such as Uber and Deliveroo are arguably the more radical examples of this trend.

Nudging, especially if viewed through the lens of its application in the context of digital industries, can thus be described as an alignment between evidence-based economics and behavioral economics (cf. Thaler, 2015, p. 348f.). Furthermore, it can be understood as a conflation between organizational experimentation, big data, and a continuous process of improvement. In this regard, nudging combines various aspects of Lewin's, Drucker's and Beer's organizational agendas. It focuses on promoting autonomy and a greater sense of responsibility while installing a frame wherein "freedom" is to be pursued. Moreover, it fosters groupwork while lowering communicative tensions, whereby the firm is conceived of as a systemic whole that partly relies on self-regulation. Indeed, according to Thaler, the explicit aim is to enable "creative evidence collection" (2015, p. 353). This is combined with the forms of self-induced adaptation on the basis of continuous learning.

As Ulrich Bröckling explains, such (neo)cybernetic mechanisms are linked to a significant paradigm shift. What Michel Foucault had still characterized as the disciplinary formula "une aptitude majorée et une domination accrue [an increased aptitude and an enhanced domination]" (Foucault 1977, p. 138) is in applied nudging theory replaced by "*docilité/docility*, the capacity and willingness to learn and to behave according to social demands." According to Bröckling, thereby "steerability replaces obedience" (2017, p. 182, transl. by the authors). In this regard, the permanent promotion of adaptation can be envisioned as a steady feedback loop, a way of constantly mediating between ought and is, potentiality and actuality. The working individual is thus described as a flexible self. Flexibility, however, is defined merely as the imperative to adapt and react to external feedback. It delineates the need to optimize oneself via navigating through the interfaces of options to maximize the outcomes of the whole organization. As such, individuals find themselves steadily within mechanisms of observation, attention, and mutual assessment. As Richard Thaler (2015, p. 357) himself notes affirmatively, "The ideal organizational environment encourages everyone to observe, collect data, and speak up."

In this process, the central figure remains—albeit faceless and invisible—the choice architect. This is a figure of subtle consultancy, occupying a place at a distance from things and the individuals that he or she is attempting to shape. At the same time, choice architects also intervene in the internal processes to decisively cocreate them—starting from algorithmic automation to the development of facilities. Through this, the organization is often redesigned in the mode of trial and error—or, as Pentland terms it, it is restructured as a "living laboratory" to detect "behavior patterns" (2014, p. 218). However, in the long run, the choice architect ideally becomes superfluous: Any employee should become an observer not only of himself or herself but also of his or her environment to the point that external regulation is no longer needed.

What is often presented as a process of decentralization and emancipation, as a "democratized panoptism," can thus be equally viewed as quite the opposite, as a form of "enhanced domination" (Bröckling, 2017, p. 182, transl. by the authors). Freedom thus equals, quietly reminiscent of Beer's concept of a programmable liberty, the freedom to adapt oneself. In line with this, freedom of choice merely entails the "freedom" to choose more rationally. Bearing in mind the aforementioned applied nudges of Uber and Deliveroo, it seems obvious that behavioral economics thus tends to radicalize techniques of bio- and psychopolitical self-control and self-regulation. Indeed, behavioral economics explicitly considers new digital technologies as a fruitful basis for its approach.[8] Especially given the contemporary cybernetic-capitalist frames of application, it reinforces not a turning away but rather a radicalization of the marketization and cybernetization of human relations in general and those in the organization in particular. It is specifically regarding new forms of data collection that applied behavioral economics enables a new professional management of the self, a form of Big Nudging, which reframes the "good shepherd" as a "utopia of machines" (2017, p. 193) and materializes as a never-ending process, an endless feedback loop that permanently moves on. Precisely, this horizon is alluded to by Sunstein and Thaler when they portray the ultimate aim of nudging as providing people with "automatic systems without getting into terrible trouble" (2008, p. 83). Indeed, the aim of such a system is fundamentally cybernetic: to maintain an ultrastable homeostatic balance.

ii. *Social Physics: Changing the social fabric by influencing "peer-to-peer behavior"*

To finally turn our focus to an arguably even more radical and timely neo-cybernetic agenda, the MIT professor and consultant (among others, for Google) Alex Pentland has cultivated the influential[9] approach of what he terms "network science," which—and this is very close to Beer's focus on the dynamics of a system—"tries to understand people in the context of their social networks rather than viewing them as isolated individuals" (2008, p. x; cf. Schaupp, 2017). Individuals are thus considered in the larger context of their milieus. In contrast to Auguste Comte's "physique sociale," which is often considered the origin of sociology, Pentland's social physics does not stop at merely understanding and examining behavior. As we will argue subsequently, his focus is rather on changing it (cf. Zuboff, 2019, p. 416ff.; cf. Maschewski & Nosthoff, 2019c, pp. 39–63).

Consider, however, first, the parallels to cybernetics: Pentland draws analogies between animal and human behavior, as well as between corporations and nervous systems that are, in the first place, self-regulating. This is very similar to Beer's cybernetic focus on organisms. Moreover, Pentland focuses on measuring what he terms biological "honest signals" (four examples of which are influence, mimicry, activity, and consistency). According to him, honest signals are secret insofar as they can be measured and—this again is a cybernetic motif—"used to control behavior" (p. xiii). These signals are unconscious yet detectable with the help of big data and digital tools such as "sociometers"[10] and computerized feedback systems. A practical example of their use is the prediction of the outcome of salary negotiations and forms of group behavior. The aim is to develop the capacity to read social signaling to better "govern[ing] ourselves" and to be able to anticipate "when the group is moving towards problems like groupthink and polarization" (p. 51). In other words, the prior motif is to decrease the likelihood of unwanted behavior occurring while reducing undesired interruptions to basically guarantee the functioning of the whole. Pentland's general advice to managers sums this up as follows:

> If you want to make wise decisions, then be sure to spend time reading your organization's network intelligence. Create an open environment through the face-to-face promotion of trust and empathy so that it becomes easy to read the signaling. Spend time reading your group's signaling around each issue, taking care to adjust for the problems of idiots and gossip. By utilizing your group's inherent network intelligence, you can reliably make better decisions than you could on your own. (p. 68)

In addition, Pentland claims that honest signals lead to increased interest and engagement and to more trust and empathy, thus fostering overall performance. Similar to Beer, control here emerges from installing sociometric devices in a decentralized manner and via promoting processes of self-learning based on positive feedback, that is, a form of signal-response mechanism that reinforces desired forms of behavior while weakening unwanted patterns. With this in mind, Pentland's intentions seem similar to Thaler's and Sunstein's intentions. However, Pentland's focus is on influencing the interrelations *between* humans and not so much on changing the choice architecture. His aim is to shape the social fabric by implementing quantifiable incentives that modify interactions. Such a focus on the network and on "peer-to-peer behavior" as distinct from "individual behavior" is, according to him, at least twice as efficient as mainly focusing on the isolated self. The former largely rests on adaptation, a term that became extremely popular during the rise of cybernetics as a science (for instance, in the works of W. Ross Ashby or Norbert Wiener).[11]

One of Pentland's experimental examples of adjusting "peer-to-peer behavior" refers to the attempt to raise the overall activity level of a group during a lazy winter. There were two groups: one in which people were rewarded with a specific amount of money according to their activity level and a second one in which people were assigned buddies. In the second group, a reward was given not in the case that one had maximized one's own activity level but if one's buddy increased his or her activity. In other words, an individual's assigned buddy got rewarded for the individual being active. Pentland's experimental results showed that the second group was far more effective due to the extent of interactions between people and the structures of mutual control and responsibility established between them (cf. 2014).

Pentland here indeed radicalizes what Lewin had envisioned decades before him—promoting the "healthy signaling" of the "social circuitry of a work group" (2008, p. xi), albeit now with the help of smart devices allegedly providing us with a "'God's eye' view of ourselves" (p. x). Thus, although the entire mechanism described here works on the basis of self-regulation, the overall aim is to be able to maintain control of the process of the whole by creating visibility, metric transparency, and foreseeability. In this vein, it is hardly surprising that autonomy or freedom of choice plays next to no role in Pentland's model given that his entire approach explains human behavior as based on imitation and mimicry as opposed to reasonable choice and deliberate purpose—the model of which is, as he puts it, the "homo imitans." Against this background, it can be argued that Pentland even radicalizes Thaler's and Sunstein's agenda, as his anthropological premise of the homo imitans leaves even less room for the conception of freedom.

As we will now argue in a concluding paragraph, what emerges here is a form of integral power that rests on the picture of the individual being adjustable and regulatable. Therefore, techniques that the Californian counterculture has in particular understood to be potentially liberatory (cf. Turner, 2006), in the sense that they promise to allow broader participation and greater organization from the bottom-up and thus greater freedom, are often entangled with forms of control that, as we claim, need to be taken into account when addressing the question of emancipation in the era of digitization, particularly when examining the scales and dimensions of emancipation in the digital industries. Thus, now that we have examined the current renaissance of the basic cybernetic concepts implicit in current approaches to organizational thought, we conclude by briefly analyzing the concept of the individual that they rely upon and tacitly reproduce when implemented in the industrial context. We then conclude with a brief reflection on what this transformation of subjectivity means for a praxis of emancipation.

Self-Control as Emancipation? On a New Form of Integral Power

Just as early management cybernetics and systems thought implicitly left behind the picture of the rational decider, neocybernetic approaches to organization now explicitly leave behind *homo oeconomicus*. As is particularly exemplified by the thought of Alex Pentland, neocybernetic approaches are based on the supposition of a highly flexible, adaptive individual. Thus, the individual is considered capable of repositioning himself or herself in milieus of changing circumstances by responding to them in an anticipatable manner. Eventually, a subject thus emerges that develops by constantly responding to external feedback, a subject that becomes manifest through the imperatives of self-learning and incentive-based adaptation. Arguably, the neoliberal intensification of competitive structures only accelerates this development.[12] Not surprisingly, the aforementioned cyberneticist Stafford Beer already pictured a similar shift: from homo faber to what he termed “homo gubernator” (1994b, p. 35), i.e., an individual who is capable of regulating and steering himself or herself.

Eventually, these critical developments raise the question of whether the notion of a controllable or “programmable” freedom allows for any emancipation at all, if understood in the sense of a reduction of domination. Rather than paralleling decentralization with a necessary simultaneous increase in freedom in the sense proposed by both cybernetic and neocybernetic systems, it could be argued that what we are currently confronted with is rather a new type and form of domination. This form of domination is based on the interdependence between participation, viz. freedom, and control. In fact, this aporetic relation lies, as we have shown with regard to earlier cybernetic theories, at the very heart of cybernetic organizational thinking per se.

Relying on Günther Anders's early critique of cybernetics, it could be argued that we are currently witnessing a vast expansion of a form of *integral* domination. Thus, *integrality* delineates both the mathematical frame imposed upon the cybernetic subject in industrial contexts (through techniques of quantification and evaluation in real time, "HR Analytics," "people operations" as well as nudges in the workplace such as the exploitative techniques of Amazon, Uber, and Deliveroo) as well as the cybernetic tendency to force adaptation and integration through constant feedback. As Anders foresaw, "integral power" is effective while preserving the illusion of freedom. It operates on the basis of invisibility (cf. Maschewski & Nosthoff, 2019b). As he writes in the typically radical tone of his philosophy, a philosophy that presumes that truth can only be expressed in the mode of exaggeration,

> Of course, where commands and prohibitions are no longer necessary, the impression emerges that commands and prohibitions are no (longer) there: that is, the illusion of freedom. This illusion is the great chance of those who are interested in the production of perfect unfreedom. And one cannot say that they leave the opportunity unseized. In fact, the deprivation of liberty of a person goes hand in hand with the ideology of freedom; and the abolition of freedom takes place in the name of freedom. (Anders 1998, p. 195; transl. by the authors)

Thus, control is internalized and delegated to the self, an approach that dates back to Drucker and that became radicalized throughout the works of Stafford Beer, culminating in Pentland's timely notion of self-regulatory "social physics." Through this what Deleuze had depicted as "ultrarapid forms of free-floating control" (1992, p. 4) are installed, whereby not only norms but also any explicit external objectives become (partly) superfluous. While Thaler and Sunstein still rely on the intervention of a choice architect to increase the likelihood of a specific behavior occurring, Pentland's approach works solely on the basis of mutual adaptation. What Beer had characterized as the main principle of a functioning system is thereby revitalized, i.e., an external, regulating power intervenes only "by exception." Andreas Bernard (2017, p. 198; transl. by the authors) refers to this as "a power of internalization," reinforcing a condition in which "archives of registration and normative conceptions of life are no longer enforced by an external authority but are collectively internalized." According to him, the imperatives thus enforced subsequently "go without saying," as "they have transformed from instructions to desires."

Taking these developments into account, a praxis of emancipation is confronted with the problem that the boundaries between decentralization and centralization, freedom and regulation are not easily detectable. Rather, they are inscribed into the very structures on the basis of which dynamic and flexible organizations operate. Indeed, what can be witnessed is a decisive shift from the (precybernetic) power of the powerful—a form of centralized power—to the (cybernetic) power of processes. Thus, control is installed rather decentralized and emerges through self-regulation practices. A second difficulty in the context of digital industries is, therefore, the aporetic entanglement between participation and control, whereby any new data and any additional information tend to easily become a helpful tool within a greater agenda of workplace surveillance. As Wendy Chun has recently argued, paradoxically enough in the era of Big Data, "constant participation grounds surveillance" (2016, p. 367). As we have shown in this article, this relation is reflected in some problematic conflations that have already dominated early cybernetic concepts of organizations, in particular, between freedom and control. These are currently being revitalized in neocybernetic theories, some of which are designed to be practically implemented in the digital industrial workplace of the twenty-first century. As such, the forms of nudging applied in this context are, for the most part, not freedom preserving but rather flexible dispositifs of control influencing the unconscious. Indeed, as Sunstein himself critically highlights, certain forms of "nudging" need to be characterized as "not sufficiently engag[ing] or appeal[ing] to their [the nudged individuals'] capacity for reflection and deliberation" and are thus illegitimate (2016, p. 82).

Thus, such techniques are posing challenges to the emancipatory praxis understood not only in its classical Enlightenment articulation, i.e., as based on autonomy, on giving oneself one's own laws independent of external guidance. It also holds in view of more recent definitions, such as that provided by Jacques Rancière, who understands emancipation as a different way of inhabiting a collectively shared sensible world, provoking a "rupture in the order of things" (2003, p. 219). Indeed, neocybernetic techniques such as nudging pose challenges to emancipation precisely because they are *integral*. As such, they run through the individual without necessarily having to be consciously internalized at all. Consequently, the resulting process of adaptation is no longer dependent on imperatives that are explicitly addressed to the self. Indeed, Pentland (2014) claims that his experiment to increase the activity of peer-to-peer-groups at some point did not even require any active setting of incentives on behalf of the experimenters anymore. For "being active" had become not only a "topic of conversation" but also "a topic of social pressure, of prestige, of interest." That is, the "social fabric" had fundamentally changed in the long term—the network finally reached the stage of succeeding self-regulation, whereby external interference had become entirely superfluous.

More than half a century ago, Max Horkheimer (cf. 1947) detected the emergence of a form of instrumental rationality as the greatest challenge for a reasonable praxis of emancipation in an increasingly technical age. In our current neocybernetic era of postindustrial governmentality, this challenge is additionally confronted with the expansion of algorithmically enforced forms of adaptive behavior. Their purpose is collective and reproductive self-regulation, or to put it in cybernetic terms, ultrastability maintained through flexible adjustment. Relying on Dieter Mersch's (2017) critical analysis regarding the digital condition, what is currently needed, above all, as a first step in the development of a novel praxis of emancipation—such as the building of alternative "organized networks" (cf. Lovink, 2016)—is a new "critique of algorithmic reason":

> New, different, and substantiated positions or creative answers must instead be found that are capable of prompting paradigm changes, but that can't be covered statistically because they don't correspond to the norm. [...] We really need an analysis of algorithmic conditions and their paradoxes and ambiguities that gives them an adequate framework and horizon. But instead we currently seem to be finding an algorithmic solution of the algorithmic [...]. This tends to result in a circularity that leaves the drawing of boundaries and raising of barriers solely to programming, instead of restoring them to our ethical conscience and understanding of what the social could mean today.

Notes

1. This particularly holds if emancipation is understood not only in a classically Kantian sense, i.e., as the self-determined use of one's own reason, but also in Rancière's (cf. 2010) sense as the provocation of fissures and ruptures in the shared social fabric that we inhabit. As such, emancipation is, in the following, understood in the first place as a social praxis seeking to reduce domination.
2. It is probably not insignificant to mention that Lewin was among the participants of the famous Macy Conferences at the beginning of the 1940s in New York, together with, among others, several of the most prominent figures in cybernetics that Lewin was closely related to: Gregory Bateson, Norbert Wiener, and Margaret Mead.
3. HR analytics encompasses a series of tools to enhance the overall productivity of organizations, e.g., algorithmic predictions of future employer behavior and satisfaction, and the use of artificial intelligence to select suitable candidates for a firm based on the analysis of speech, gestures, body language, and voice tone via sociometric badges to predict performance factors within teams. Google is one of the leaders in this area, as HR is reinvented there under the rubric of "people operations." According to Sullivan (2013), Google "doesn't dictate, it convinces with data," it "influences people to change" in the workplace on the basis of algorithmically predicting which candidates have "the highest probability of succeeding after they are hired."
4. As Sinha et al. (2012) write regarding "Social Media Analytics," "Organizations adopt Social Media Analytics to engage employees by fostering collaboration resulting in productivity enhancements. According to IBM (…), social media analytics enables organizations to gain deeper insights not only into customers but also into employees' sentiments."
5. While Thaler and Sunstein do not explicitly draw analogies between nudging and cybernetics, nudging implicitly revitalizes a cybernetic logic, as it intends to increase the probability of a desired behavior occurring. In this vein, it can be interpreted as a mechanism to decrease future complexity and entropy. Moreover, the early behavioral economist Herbert Simon, one of Thaler's predecessors, explicitly suggested feedback as a model for human behavior (cf. Richardson, 1991, p. 3). Furthermore, Felix Stalder (2017, p. 170) reads nudge theory as analogous to what Tiqqun (2001) termed the "cybernetic hypothesis". According to him, similar to the cybernetic model of the individual, a nudge conceptualizes the subject as a black box where what matters are solely the inputs and outputs, i.e., the stimuli and the reactions provoked by them: "By the term 'liberal hypothesis,' Tiqqun meant the assumption, stemming from the time

of the Enlightenment, that people could improve themselves by applying their own reason and exercising their own moral faculties, and could free themselves from ignorance through education and reflection. (...) The liberal hypothesis is based on human understanding. The cybernetic hypothesis is not. Its conception of humans is analogous to its conception of animals, plants, and machines; like the latter, people are organisms that react to stimuli from their environment."

6. Tiqqun (2001) defines the "cybernetic hypothesis" as the epistemic suggestion to "conceive biological, physical, and social behaviors as something integrally programmed and re-programmable. More precisely, it conceives of each individual behavior as something 'piloted,' in the last analysis, by the need for the survival of a 'system' that makes it possible, and which it must contribute to."
7. Tom Poljanšek defines the nudge in reference to David Eugster (2013, p. 57) as a "micro dispositif": "Microdispositifs are small elements such as buildings, rooms, devices and practices that, as Agamben explains regarding the mobile phone, influence the gestures and forms of behavior of individuals" (2017, p. 23).
8. To name one prominent example in this context, Cass R. Sunstein euphorically refers to the possibilities offered by new digital technologies: "We can imagine a whole universe of behavioral apps, specifically designed to help people to counteract the mistakes to which they are prone" (2014, p. 10).
9. As Zuboff (2019, p. 417f.) points out, Pentland's MIT Lab is financed by, among others, Google, Cisco, IBM, Deloitte, Twitter, and Verizon while more than 50 of Pentland's former PhD candidates are now working in the fields of data analytics and behavioral sciences, applying his theories to the workplace, organizations, and/or cities.
10. Sociometers is short for "sociometric badges," i.e., instruments that are worn by employees to capture data, such as their physical interactions in an enterprise. According to Pentland, the aim is to make employees aware of instances when they "aren't interacting correctly" (Pentland as cited in Berman, 2016) and thus allegedly making "bad decisions."
11. On the adaptive conception of the individual in early cybernetic thinking, see for instance Bigelow, Rosenblueth, and Wiener (1943) as well as Ashby's *Design for a Brain* (1966).
12. Competitiveness is increased not least by engaging in practices of gamification; i.e., it is also *technologically* reinforced (cf. Dymek & Zackariasson, 2017).

Bibliography

Ajunwa, I., Crawford, K., & Schultz, J. (2017). Limitless Worker Surveillance. *California Law Review, 105*, 735–776.

Anders, G. (1998). *Die Antiquiertheit des Menschen, Bd. II. Über die Zerstörung des Lebens im Zeitalter der dritten Revolution*. Munich: C.H. Beck.

Ashby, W. R. (1966). *Design for a Brain: The Origins of Adaptive Behavior*. London: Chapman & Hall.

Beer, S. (1959). *Cybernetics and Management*. New York: Wiley.

Beer, S. (1966). *Decision and Control: The Meaning of Operational Research and Management Cybernetics*. New York: Wiley.

Beer, S. (1973). *Fanfare for Effective Freedom. Cybernetic Praxis in Government*. Brighton: Brighton Polytechnic.

Beer, S. (1981). *Brain of the Firm*. New York: Wiley.

Beer, S. (1990). *Diagnosing the Systems for Organisations*. New York: Wiley.

Beer, S. (1994a). *Designing Freedom*. New York: Wiley.

Beer, S. (1994b). *Platform for Change*. New York: Wiley.

Berman, A. E. (2016). MIT's Sandy Pentland: Big Data Can Be a Profoundly Humanizing Force in Industry. *Singularity Hub*. Retrieved from https://singularityhub.com/2016/05/16/mits-sandy-pentland-big-data-can-be-a-profoundly-humanizing-force-in-industry/#sm.000013ul87680cdccw6vixh-d467rr.

Bernard, A. (2017). *Komplizen des Erkennungsdienstes. Das Selbst in der digitalen Kultur*. Frankfurt a.M.: S. Fischer.

Bigelow, J., Rosenblueth, A., & Wiener, N. (1943). Behavior, Purpose, Teleology. *Philosophy of Science, 10*(1), 18–24.

Braun, C., Cornelissen, N. I., & von Hehn, S. (2015). *Kulturwandel in Organisationen. Ein Baukasten für angewandte Psychologie im Change-Management*. Berlin and Heidelberg: Springer.

Bröckling, U. (2016). *The Entrepreneurial Self: Fabricating a New Type of Subject*. London: Sage.

Bröckling, U. (2017). *Gute Hirten führen sanft. Über Menschenregierungskünste*. Berlin: Suhrkamp.

Chun, W. (2016). Big Data as Drama. *ELH, 83*(2), 363–382.

Cummings, S., Bridgman, T., & Brown, K. G. (2016). Unfreezing Change as Three Steps: Rethinking Kurt Lewin's Legacy for Change Management. *Human Relations, 69*(1), 33–60.

Deleuze, G. (1992). Postscript on the Societies of Control. *October, 59*, 3–7.

Drucker, P. (1993). *Management* (rev. ed.). New York: HarperCollins.

Drucker, P. (2001). *The Essential Drucker*. Oxford: Butterworth-Heinemann.

Drucker, P. (2006). *The Practice of Management*. New York: HarperCollins.

Dyer-Witheford, N. (2017). *Cyber-Proletariat: Global Labour in the Digital Vortex*. London: Pluto.

Dymek, M., & Zackariasson, P. (Eds.). (2017). *The Business of Gamification: A Critical Analysis*. London: Routledge.

Eugster, D. (2013). Mikrodispositive: Die kurze Geschichte eines Automatenladens. In J. Caborn Wengler, B. Hoffarth, & Ł. Kumięga (Eds.), *Verortungen des Dispositiv-Begriffs. Analytische Einsätze zu Raum, Bildung, Politik* (pp. 57–72). Wiesbaden: Springer.

Felin, T. (2014, November 13). *Nudge: Manager as Choice Architect* (Oxford Said Business School Working Paper 2014–13). Retrieved from https://papers.ssrn.com/sol3/papers.cfm?abstract_id=2523922.

Foucault, M. (1977). *Discipline and Punish: The Birth of the Prison*. New York: Pantheon Books.

Galison, P. (1994). The Ontology of the Enemy: Norbert Wiener and the Cybernetic Vision. *Critical Inquiry, 21*(1), 228–266.

Horkheimer, M. (1947). *Eclipse of Reason*. Oxford: Oxford University Press.

Hörl, E., & Hagner, M. (Eds.). (2008). *Die Transformation des Humanen: Beiträge zur Kulturgeschichte der Kybernetik*. Berlin: Suhrkamp.

Kotter, J. P. (1996). *Leading Change*. Boston: Harvard Business School Press.

Krüger, W., & Bach, N. (2015). *Excellence in Change: Wege zur strategischen Erneuerung*. Wiesbaden: Springer.

Lewin, K. (1947a). Frontiers in Group Dynamics: Concept, Method and Reality in Social Science; Social Equilibria and Social Change. *Human Relations, 1,* 5–41.

Lewin, K. (1947b). Frontiers in Group Dynamics, Part II-B: Feedback Problems of Social Diagnosis and Action. *Human Relations, 1,* 147–153.

Lovink, G. (2016). *Social Media Abyss: Critical Internet Cultures and the Force of Negation*. Cambridge: Polity.

Malik, F. (2004a). *Systemisches Management, Evolution, Selbstorganisation – Grundprobleme, Funktionsmechanismen und Lösungsansätze für komplexe Systeme*. Bern: Haupt.

Malik, F. (2004b). Konservatismus und effektives Management: Wege aus der Orientierungskrise. In P. F. Drucker & P. Paschek (Eds.), *Kardinaltugenden effektiver Führung* (pp. 25–40). Heidelberg: Redline.

Malik, F. (2013). *Strategy: Navigating the Complexity of the World*. Chicago: University of Chicago Press.

Maschewski, F., & Nosthoff, A. (2018, September 27). *Das Silicon Valley schafft die Freiheit ab – im Namen der Freiheit*. Retrieved from https://www.republik.ch/2018/09/27/das-silicon-valley-schafft-die-freiheit-ab-im-namen-der-freiheit.

Maschewski, F., & Nosthoff, A. (2019a). 'We Have to Coordinate the Flow' oder: Die Sozialphysik des Anstoßes. Zum Steuerungs- und Regelungsdenken neokybernetischer Politiken. In A. Friedrich et al. (Eds.), *Jahrbuch Technikphilosophie 2019, Steuern und Regeln* (pp. 31–46). Baden-Baden: Nomos.

Maschewski, F., & Nosthoff, A. (2019b). The Obsolescence of Politics: Rereading Günther Anders's Critique of Cybernetic Governance and Integral Power in the Digital Age. *Thesis Eleven, 153*(1), 75–93.

Maschewski, F., & Nosthoff, A. (2019c). *Die Gesellschaft der Wearables. Digitale Verführung und soziale Kontrolle*. Berlin: Nicolai Publishing & Intelligence.

Mau, S. (2017). *Das metrische Wir. Über die Quantifizierung des Sozialen*. Berlin: Suhrkamp.

Meißner, S. (2015). *Techniken des Sozialen. Gestaltung und Organisation des Zusammenarbeitens in Unternehmen*. Wiesbaden: Springer.

Mersch, D. (2017, October 12). *Digital Criticism: A Critique of 'Algorithmic' Reason*. Retrieved from https://www.diaphanes.net/titel/digital-criticism-5313.

Moore, P. V. (2017). *The Quantified Self in Precarity: Work, Technology and What Counts*. London: Routledge.

Morozov, E. (2014, October 6). *The Socialist Origins of Big Data*. Retrieved from https://www.newyorker.com/magazine/2014/10/13/planning-machine.

Nachtwey, O., & Staab, P. (2016, April 29). *Die Digitalisierung der Dienstleistungsgesellschaft*. Retrieved from http://www.bpb.de/apuz/225692/die-digitalisierung-der-dienstleistungsarbeit?p=all.

Pentland, A. (2008). *Honest Signals: How They Shape Our World*. Cambridge, MA: MIT Press.

Pentland, A. (2014, March 7). *Social Physics: How Good Ideas Spread*. Retrieved from https://talksat.withgoogle.com/talk/social-physics.

Pentland, A. (2015a). *Social Physics: How Social Networks Can Make Us Smarter*. London: Penguin Books.

Pentland, A. (2015b, April 25). *Social Physics Can Change Your Company (and the World)*. Retrieved from https://www.wnyc.org/story/401-social-physics-can-change-your-company-and-the-world/.

Pias, C. (2004). Unruhe und Steuerung. Zum utopischen Potential der Kybernetik. In J. Rüsen (Ed.), *Die Unruhe der Kultur. Potentiale des Utopischen* (pp. 301–325). Weilerswist: Velbrück.

Poljanšek, T. (2017). Die Vorstrukturierung des Möglichen – Latenz und Technisierung. In A. Friedrich et al. (Eds.), *Jahrbuch Technikphilosophie 2017, Technisches Nichtwissen* (pp. 17–40). Baden-Baden: Nomos.

Rancière, J. (2003). *The Philosopher and His Poor*. Durham and London: Duke University Press.

Rancière, J. (2010). *Dissensus: On Politics and Aesthetics*. London: Continuum.

Richardson, G. P. (1991). *Feedback Thought in Social Science and Systems Theory*. Philadelphia: University of Pennsylvania Press.

Rothman, J. (2014, June 3). *Big Data Comes to the Office*. Retrieved from https://www.newyorker.com/books/joshua-rothman/big-data-comes-to-the-office.

Schaupp, S. (2016a). *Digitale Selbstüberwachung. Self-Tracking im kybernetischen Kapitalismus.* Münster: Verlag Graswurzelrevolution.

Schaupp, S. (2016b). 'Wir nennen es flexible Selbstkontrolle': Self-Tracking als Selbsttechnologie des kybernetischen Kapitalismus. In S. Duttweiler et al. (Eds.), *Leben nach Zahlen: Self-Tracking als Optimierungsprojekt?* (pp. 63–86). Bielefeld: transcript.

Schaupp, S. (2017). Vergessene Horizonte. Der Kapitalismus und seine Alternativen. In P. Buckermann et al. (Eds.), *Kybernetik, Kapitalismus, Revolutionen* (pp. 51–74). Münster: Unrast.

Scheiber, N. (2017, April 2). *How Uber Uses Psychological Tricks to Push Its Driver's Buttons.* Retrieved from https://www.nytimes.com/interactive/2017/04/02/technology/uber-drivers-psychological-tricks.html?_r=0.

Seibel, B. (2016). *Cybernetic Government: Informationstechnologie und Regierungsrationalität von 1943–1970.* Wiesbaden: Springer.

Sinha, V., et al. (2012). The Contemporary Framework on Social Media Analytics as an Emerging Tool for Behaviour Informatics, HR Analytics and Business Process. *Management, 17*(2), 65–84.

Solon, O. (2018, February 1). *Amazon Patents Wristband That Tracks Warehouse Workers' Movements.* Retrieved from https://www.theguardian.com/technology/2018/jan/31/amazon-warehouse-wristband-tracking.

Stalder, F. (2017). *The Digital Condition.* London: Polity.

Sullivan, J. (2013, February 26). *How Google Is Using People Analytics to Completely Reinvent HR.* Retrieved from https://www.tlnt.com/how-google-is-using-people-analytics-to-completely-reinvent-hr/.

Sunstein, C. R. (2014). *Why Nudge? The Politics of Libertarian Paternalism.* New Haven: Yale University Press.

Sunstein, C. R. (2016). *The Ethics of Influence: Government in the Age of Behavioral Science.* New York: Cambridge University Press.

Sunstein, C. R., & Thaler, R. H. (2008). *Nudge: Improving Decisions About Health, Wealth, and Happiness.* New Haven: Yale University Press.

Tiqqun. (2001). *The Cybernetic Hypothesis.* Retrieved from http://theanarchistlibrary.org/library/tiqqun-the-cybernetic-hypothesis.

Thaler, R. H. (2015). *Misbehaving: The Making of Behavioral Economics.* New York: W.W. Norton & Company.

Traue, B. (2010). *Das Subjekt der Beratung. Zur Soziologie einer Psycho-Technik.* Bielefeld: transcript.

Turner, F. (2006). *From Counterculture to Cyberculture: Stewart Brand, the Whole Earth Network and the Rise of Digital Utopianism.* Chicago and London: The University of Chicago Press.

Vehlken, S. (2004). *Environment for Decision – Die Medialität einer kybernetischen Staatsregierung*. Retrieved from http://homepage.univie.ac.at/sebastian.vehlken/files/2007_04_04_Magisterarbeit%20Cybersyn%20Sebastian%20Vehlken.pdf.

Wiener, N. (1948). *Cybernetics: Or Control and Communication in the Animal and the Machine*. Cambridge, MA: MIT Press.

Zuboff, S. (2019). *The Age of Surveillance Capitalism: The Fight for a Human Future at the New Frontier of Power*. London: Profile Books.

CHAPTER 5

It's All in the Game: Emancipation in Digitalized Working Environments

Janosch Schobin and Philipp Staab

Introduction

Much of the discussion on autonomy and emancipation in digital environments—be it in commercial or non-commercial parts of the Internet—has focused on the character of digital publics. While techno-enthusiasts claim that digitalization offers new ways of participation, broader inclusion in decision making, and more democratic control (e.g., Dahlberg, 2011), critics focus on the commercialization, fragmentation, and expansion of political control over the Internet (e.g., Gunitsky, 2015).

With an increase in the digitalization of work spaces, this discussion has reached the shop floor. We argue that, in the case of emancipation at work, the distinction between non-commercial environments as emancipation and autonomy friendly vs. commercial environments as hostile to it needs modification. Capitalist work is by definition a site of commercialization, first of all of labor itself. Therefore, the question about the possibilities of emancipation in digitalized work environments needs to be addressed in a different way compared to the question of the defense

J. Schobin (✉) · P. Staab
University of Kassel, Humboldt University, Berlin, Germany
e-mail: jschobin@uni-kassel.de

U. Meyer et al. (eds.), *Digitalization in Industry*,
https://doi.org/10.1007/978-3-030-28258-5_5

and expansion of the digital commons against the appropriation and monopolization of the Internet by commercial entities.

We argue that an ontological approach is helpful in evaluating the potential of emancipation in digitalized workplaces. In our view, digitization is in many ways gamification (i.e., the introduction of game routines and game elements into non-gaming contexts). We argue that the success in applying digital technologies (especially software) to the working world, roughly from the 1980s to the present, is based on their ability to offer gamified interfaces to users. As sociology of technology has shown time and time again, the application of new technologies regularly meets resistance (be it direct opposition or forms of misuse) from users (e.g., Degele, 1994; Latour, 1996). Gamification can be understood as a strategy to ensure cooperation from users.

This observation begs the question of how digital games and game elements fit into the regulation and the control of work processes. Roughly observed gamification practices can be linked to both: to an intensification of direct modes as well as to the broadening of indirect modes of labor process control.

However, this observation should be taken with a grain of salt. While the "control gap" (Raffetseder, Schaupp, & Staab, 2017) in the regulation of labor processes has probably diminished over the past decade, due to the implementation of systems of algorithmic control, the historical observation of the adaption of gamified digital technologies offers evidence for the assumption that users still manage to develop certain amounts of autonomy in gamified contexts by applying specific strategies. We argue that the level of user autonomy achieved in gamified work situations can be described in three skill steps, listed below.

- Adaption: the ability to play the game with few capabilities of leaving the game's formal frame;
- Mastery: the ability to play the game well, therefore offering opportunities for autonomy beyond the game;
- Subversion: the ability to change the rules of the game, thereby offering opportunities for autonomy inside the game.

Thus, a digitally highly skilled workforce will not only be able to adapt to digitalized and, therefore, gamified modes of control. They will be able to change the "rules of the game" (e.g., by tampering with code or by rearranging the use of digital systems) and, by this, substantially widen the control gap. Foreseeably, the reaction of management to workers' mastery and subversion skills will be to install even more complex systems of recursive control. Recursive control—enabled by the constant feedback of user experience into the control system—can be understood as the attempt to include every strategy of mastery and subversion into the overall goals of the gamified system, which means a tighter control of management over labor. We argue, therefore, that the social conflict particular to digitalized work situations develops around the conflicting principles of recursive control vs. emancipation through mastery and subversion. It will, thus, be strongly shaped by the accumulation and distribution of digital competency and literacy throughout the workforce.

Early Digitalization as a Gamification Process

Since the early 1990s, sociology has been intensively working on the question of why computers suddenly became a common everyday object in the mid-1980s (Degele, 1994, 1996; Rammert et al., 1991; Wehner & Rammert, 1990). From the very beginning, sociological research in technology has been directed against the popular notion in economics that the spread of computers was due to a combination of tendencies toward rationalization in companies and the resulting qualification needs within the private sector.

The rationalization hypothesis still applies today. The intensive, ongoing debate about whether computers have contributed to increasing the productivity of modern capitalist enterprises is not just confined to sociology (Acemoglu, Autor, Dorn, Hanson, & Price, 2014; Brynjolfsson, 1993). "You can see the computer age everywhere but in the productivity statistics," said American Nobel Prize winner Robert Solow, summarizing the empirical findings from an economic perspective as long ago as the late 1980s (Solow, 1987). In the context of the so-called secular stagnation thesis, economist Robert Gordon currently argued that the productivity gains made by computer technology have been falling sharply since the end of the "dot.com" era (Gordon, 2015).

On the other hand, hope is articulated in many places for delayed rationalization gains on the basis of an understanding of digital technology as a basic technology, and this viewpoint is prominently represented by Frey and Osborne (2013), for example. They justify the lack of the great rationalization wave caused by computer technology with a recurring pattern in industrial development: As a rule, rationalization gains from new basic technologies do not become apparent until decades after their invention, once a certain market maturity has been reached. The overall social structure into which a new technology has to be integrated is often too sluggish to implement it within efficient organizational and work processes in just one generation (Frey & Osborne, 2013). Brynjolfsson and McAfee (2014) argue in a similar way, pointing out that the rationalization effects of computer technology will only gradually become apparent through the exponential increase in computing capacity and the constant build-up of complexity by recombining algorithms.

Whether or not this delayed rationalization gain hypothesis is valid will become apparent in the coming decades. However, hardly anyone would argue that the epochal success that PCs and their derivatives had in the 1980s and early 1990s can be explained by certain long-term productivity gains that computer technology may eventually bring about. Such an argument presupposes a strong technical determinism, which at least in the sociology of technology, work, and economics was considered obsolete by the mid-1980s (Lutz, 1986; Pfeiffer, 2010; Rammert, 2006). Even entrepreneurs, shareholders, and markets are hardly so patient and forward-looking, and the acquisition of technology in work and economic processes rarely follows primarily functional orientations with long-term horizons. Rationalization rhetoric is, therefore, easy to understand, especially for the early computerization processes of the 1980s and 1990s, as a strategy for increasing sales of computers. In practice, however, processes often became slower and more expensive when computers were first introduced (Acemoglu et al., 2014). The rationalization hypothesis, therefore, does not explain how computers were able to reach a critical mass.

It is far more plausible to explain the first widespread successes of the calculating machine as an effect of gamification processes. Gamification can be understood as the transfer of game design elements into non-gaming social processes (Deterding, Dixon, Khaled, & Nacke, 2011).[1] Computers became popular primarily because the interaction design of their user interfaces in the early 1980s was closely related to the interaction design of computer games. A series of observations can best illustrate this. In media studies, for example, many of the most widespread computer games of the early 1980s are now regarded as instruments of socialization, which made it possible to "practice in a new world increasingly shaped by virtualisation" (Freyermuth, 2015). To give a succinct example, Microsoft included the game Solitaire in its Windows operating system primarily to make it easier for new users to learn how to use the computer mouse (deWinter, Kocurek, & Nichols, 2014). Computer games were, therefore, not least a format in which people could learn how to interact in computer-controlled social situations.

However, learning how to interact with the computer was just one of the ways that computer game design elements encouraged computerization and, thus, digitalization processes.[2] The increase in the user friendliness of man–machine interfaces has also been achieved historically by orienting these along the lines of computer games: New interaction design ideas were first tested in games, popularized through games and only then adopted in "serious" software. Many of the most basic interaction design strategies used today on any website, any graphical user interface, and in any office program originally came from computer games. As long ago as the early 1980s, key pioneers of user interface design transferred design lessons from games to graphical user interfaces and computer applications. This project can be illustrated with an example from Tom W. Malone's (1982) study "Heuristics for designing enjoyable user interfaces: lessons from computer games" (Malone, 1982, p. 63). Malone, then an employee at the Xerox Research Center in Palo Alto, asked himself two questions: "(1) Why are computer games so captivating? and (2) How can the features that make computer games captivating be used to make other user interfaces interesting and enjoyable to use?" One of the empirical results of his study was that computer games were so interesting and pleasant compared to conventional user interfaces because they formulated challenges, because they stimulated the imagination through metaphors and narratives, and because they presented information in such a way as to arouse curiosity (Malone, 1982, p. 65). Malone translated this insight into user interface design strategies. In the early 1980s, therefore, the practice of orienting computer dialogues with the user on narrative patterns and organizing these dialogue groups in such a way that they thematically linked to form "stories" arose in the context of gamification processes.

At the same time, John Carroll, an IBM employee and one of the developers of the influential "Minimalist Design" approach, transferred design lessons from the Atari game Adventure to word processing programs. Adventure is one of the pivotal games in computer game history, and one which has spawned its own computer game genre, so-called action adventures. In the game, a block-shaped avatar is sent through labyrinths to find an enchanted chalice. Keys and arrows need to be found to open gates and hunt hungry pixelated dragons. If the avatar is eaten by a dragon, the game does not restart, but the score is kept at that level. For example, the objects used, such as keys and arrows, can be found where they were left behind (Carroll, 1982, p. 53). Therefore, one of the central requirements for user interfaces, which Carroll derived from his observations of Adventure, was that they should be tolerant of user errors. They should also provide an "exploratory environment"—an explorable, graphically represented environment (Carroll, 1982, p. 54). Suspending the consequences of errors, which can be found in the "restore" function that most Word users are familiar with, are just as much a technology transfer from an Atari game as the open interface (e.g., desktop) on which things can be found, stored, arranged, and manipulated and that every popular operating system offers today.

Thus, in summary, it may be said that graphical user interfaces are designed to create interaction routines and logics similar to those of computer games. Ultimately, these are computer games whose character as a game has been distorted, but which retain specific structural elements from the original computer game. Our hypothesis is, therefore, that the interaction design of all everyday software being used today is gamelike. Without graphical user interfaces, the popularization of the PC and its derivatives in the 1980s is just as unthinkable as the current surge in digitalization in work and industry. They are a *conditio sine qua non* of digitalization. Therefore, all computer programs today that are not developed for a very narrow class of technical experts with programming skills—meaning almost all of them—show essential traits of Huizinga's (1949) definition of the game: They feature a "playground" with a distinctive delimiting temporal and spacial structure. Their interaction design aims to generate excited attention, and the interaction with the software opens up along control systems (in the sense of an interconnected set of generative rules) with different levels of flexibility, which need to be explored by the user during use. They can and should be modified and adapted to the needs of the user. Only the latent play that graphical user interfaces offer made and makes computers feasible as ubiquitous tools for working and learning.

Gamification and the Strengthening of Digital Work Process Control Since the 2000s

The incorporation of game routines and abstracted game elements into software was not only an enabler of the computerization of everyday life in the early 1980s and 1990s. Our hypothesis is stronger: We view gamification as an essential structural element of all digitalization processes. It guarantees the compatibility of man and computer and stabilizes the interaction between the two.[3] But, even if this argument should be disputed, for us it remains obvious that since the mid-2000s, more and more openly declared game elements have been integrated into software to better motivate users.

It is this particular normatively charged technocratic practice that around 2010 inspired the conceptual term *gamification*.[4] The practice itself is not subject to the boundaries of any software genre (Deterding & Walz, 2015). The aim of this type of *gamification* is to mobilize human effort for non-gamelike social processes on a large scale (McGonigal, 2011). At its core is the technical stabilization of a hybrid type of activity, half of which is part of a digital game (or a gamelike routine) and the other half of which is a non-gamelike process. The gamelike aspect should motivate participants to over-perform, and this over-performance is then used by the non-gamelike part of the activity—like waste heat, so to speak (Rigby, 2015).[5]

In this discourse, the positions that want to use technocratic gamification to improve consumption and production processes are dominant.[6] From a broader, more historically informed perspective, the strong gamelike aspect of digital infrastructures thus has to be analyzed as part of a complex that has been focused upon by work and industry sociology since the mid-2000s: The strengthening of social control and surveillance by digital infrastructures within the framework of a changing capitalist production model referred to by some as "digital capitalism" (Schiller, 2000, 2014; Staab, 2016; Staab & Nachtwey, 2016). Technocratic gamification can be associated with both new modes of establishing direct control and with new forms of enforcing indirect controls. This direct control is defined as the closely meshed guidance, monitoring, and sanctioning of employees during the work process. It aims, above all, at the direct control of labor actions, but not at procuring the willingness of employees to cooperate and perform beyond the context of their specific working task (Marrs, 2010, p. 335). Highly gamified software, such as Salesforce, a digital customer relationship management system, fits well into this picture. This produces a system of close monitoring in which a large proportion of the employees' activities are recorded and algorithmically evaluated. The system constantly updates the employees' key performance indicators and aggregates them with additional external information showing the employees the success of their "gaming activities" (Raffetseder et al., 2017).

On the other hand, technocratic gamification strategies can also be linked to the strengthening of the control strategy of so-called responsible autonomy (Friedman, 1987). These strategies can be understood as control modes that are primarily aimed at procuring the willingness of employees to cooperate and perform, without closely monitoring the work process (Marrs, 2010). Here, the common thread is that all forms of control through responsible autonomy rely on target agreements. Coarsely summarized, it does not matter how and when the work is done; it is important that the result is correct. The only thing that needs to be ensured is that the executing authority has sufficient resources, such as the motivation, tools, and skills, to achieve its goal (Marrs, 2010, p. 336). Gamified crowdworking platforms, such as Upwork (formerly oDesk) and Freelancer, fit well into this picture. They provide a forum where workers can apply for work packages and negotiate the price for their work independently. Furthermore, they "nudge" their "clickworkers" and "digital nomads" with small, sometimes immaterial incentives, such as pennants and performance metrics, to keep them motivated (Caraway, 2010).

Digital Literacy and Digital Domination

After what has already been said, one obvious thesis is that the algorithmic regulation of work processes by means of gamified digital technologies will further reduce the control gap (Raffetseder et al., 2017).[7] The gamification hypothesis not only answers the question of what social format computers offer in order to create and stabilize human–machine interaction; it also explains why the implementation of work processes using digital control infrastructures meets comparatively little resistance. However, a word of warning has to be given in that the trend toward digital monitoring and control in the last 10–15 years should not be used as a direct indicator of their long-term, anti-emancipative effects on digital work process controls. In order to assess the situation correctly, it is necessary to take into account the medium and long-term dynamics that arise during the appropriation, usage, and disuse of digital systems. Software is not simply integrated into business processes and then used in the same way for all of its lifecycle. It is gradually being exploited by employees, who today are usually involved both in further development of its use and also in its continuous further development within the framework of user-centered software development. Users at the workplace, therefore, work toward adapting and using digital systems in several concrete ways (e.g., D'Adderio, 2001; Orlikowski, 2000; Pentland, 1997). Also, it is usually personnel from the employee group who administer the systems, configure them locally, and evaluate their data. With gamified digital systems, every management team tends to install a black box between itself and the shop floor, over which the team has only mediated control. In this context, it can be assumed that, in addition to questions on the social organization of employees, the accumulation and distribution of digital competence among employees are decisive in determining who can assert which interests by which means in the long run.

Here, digital competence should not only mean formal IT knowledge. Rather, it should also encompass complex experiential knowledge that is primarily acquired when using the computer and in interactions with other users. Digital competence, therefore, also includes determining when using digital technology is ineffective, not expedient, inefficient, or harmful and knowing how software can be reused, misused, or sabotaged. Sociology of technology impressively points out that the use of software and software-driven machines creates complicated trajectories (e.g., Schulz-Schaeffer, 1996; Weyer, 2008), because human–machine systems—and the interaction with computers via gamified software is nothing other than that—are both enormously complex and enormously dynamic.

At this point, the arc stretches from gamification to gaming competence: User interface development pioneers, such as Carroll (1982) and Malone (1982), had the goal of simplifying the adoption of software by directly interacting with it, because users apparently learned it all by themselves in computer games. In contrast, though, no matter how detailed the user manual was, users despaired when confronted with the standard user interfaces of the late 1970s (Carroll, 1982). In order to simplify the use of computers, not only did their use have to change, but also learning how to use them had to change. The gamification of graphical user interfaces solved this problem. The new graphical user interfaces used interaction formats that were abstractly based on children's games, which meant that users had to work out the rules, which offered a high degree of interpretative openness.

Children's play constantly created new micro-games through children negotiating among themselves, with these micro-games usually being unstable and only gradually condensing into repeatable rule games within the framework of the children's interaction history (Broadhead, 2004; Caillois, 1967; Flitner, 1976). Moreover, that is exactly what interaction with graphical user interfaces still does today. In particular, the computer offers a playing field and a playing framework. What is played there and exactly how it is played is left to the users, who develop their routines and, in interaction with the algorithmic agents of the playground, constantly assemble new action patterns (micro-games). The abstracted game, which is built into any graphical user interface, makes the system easy to learn. The users only need to "play around" for a while so that it becomes self-explanatory what the system is good for. In other words, the use of the system is discovered and produced in this process. What attributes do users need to be able to develop to make use of such systems and become competent users in the course of their use? The answer is simple, but there may already be a whole concept of digital competence at its core: They must understand how to play with the computer and its software and how to influence the design of the game. Digital competence is not least gaming competence.

The Three Levels of Digital Gaming Competence

The first and basic level of digital competence can be described as a gamelike development competence in which the possibilities and limitations of a digital system are explored through trial and error. This is the ability to adapt to the game to gain knowledge of how to play the game. Users at this level gradually adapt their behavior to its rules due to the sequence of positive and negative experiences with the system.

However, users who an external observer would describe as competent have usually done more than simply learn the rules of a system. Rather, over time and often through communication with other users, they develop skills in the course of creative use of such systems that go beyond simple rule-following and rule-conform use. In terms of the gamelike aspect of the systems, this ability is about the important aspect of their generative openness. Playing—except in the case of classical plays—is open-ended. Games, or sequences of legitimate playing behavior, are usually generated according to very simple rules, but the combinatorics of simple playing moves makes the development of a game seem indeterminate across the various playing behaviors. This generates a specific scope in the game, which can be distinguished from the simple ability to play. "Good" (i.e., more competent) players differ from "bad" (i.e., less competent) players precisely in the fact that they know how to make better use of the wide range of combinatorial possibilities that the respective game opens up for their purposes. This second level of gaming competence in dealing with digital systems is, therefore, well described by the word *mastery*. Mastery is realized in the ability to construct new action patterns from the respective possibilities of the digital system, which are usually provided by software, and to condense them into effective action routines.

The third level of digital gaming competence concerns the ability to modify the rules of the game. Recent cultural sociological work on games suggests that it is a categorical mistake to see games as almost timeless, formal systems of rules and to play by following the rules (Malaby, 2007; Miller, 2008). For instance, in children's play it can be easily seen that the rules of the game between the players can be negotiated again and again and, in many cases, also need to be negotiated (Broadhead, 2004; Caillois, 1967; Flitner, 1976). This observation also applies to a large extent to modern computer games, of which it is often claimed that negotiating rules plays no role by virtue of the fact that these are "hard" coded by the software in the sense of being unavailable to the players. Contrary to this assumption, it is organic to many games today—the very successful game Minecraft is a good example of this—that the players themselves alter the game code via *modding*[8] in order to open up new game possibilities for themselves and their fellow players. There are mods, for instance, that transform Minecraft from a game where you cooperatively build a world with bricks into an ego-shooter or a family simulator. The life cycle and appeal of computer games increasingly depend directly on the users' free meta-gaming with the code, which is to be understood as an essential possibility to change the rules of the basic game.

From this observation, a third level of digital gaming competence can be derived: the ability to change the rules of the game. We call this *subversion*, because only by realizing this are the users of digital systems given the essential possibility to transform and rebel against digital systems.[9] There are two types of digital system subversion. The first can be described as inner or sudden subversion. In inner subversion, the rules of the game are changed directly by the user at the program code level. Special programming skills are still needed to be able to modify the rules of a digital system in specific terms, at least as things stand today. The hurdle posed by this need steadily decreased from the early 1950s to the early 1990s due to the development of higher programming languages. Since the early 1990s, however, there has been no further significant simplification of the most important commercially used programming languages. Python, the language developed in the late 1980s, is still the height of simplicity when it comes to programming. Today, visual programming modules are increasingly being provided as part of commercial programs, which make the respective program programmable to a certain degree by the arrangement of visual program components. However, such programming modules presented as graphical user interfaces are generally very limited in their possibilities. Flexible visual programming languages, such as Scratch and Snap!, which can be programmed relatively intuitively and playfully, can still be found today, especially in the learning area. To a certain extent, they themselves are games that are hardly used in the commercial sector and, therefore, play no role in work design. Thus, it should be noted that anyone who wants to "play around" with code in order to change the rules of a digital system today still usually has to acquire programming skills that require a considerable degree of technical education and that must be acquired well within the framework of formal learning opportunities. Thus, the possibility of internal subversion of digitally controlled work processes depends, at least at present, on the availability of formal IT knowledge among employees—while it remains an empirical question in how far such subversive strategies can actually be applied in work contexts given that organizational rules might forbid workers from engaging with algorithms in such a way. Our tentative guess would be that the higher up the occupational ladder one goes the bigger the possibilities of effective subversion should be. This hypothesis is justified by the consideration that a higher position in the organizational hierarchy should coincide with a higher degree of authority over the implementation and application of new code as well with a higher degree of formal IT training.

However, it should be noted that direct modification of the code is neither the only nor the most important path of subversion of the digital system. Forms that are referred to in the following as external or mediated subversion are much more common in practice: Human–computer systems are not simply systems in which atomized users use software via a user interface. Their social involvement is far more complex. On the one hand, users often interact with each other. On the other hand—and this is, admittedly, also a gross simplification—in addition to the role of the users, most of the time there are people in human–computer systems who play the role of administrators and developers of the system's software. This group usually has far greater technical expertise than the group of users and belongs often, but not always, to the group of employees. The subversion of software can, therefore, also be mediated by the users who influence the administrators and developers. It is plausible to assume that this is currently the usual way for digitally competent employees to influence the design of digital systems, even if they themselves have adequate programming skills. This type of subversion can happen in an organized fashion (e.g., through employee representatives), by informal request, or even simply by generating enough "trouble" for the administrators and developers. It is well known, for example, that users in companies often "vote with their feet" on software by simply ceasing to use it or not even starting to use it (Charette, 2005). In the context of agile software development, it has, therefore, become common practice to continuously develop and update software in contact with users (Drury, Conboy, & Power, 2011, 2012). Subversion competence is imparted in this context through expert groups of administrators and developers who develop the software further by dealing with digitally competent users, which in this case means with those who know the current rules of the game and their expert use. Furthermore, the adaptation of software based on user feedback has become common in the post-production phase. Software is no longer simply delivered; it is becoming faster and is being adapted and changed more and more often (McIlroy, Ali, & Hassan, 2016). Constant feedback in reaction to the needs of the users is crucial (Pagano & Bruegge, 2013), as it serves as a primary source of information not only about strengths and weaknesses, but also about the software's further potential development possibilities. Modern software development has become inconceivable without user innovations. This is also evident from the fact that digital innovation paradigms are strongly oriented toward the practices of the open-source movement (Gambardella, Raasch, & Hippel, 2017; Hippel, 2005; Krogh & Hippel, 2006). Open source projects not only include users in the continuous development process of the software, but also tend to also propagate knowledge about its use among the community. Having an "ear" for the user community is considered indispensable for successful software design today, because, as a rule, the practical use of the software can only be developed there and discovered in collectively distributed appropriation processes. In this respect, practical subversion (i.e., user action that does not correspond to the original intention of the respective software) is an essential source for the redesign of digitally regulated work processes. Therefore, the availability of variation and subversion competence is an important key for the correct assessment of systematic opportunities for the freedom of employees in digitally controlled work processes.

Conclusion: META or Digital Competence and the New Game About the Power Gap

An objection to this description of subversion competence is already obvious on the basis of the given description. The fact that users are involved in the continuous further development and adaptation of software must in itself be reconstructed into a certain form of rule. This is, after all, about the very obvious introduction of close-meshed feedback loops into the development trajectories of digital labor control systems. These are, therefore, forms of recursive, cybernetic self-correction mechanisms of labor control systems (Raffetseder et al., 2017). In this way, practical subversion indirectly serves the increasingly comprehensive control of employees, because it constantly integrates their skillful variations and subversion attempts at a higher level into the control system by translating these into code. Management should always be particularly keen to integrate the implicit knowledge, the skillful use of the software into the code as knowledge capital, while it will seek to prevent subversion (i.e., the misuse and restructuring of the labor control software for the benefit of the employees). To the extent that code becomes capital, the subversive actions of employees themselves are integrated into value creation and, in this respect, into part of the production model of digital capitalism. This objection is not easy to dismiss and is probably correct in its essence. User innovations are an important part of the value-added chain within software development. Why should this be different in digitally controlled work processes? However, the pessimistic attitude essentially depends on the hypothesis that management always manages to organize sufficient digital competence on the adaptation side of the system, so that the continuous adaptation of the system primarily serves to accumulate capital. On the one hand, this evokes the emergence of a new class of cybernetic managers and the complete change in the function of IT departments in companies, though neither is yet in sight. The role of computer scientists in companies is usually that of service providers. IT departments are subordinate cost centers in most companies. Real social computer scientists—if needed—are still a rare species. Furthermore, the pessimistic thesis underestimates the self-reinforcing effect of the accumulation of digital knowledge among employees. As an example, a process that determines the business of virtually every major massively multiplayer online game (MMOG) is the constant need to "rebalance" the game (Kou & Nardi, 2014). In games such as League of Legends (LOL), a competitive e-sports game with a community of several million players, the code of the game has to be constantly adapted, because the players develop a new most effective tactic available (META) in a short time, which makes the game predictable and boring. The game must, therefore, be constantly "rebalanced" by adding new characters, new equipment, new skills, and changed avatar attributes to the game. In this process, so-called swarm intelligence plays an important role; the mass of competent players apply their variation skills millions of times in a short time to the problem of how to play the game most effectively. Near-optimal solutions are, therefore, found very quickly. This, however, is only half the story. The players develop theories for games such as LOL. They produce an extremely complex meta-knowledge about the game, often accessible in wikis (Donaldson, 2017). The depth and complexity of these new theories is breath-taking and can be compared to the theoretical knowledge that mankind has developed over centuries on very complex games such as Go or chess. The lesson to be learned from this example is that it is not only the company producing the game that accumulates knowledge in the form of code. The player community accumulates knowledge in its collective network to at least an equivalent extent. In our view, therefore, the question as to who will ultimately prevail in the power gap game in digitally controlled work systems is anything but decided.

Notes

1. In line with Huizinga (1949), we understand a game as a social activity that is pursued as an end in itself and in which participation is voluntary at all times (Huizinga, 1949, pp. 13–19). Moreover, games unfold in a specially delimited space have a distinctive delimiting temporal structure, and the actions inside the game follow a set of socially shared, albeit often negotiable rules. Last, it is a distinctive feature of games that they are carried out with a special consciousness that marks them as separate from ordinary life (the so-called magic circle) and a special emotional state often described as a heightened type of cognitive tension and elation. It is also customary in sociological theories of games to distinguish between types of games, in which the rules of the game are rather ephemeral and emerge as a product of playing (often described in the terms of Caillois [1967] as *Paidia* or child's play) and games where the rule structure is institutionalized (i.e., rather static in time and non-negotiable during playtime, often referred to as *Ludus* or organized game). Beyond this main distinction social sciences and games, studies have developed many competing taxonomies of digital as well as of non-digital games and game elements, which go beyond the scope of this paper. Given the complexity of the concept of game and the game related taxonomies the concept of gamification addresses a very heterogeneous group of phenomena. In its most narrow technical and descriptive interpretation it just refers to the use of abstracted *digital* game elements typically found in computer games such as points, badges, narrative strategies, game loops (repeating game typical tasks), and so on in non-gaming software. The term *abstracted* in this definition points to the fact that it is typical of gamification that the transformed activity is not framed as a gaming/playing situation (i.e., the characteristic of marking an activity as being separate from ordinary life is subtracted from it). This is the meaning we adopt primarily in this paper. Nevertheless, in the sociological discussion of gamification a wider interpretation is often in use (e.g., Fuchs, Fizek, Ruffino, & Schrape, 2014; Woodcock & Johnson, 2017). In this later conceptual context, as Woodcock and Johnson (2017) point out, the difference between "Gamification-from-above" and "Gamification-from-below" is of special importance. On this also see Walz and Deterding's (2015) similar distinction between liminal and liminoid types of gamification. This wider concept of gamification focusses less on the technical migration of game elements into software, and more on the appropriation process by those that 'play' gamified activities. Therefore, it is much more centered on questions of agency: Who gamifies what, how and to what ends und who 'plays' (at) it? (Woodcock & Johnson, 2017, p. 545) We believe that

for our purposes it is simpler to discuss questions of agency separate from the descriptive term gamification, that we identify as a structural pattern of digitalization independent of the intentions of its proponents, designers, users, and so on.

2. When we refer to digitalization, we primarily focus on the spread and adoption of ICT in everyday work and life situations from the late 1970s onwards. In particular, we regard gamification as a pattern of structuration of individual digitization practices. For the purpose of disambiguation, we, therefore, exclude the implementation of physical infrastructure necessary for this process from our definition of digitalization.
3. To show this argument in detail is out of the scope of the present paper. It has to be noted that the history of the transference of central innovations of games into "serious' software" did not end with graphical user interfaces. It extends to the main characteristics of all software that was labeled as the "Web 2.0." In particular, the emergence of massive online cooperation and content production, as well as the persistence of shared online worlds, is a salient feature of early role-playing games (RPGs). For a detailed discussion of this hypothesis and its techno-sociological implications see Schobin (2017).
4. The gamification concept that emerged in this particular context corresponds to what Woodcock and Johnson (2017, pp. 545–548) would term, "gamification-from-above," and Walz and Deterding (2015) would call liminal forms of gamification: types of gamification that are primarily designed to channel the activities of the "players" to serve the predefined necessities of those designing the gamified system. We refer to this type of gamification as technocratic gamification.
5. This idea goes back, as Deterding (2014) notes, to Mihaly Csikszentmihalyi's influential flow theory (Deterding, 2014, p. 305).
6. From the perspective of the technocratic gamification industry see Herger (2014), Zichermann and Linder (2010, 2013), Deterding (2014) takes a critical look at the typical goals of professional gamifiers.
7. The term "control gap" refers to the difference between the capacity of management to coerce employees into compliance and the capacity of employees to evade such coercion. The control gap can, therefore, be viewed as a descriptive term that notes that the magnitude of the transformation problem varies across labor contexts.
8. A *mod* is an extension of an already existing computer game by program code that is usually written by players or by non-professional game developers and made available for free.
9. Following in Labour Process Theory (Braverman, 1998; Burawoy, 1979), there is of course a difference between agreeing to follow or not following certain rules and acting according the strategies of control implied in these

rules (transformation problem). Rule bending (such as "working to rule" for instance) and rule breaking can even support hegemonic modes of control, as Burawoy (1979) has shown with great detail. On this account, we conclude that resistance to labor control is not necessarily the same as subversion. We understand the later as an actual transformation of the regulatory framework that controls labor and not just as the bending or deliberate breaking of its rules.

References

Acemoglu, D., Autor, D., Dorn, D., Hanson, G., & Price, B. (2014). *Return of the Solow Paradox? IT, Productivity, and Employment in U.S. Manufacturing*. Cambridge, MA: National Bureau of Economic Research.

Braverman, H. (1998). *Labor and Monopoly Capital: The Degradation of Work in the Twentieth Century*. New York: New York University Press.

Broadhead, P. (2004). *Early Years Play and Learning: Developing Social Skills and Cooperation*. London: Psychology Press.

Brynjolfsson, E. (1993). The Productivity Paradox of Information Technology. *Communications of the ACM, 36*(12), 66–77.

Brynjolfsson, E., & McAfee, A. (2014). *The Second Machine Age: Work, Progress, and Prosperity in a Time of Brilliant Technologies*. New York: W.W. Norton.

Burawoy, M. (1979). *Manufacturing Consent: Changes in the Labor Process Under Monopoly Capitalism*. Chicago: University of Chicago Press.

Caillois, R. (1967). *Les jeux et les hommes. Le masque et le vertige*. Paris: Gallimard.

Caraway, B. (2010). Online Labour Markets: An Inquiry into oDesk Providers. *Work Organisation, Labour and Globalisation, 4*(2), 111–125.

Carroll, J. M. (1982). The Adventure of Getting to Know a Computer. *Computer, 15*(11), 49–58.

Charette, R. N. (2005). Why Software Fails [Software Failure]. *IEEE Spectrum, 42*(9), 42–49.

D'Adderio, L. (2001). Crafting the Virtual Prototype: How Firms Integrate Knowledge and Capabilities Across Organisational Boundaries. *Research Policy, 30*(9), 1409–1424.

Dahlberg, L. (2011). Re-constructing Digital Democracy: An Outline of Four Positions. *New Media & Society, 13*(1), 1–18.

Degele, N. (1994). *Der überforderte Computer. Zur Soziologie menschlicher und künstlicher Intelligenz*. Frankfurt am Main and New York: Campus Verlag.

Degele, N. (1996). Die Entwicklung und Nutzung von Software. Zur Genese informationstechnischen Handelns. *Zeitschrift für Soziologie, 25*, 1.

Deterding, S. (2014). Eudaimonic Design, or: Six Invitations to Rethink Gamification. In M. Fuchs, S. Fizek, P. Ruffino, & N. Schrape (Eds.), *Rethinking Gamification*. Lüneburg, Germany: Meson Press.

Deterding, S., Dixon, D., Khaled, R., & Nacke, L. (2011, September). From Game Design Elements to Gamefulness: Defining gamification. In *Proceedings of the 15th International Academic MindTrek Conference: Envisioning Future Media Environments* (pp. 9–15).

Deterding, S., & Walz, S. P. (2015). An Introduction to the Gameful World. In S. P. Walz & S. Deterding (Eds.), *The Gameful World: Approaches, Issues, Applications*. Cambridge: MIT Press.

deWinter, J., Kocurek, C.A., & Nichols, R. (2014). Taylorism 2.0: Gamification, Scientific Management and the Capitalist Appropriation of Play. *Journal of Gaming & Virtual Worlds, 6*(2), 109–127.

Donaldson, S. (2017). Mechanics and Metagame: Exploring Binary Expertise in League of Legends. *Games and Culture, 12*(5), 426–444.

Drury, M., Conboy, K., & Power, K. (2011). Decision Making in Agile Development: A Focus Group Study of Decisions and Obstacles. In *2011 AGILE Conference*.

Drury, M., Conboy, K., & Power, K. (2012). Obstacles to Decision Making in Agile Software Development Teams. *Journal of Systems and Software, 85*(6), 1239–1254.

Flitner, A. (1976). *Das Kinderspiel. Texte* (3rd ed.). München: Piper.

Frey, C. B., & Osborne, M. A. (2013). *The Future of Employment: How Susceptible Are Jobs to Computerisation*. Retrieved September 7, 2013.

Freyermuth, G. S. (2015). Der Weg in die Alterität. Skizze einer historischen Theorie digitaler Spiele. In B. Beil, G. S. Freyermuth, & L. Gotto (Eds.), *New Game Plus: Perspektiven der game studies. Genres - Künste – diskurse*. Bielefeld, Germany: Transcript.

Friedman, A. (1987). Managementstrategien und Technologie. Auf dem Weg zu einer komplexen Theorie des Arbeitsprozesses. In E. Hildebrandt & R. Seltz (Eds.), *Managementstrategien und Kontrolle. Eine Einfürung in die Labour Process Debate*. Berlin: Sigma.

Fuchs, M., Fizek, S., Ruffino, P., & Schrape, N. (2014). Introduction. In M. Fuchs, S. Fizek, P. Ruffino, & N. Schrape (Eds.), *Rethinking Gamification*. Lüneburg, Germany: Meson Press.

Gambardella, A., Raasch, C., & von Hippel, E. (2017). The User Innovation Paradigm: Impacts on Markets and Welfare. *Management Science, 63*(5), 1450–1468.

Gordon, R. J. (2015). Secular Stagnation: A Supply-Side View. *American Economic Review, 105*(5), 54–59.

Gunitsky, S. (2015). Corrupting the Cyber-Commons: Social Media as a Tool of Autocratic Stability. *Perspectives on Politics, 13*(1), 42–54.

Herger, M. (2014). *Enterprise Gamification. Engaging People by Letting Them Have Fun*. CreateSpace Independent Publishing Platform.

von Hippel, E. (2005). Democratizing Innovation: The Evolving Phenomenon of User Innovation. *Journal für Betriebswirtschaft, 55*(1), 63–78.

Huizinga, J. (1949). *Homo Ludens: A Study of the Play-Element in Culture.* London, New York, and Henley: Routledge and Kegan Paul.

Kou, Y., & Nardi, B. (2014). *Governance in League of Legends: A Hybrid System.* https://www.researchgate.net/profile/Yubo_Kou/publication/309738489_Governance_in_League_of_Legends_A_Hybrid_System/links/5821417808ae40da2cb53911.pdf. Accessed 17 May 2018.

von Krogh, G., & von Hippel, E. (2006). The Promise of Research on Open Source Software. *Management Science, 52*(7), 975–983.

Latour, B. (1996). *Aramis, or the Love of Technology.* Cambridge, MA: Harvard University Press.

Lutz, B. (1986). Das Ende des Technikdeterminismus und die Folgen: soziologische Technikforschung vor neuen Aufgaben und neuen Problemen. In B. Lutz & Deutsche Gesellschaft für Soziologie (Eds.), *Technik und sozialer Wandel: Verhandlungen des 23. Deutschen Soziologentages in Hamburg 1986.* Frankfurt am Main: Campus.

Malaby, T. M. (2007). Beyond Play: A New Approach to Games. *Games and Culture, 2*(2), 95–113.

Malone, T. W. (1982). Heuristics for Designing Enjoyable User Interfaces: Lessons From Computer Games. In J. A. Nichols & M. L. Schneider (Eds.), *Proceedings of the 1982 Conference on Human Factors in Computing Systems* (pp. 63–68).

Marrs, K. (2010). Herrschaft und Kontrolle in der Arbeit. In F. Böhle, G. G. Voß, & G. Wachtler (Eds.), *Handbuch Arbeitssoziologie.* Wiesbaden: VS Verlag für Sozialwissenschaften.

McGonigal, J. (2011). *Reality Is Broken: Why Games Make Us Better and How They Can Change the World.* New York: Penguin Press.

McIlroy, S., Ali, N., & Hassan, A. E. (2016). Fresh Apps: An Empirical Study of Frequently-Updated Mobile Apps in the Google Play Store. *Empirical Software Engineering, 21*(3), 1346–1370.

Miller, V. (2008). New Media, Networking and Phatic Culture. *Convergence, 14*(4), 387–400.

Orlikowski, W. J. (2000). Using Technology and Constituting Structures: A Practice Lens for Studying Technology in Organizations. *Organization Science, 11*(4), 404–428.

Pagano, D., & Bruegge, B. (2013). User Involvement in Software Evolution Practice: A Case Study. In *2013 35th International Conference on Software Engineering (ICSE).*

Pentland, B. T. (1997). Bleeding Edge Epistemology: Practical Problem Solving in Software Support Hotlines. In S. R. Barley & J. E. Orr (Eds.), *Between Craft and Science: Technical Work in U.S.* New York, NY: Cornell University Press.

Pfeiffer, S. (2010). Technisierung von Arbeit. In F. Böhle, G. G. Voß, & G. Wachtler (Eds.), *Handbuch Arbeitssoziologie.* Wiesbaden: VS Verlag für Sozialwissenschaften.

Raffetseder, E.-M., Schaupp, S., & Staab, P. (2017). Kybernetik und Kontrolle. Algorithmische Arbeitssteuerung und betriebliche Herrschaft. *Prokla, 187,* 229–247.

Rammert, W. (2006). *Technik, Handeln und Sozialstruktur. Eine Einführung in die Soziologie der Technik.* https://www.ts.tu-berlin.de/fileadmin/fg226/TUTS/TUTS_WP_3_2006.pdf. Accessed 13 March 2017.

Rammert, W., Böhm, W., Olscha, C., & Wehner, J. (1991). *Vom Umgang mit Computern im Alltag. Fallstudien zur Kultivierung einer neuen Technik.* Wiesbaden: VS Verlag für Sozialwissenschaften.

Rigby, C. S. (2015). Gamification and Motivation. In S. P. Walz & S. Deterding (Eds.), *The Gameful World: Approaches, Issues, Applications.* Cambridge: MIT Press.

Schiller, D. (2000). *Digital Capitalism: Networking the Global Market System.* Cambridge, MA and London: MIT Press.

Schiller, D. (2014). *Digital Depression: Information Technology and Economic Crisis.* Urbana and Chicago: University of Illinois Press.

Schobin, J. (2017). Vom Spiel getrieben? Die Digitalisierung des Alltags als Ludifizierungsprozess. *Leviathan, 45*(3), 309–334.

Schulz-Schaeffer, I. (1996). Software-Entwicklung zwischen Ingenieur- und Designwissenschaft: Überzeugungskraft und nützliche Widersprüchlichkeit von Software-Engineering und Software-Gestaltung. In H. D. Hellige (Ed.), *Technikleitbilder auf dem Prüfstand: Leitbild-Assessment aus Sicht der Informatik- und Computergeschichte.* Berlin: Ed. Sigma.

Solow, R. (1987). We'd Better Watch Out. *New York Times Book Review, 1987,* 36.

Staab, P. (2016). *Falsche Versprechen. Wachstum im digitalen Kapitalismus.* Hamburg: Hamburger Edition, HIS.

Staab, P., & Nachtwey, O. (2016). Market and Labour Control in Digital Capitalism. *Triple C. Communication, Capitalism, Critique, 14*(2), 457–474.

Walz, S. P., & Deterding, S. (2015). An Introduction to the Gameful World. In S. P. Walz & S. Deterding (Eds.), *The Gameful World: Approaches, Issues, Applications.* Cambridge: MIT Press.

Wehner, J., & Rammert, W. (1990). Zum Stand der Dinge: Die Computerwelt und ihre wissenschaftliche Beobachtung. In W. Rammert (Ed.), *Computerwelten - Alltagswelten. Wie verändert der Computer die soziale Wirklichkeit?* Opladen: Westdt. Verl.

Weyer, J. (2008). *Techniksoziologie: Genese, Gestaltung und Steuerung sozio-technischer Systeme.* Beltz: Juventa.

Woodcock, J., & Johnson, M. R.(2017). Gamification: What It Is, and How to Fight It. *The Sociological Review, 66*(3), 542–558.

Zichermann, G., & Linder, J. (2010). *Game-Based Marketing: Inspire Customer Loyalty Through Rewards, Challenges, and Contests.* Hoboken, NJ: Wiley.

Zichermann, G., & Linder, J. (2013). *The Gamification Revolution: How Leaders Leverage Game Mechanics to Crush the Competition.* New York: McGraw-Hill.

PART II

Promises of Emancipation Through Digital Fabrication

CHAPTER 6

Concrete Utopias of Digitalization Compared: The Case of the Post-Work and the Maker Movements

Philipp Frey and Christoph Schneider

The relationship between emancipation and technology is multifaceted. In our chapter, we shall approach this complex in the context of the digitalization of work. We shall start out by reconstructing Marx's early writings on emancipation in the field of work as a conceptual framework for our analysis. We will bring this classic framework into contact with contemporary approaches to study innovation and sociotechnical change through the lens of imaginations of sociotechnical futures. This combination will help us grasp two empirical cases where the complex relationships of technology, emancipation, and work have been prominently enacted in recent times. In these cases—the maker and the post-work movement—collective actors are working on projects of emancipation in entanglement with technological changes. The combination of Marx and a social-constructivist framework of technology helps us to address how these projects configure specific versions of "emancipation" and "technology" and their relationship. We argue at the end that the attention

P. Frey (✉) · C. Schneider
Karlsruhe Institute of Technology, Karlsruhe, Germany
e-mail: philipp.frey@partner.kit.edu

U. Meyer et al. (eds.), *Digitalization in Industry*,
https://doi.org/10.1007/978-3-030-28258-5_6

to such projects of sociotechnical imagining can help us better understand and appreciate where emancipation today could come from, what it could look like and that the uncertainty of the sociotechnical dynamics of our present historical situation could indeed support emancipatory social change.

Marx and Sociotechnical Imagining

First, we need to derive some basic understanding of the idea of emancipation in the context of work. In the third volume of *Capital*, Karl Marx outlines a technopolitical project that, as we will show, can be helpful in making sense of today's discussion on the emancipatory potentials of technology: He starts out by distinguishing two realms of human activity: the so-called realm of freedom which "actually begins only where labor which is determined by necessity and mundane considerations ceases" and the realm of necessity which is determined by said necessity and mundane considerations. To him, emancipation in the context of socially necessary production "can only consist in socialized man, the associated producers, rationally regulating their interchange with Nature, bringing it under their common control, instead of being ruled by it as by the blind forces of Nature; and achieving this with the least expenditure of energy and under conditions most favorable to, and worthy of, their human nature" (Marx, 1894/1966, p. 820). Emancipation in the context of work to Marx, then, has to be conceptualized twofold: *Emancipation from work*, with the shortening of the working-day as its basic prerequisite, and *emancipation within work*, with the "humanization" of working conditions at its core, aspiring toward work through which people flourish.

If we take Marx's notion that the way technology is being employed in the production process "discloses man's mode of dealing with Nature, the process of production by which he sustains his life" (Marx 1867/1906, p. 406); seriously, we can conclude that from the perspective of critical, materialist social philosophy, emancipation both from and within work would require production to be based on a qualitatively different technological apparatus. Seen in this way, emancipation *from* work emphasizes the transcendence of capitalist relations of production and accelerated automation. The focus on emancipation *within* work demands to ask what the qualities of the relations between persons, organizations, technologies, and activities should be like to enable human beings to develop the best of their potential and flourish. In fact, Marx's dialectical approach to the entwinement of relations of production (e.g., ownership structures, hierarchies) and forces of production (labor power, technology, knowledge) enables a fairly complex consideration of the drivers and the qualities of change in work and technology. Already in Marx's work, it is not only capitalist relations of production determining work but he also saw the affordances of the design of machinery to have an effect on work practices.

Indeed, the forms of work, technologies and the potentials for emancipation have changed since Marx' times. Especially today, amidst high uncertainty about the future, vast changes of technologies, work, and economies are envisioned by different and sometimes very powerful actors in research, the economy, politics, and civil society. In these technovisionary times, research strands have developed with a special focus on the role of imaginations of futures within sociotechnical innovation processes. They show that imagination of futures is not mere speculation but a constituting aspect of innovation and transformation. Most of these approaches roughly follow a social-constructivist perspective onto technologies and argue that the meaning that is given to technologies and the problems that they shall solve has a huge influence over the way a technology is developed and used (see Pinch & Bijker, 1984). Meaning is given to technology through discourse and social practices. Starting in the 1990s, research following such a perspective has shown the importance of imaginations of the future on technological innovation processes. The expectations and visions that are created and circulate in entanglement with technologies and innovation processes are central to shaping the further development of these processes. In short, how actors imagine (the transformations of) technologies are very significant for what these technologies are and what they become. Different theoretical concepts have been used to inquire into these relationships: "sociotechnical imaginaries" (Jasanoff & Kim, 2009), "expectations" (Konrad et al., 2017) or "visioneering" (McCray, 2012, Sand & Schneider, 2017). Our perspective draws upon the current debates on "vision assessment" which was developed in technology assessment (TA). Here the idea is that to assess emerging technologies, which often do not have a material existence outside of research programs, you need to assess the meaning that is given to these technologies by researchers, developers, politicians, and other actors and how they struggle over the definition of desirable futures (Grunwald, 2014). This approach has recently been extended to include the analysis of the practices and social processes within which such imaginations take place (Ferrari & Lösch, 2017).

However, most of these STS studies have been overly focused on the imagining of future technologies with the socio in *socio*technical somewhat underappreciated. All the more interesting are empirical cases where radical transformations of the social are part of the imagining of futures. And indeed—somewhat analogue to the studies mentioned above—utopian strands of critical social theory have long emphasized the constituting role of positive visions and normative. The sociologist Peter Wagner (2016) has reconstructed the idea of emancipation (as part of the larger idea of progress) and its changes over the course of modernity. He shows how historically specific versions of the idea of emancipation have been part of specific social struggles. However, with old certainties of "progress" fading Wagner argues, that societal actors need to define new conceptions of emancipation to regain perspectives of societal improvement. This somewhat mirrors the Marxist philosopher Ernst Bloch's claims that every age needs its "concrete utopias" that mediate present conditions and their inherent potentials with visionary ideas of betterment and human flourishing (Bloch, 1986). Similar to the STS findings, the mentioned critical scholarship shows that particular visions of a future society are a constituting part of present practices of transformation. There is a social construction not only of technology but also of emancipation.

From these critical traditions, we can also learn that scholarship can strive to not only observe the world but to change it. Wagner, for example, argues that critique is a capacity by social actors themselves within their respective social contexts. There are, however, different capacities for critique and intellectuals can—and should—engage in fostering these capacities by providing analyses and concepts that can be useful for this. Recent, self-reflexive work in STS supports this by highlighting that social science enacts realities (Law & Urry, 2004). In our research, both of us have been engaged with the realities of the two movements we analyze, as "action researcher" and public intellectual. However, here is not the place to discuss these approaches to scientific practice and our roles in it. Here we focus on describing and analyzing the cases with a framework of emancipation.

With this conceptual approach, we will turn to two empirical cases that combine and enact imaginations of emancipation, work, and technology. We will look at how different actors engage themselves in projects and use visions as a ledger for public engagement, enabling debates that confront the current social conditions and their perpetuation with alternative futures that explore what could be possible. Furthermore, we look at the processes and practices that enable these actors to do exactly this. We will analyze them as sociotechnical practices that produce and mediate particular imaginations of the future. Our analysis will attend to both the imaginations of future transformations and the present conditions within which they take shape. Furthermore, we will inquire what understandings of work, technology, and emancipation are produced within the technopolitical projects of "post-work" and "making." In short, we look at the social construction of "technology" and "emancipation" and their relationship in these cases.

Post-Work: A Project of Reframing Automation Technologies, Politics, and Emancipation

Our first case is the debate on the automation of work, whose utopian core—the longing to be freed from labor imposed from necessity—is as we will show a time-honored one and particularly well suited to discuss the connection between emancipation and technology.[1] The pertinence and fundamental character of this connection can be illustrated by the historical extent of this debate, which can be traced back to the fourth century BC. In his *Politiká*, Aristotle discusses the prospect of instruments, "obeying or anticipating the will of others," employing mythological examples such as the statues of Daedalus or the tripods of Hephaestus, and concludes: "if, in like manner, the shuttle would weave and the plectrum touch the lyre without a hand to guide them, chief workmen would not want servants, nor masters slaves" (Aristot. Pol. 1.1253b). His technology assessment seems clear enough: The introduction of automation technologies would enable the emancipation from slavery (all the more fitting that emancipation derives from the Latin term *emancipatio*, the act of setting a slave free). This early statement was not lost on the nineteenth-century radicals in their endeavor to sketch out a postcapitalist future. Paul Lafargue, a son-in-law of Marx, directly addresses Aristotle in his seminal work "The Right to Be Lazy" (1883): "Aristotle's dream is our reality. Our machines, with breath of fire, with limbs of unwearying steel, with fruitfulness, wonderful inexhaustible, accomplish by themselves with docility their sacred labor. And nevertheless the genius of the great philosophers of capitalism remains dominated by the prejudice of the wage system, worst of slaveries.

They do not yet understand that the machine is the saviour of humanity, the god who shall redeem man from the sordidae artes and from working for hire, the god who shall give him leisure and liberty" (Lafargue 1883/1907, p. 62).[2] This techno-optimist, utopian current has seen a resurgence in the context of today's debate on the digitalization of work, with proponents of the so-called post-work debate drawing upon these earlier contributions. One of the most influential and exemplary books in the field, *Inventing the Future* by Nick Srnicek and Alex Williams, for instance, sports a chapter likewise headlined "The Right to Be Lazy."

In their book, Srnicek and Williams combine the discussion on automation-related labor market transformations with reflections on the significance of sociotechnical visions for progressive politics. They start out with an analysis of what they perceive to be decisive tendencies of the automation of work in today's capitalism: the rise of the phenomenon of jobless recoveries, the expansion of surplus population that is unable to find jobs, the deepening social polarization of society (Srnicek & Williams, 2015, pp. 85–106). This bleak prospect is met by the authors with the call for a project that employs the possibilities presented by automation to "liberate humanity from the drudgery of work, the dependence on wage labor, and the submission of our lives to a boss." While they openly refer to a long theoretical tradition, they claim that "recent developments in capitalism give renewed urgency to these issues." They are quick to point out that a post-work world would not be a world of idleness; rather it would be a world in which a specific form of labor, wage labor, which is qualified by them as "time that is not under our control, but under our [...] employers' control," would be done away with. Their call for a post-work project then is one for the rise of autonomous labor and the end of the social and material marginalization of unemployed members of society. They argue that it should be a central societal goal to build capacity for humans to act according to their desires, or, as they put it "to open up the 'realm of freedom'" (ibid., p. 85; see our discussion of Marx in the introduction).

To reach this goal, they suggest to build a broad political movement around the common vision of a post-work society, arguing that such a project could be attractive for various social groups, putting an end to the orientation on economic growth as a means to create jobs, enabling a decrease of carbon emissions, helping women's emancipation by guaranteeing their material independence and improving the social conditions of the unemployed (ibid., p. 161). The authors call for a long-term political strategy, linking up parties, unions, leftist think tanks, media organizations and other actors of civil society, with imaginations of sociotechnical futures serving as both a central tool to foster a shared identity, to coordinate and motivate actors and to build up counter-hegemony. This active and conscious engagement with sociotechnical futures as a part of political struggle follows from their conviction that "one of the most pervasive and subtle aspects of hegemony [today] is the limitations it imposes upon our collective imagination," rendering the (re-)appropriation of the future a central objective of the progressive contemporary left (ibid., p. 131).

Since the publication of their book, Srnicek and Williams have been involved in founding several think tanks on the future of work in New Zealand and Great Britain while at the same time pushing their agenda by intervening into the mass media discourse on the societal implications of automation and relentlessly giving presentations at academic conferences and research institutes. Furthermore, the techno-optimist current of the British academic left continues to display increased engagement with the Labour party ever since Jeremy Corbyn could establish himself as its head, as illustrated by various newspaper contributions and event collaborations. Labour's current Shadow Chancellor, John McDonnell, in particular forwards initiatives in this respect such as the "The New Economics" event series hosted by him and prominently featuring future- and technology-oriented proponents such as Paul Mason (2015) and Nick Srnicek (see Labour, 2018). McDonnell, in this spirit, also pledged to increase spending on infrastructure and research, describing his vision for the economy as "socialism with an iPad" (McDonnell, 2015). In recent speeches, Corbyn has taken up demands put forward by progressive researchers and unionists such as the demand for a radical reduction of working hours and the establishment of an extensive basic income scheme as well as promoting the move toward a new economy that "can be the gateway for a new settlement between work and leisure" and a "springboard for expanded creativity and culture" (Corbyn, 2017), fulfilling the emancipatory potentials of automation technologies (see Srnicek & Butler, 2018, for a more critical assessment of the relevance of the postcapitalism discourse to Corbynism, see Pitts & Dinerstein, 2017).

To summarize, the contemporary post-workists focus their activity on intervening in the broad public discourse as well as engaging with political actors, leveraging their expertise to propagate alternative imaginations of sociotechnical futures, connecting concrete policy advice and far-reaching technoutopian visions. This engagement with sociotechnical futures is actively reflected as a necessary aspect of the construction of a counter-hegemonial technopolitical project and thereby supplies further evidence for TA and STS scholars dealing with the importance of futures in societal transformation processes. On an organizational level, an expansion of the interaction between party politics and public intellectuals can be observed in the last few years as Labour moved to the left of the political spectrum; at the same time, a process of institutionalization is progressing, as illustrated for instance by the establishment of Autonomy, a UK-based progressive think tank focused on the relationship between work, technology, and emancipation.

Making: A Project of Self-Determined Creativity

Next, we turn to the so-called maker movement which gained a lot of popularity during the past decade. And although "making" has become a rather diverse issue, ideas of emancipation of the "maker" are a central aspect of this project. Somewhat different to the post-work intellectual project, making takes place largely through technological practices, to understand it as a field for concrete utopian practices and for critique we therefore need to take the sociotechnical assemblages into account that have enabled and shaped making. This includes discourse but the visionary character is also enacted in practice (Schneider, 2018).

Making is entwined with digital fabrication technologies such as 3D-printing. These technologies have a long history and combine different approaches to produce material objects with the help of digital technology. Symbolically the advances in these technologies, i.e., of the material world becoming more digitally malleable, helped to link digital fabrication to a larger narrative of Internet utopianism which sees the emergence of a new society as part of the spread of digital technology (Turner, 2006). This has not always been the case, however. Computer-controlled machines, as David Noble showed, originated in military research and were not simply a way to make machines more efficient; these technologies have also been used by management to break organized labor and deskill workers (see also Söderberg, 2014; Noble, 1984). However, with the machines becoming smaller and more capable the idea of "personal" fabrication emerged around the turn of the millennium (Gershenfeld, 2012). In analogy to the personal computer, "personal fabricators" should enable individuals to produce what they want. While first tests for personal fabrication took place within university departments the radical re-contextualization of these technologies took place in 2005. The RepRap project started that year (http://en.wikipedia.org/wiki/RepRap_Project, accessed 14.04.2015) and dramatically changed what 3D printing actually meant (Dickel & Schrape, 2017; Tech et al., 2016). Drawing on the open-source approach and a strong vision to make technology self-replicating, the project has created a large community that develops small-scale 3D printers and shares digital knowledge. RepRap dramatically lowered the cost for the creation of 3D printers. Besides this economic aspect, RepRap also pulled 3D printing out of industrial contexts, where it had been used from the 1980s onwards. The "hype" about 3D printing (around 2012 in Germany) was strongly fueled by these development since they not only showed the "technology," but also the new "social" formations that entwined with it (Alvial Palavicino, 2016): 3D printing had become the meeting point of decentralized and open Internet cultures and novel forms of material fabrication.

Therefore, making was equally fostered by novel organizational forms that drew their inspiration from open-source software development. Besides such collaborative developer platforms so-called maker spaces, novel organizations that explicitly aim to provide the infrastructures for making, were developed. In particular FabLabs, notably launched at the Massachusetts Institute of Technology (MIT), have become central organizations to foster open digital fabrication. In 2018, around 1700 such labs exist around the globe based upon the idea of providing access to digital fabrication machines for individuals. Besides this common aim, FabLabs exist in different forms, with or without formal ties to MIT, and can be found from small, volunteer-run labs with low budgets to labs hosted by a university or company with equipment worth hundreds of thousands of euros. This diversity of the labs in a way reflects the mentioned diversity of making. However, FabLabs have generally been places for enthusiasts and others alike to learn about and to experiment with digital fabrication and other technologies in settings where professionals and amateurs can be found. Central to this spread of these organizational forms, however, have been the more accessible technologies and the knowledge that has been shared online around these technologies, their usages, their design and their adoption in the new labs (Schneider, 2018). Again this could plausibly emphasize the Internet utopian idea of a new societal organization spreading along with digital technologies (Turner, 2006).

Within and as part of this assemblage, the subjectivity of the maker emerged. The term "maker" in its present connotation was popularized by O'Reilly Media, a company specialized in publications concerning (open source) software, with the launch of their "Make Magazine" in 2005. The rhetoric strategy behind the magazine's title was to address more people than with the more narrowly and partly negatively interpreted term "hacker," while still culturally drawing on the values of hacking, of self-directed technology experts that try out creative uses of technology. Yet, far from mere semantics, the magazine has been including all kinds of DIY projects, which do not only feature computers and electronics, the main fields for tinkering of hackers. And the company even started a successful series of "maker fairs," large events in the USA and beyond about all forms of DIY, combining commerce, hobby and festival (see the CEO of O'Reilly describing the history of Make Magazine: http://vimeo.com/51841691, accessed 25.06.2014; see also this press release for a further self-description of Make Magazine: http://www.oreilly.com/pub/pr/3185, accessed 25.06.2014). The maker movement builds upon cultural framings of "web 2.0" that see a new society of decentralized and networked prosumers being born (Dickel & Schrape, 2017). What has been termed the "maker movement" could also be seen as a combination of the "hacker ethic" (e.g., Himanen, 2001) of constructing and tinkering, sharing and learning with an increased diversity of the objects involved: Beyond software and electronics "everything," e.g., textiles, wood, machines, social problems in "hackathons," can and should now be "hacked," which also implies that "everyone" who tinkers can become a "maker." However, this aspect of making also resonates with older discourses of the creative and productive individual, powerfully inscribed into modernity, often as a romanticized antidote to industrial and bureaucratic realities. And more mundanely, it resonates with people simply enjoying to make stuff for themselves or together (e.g., Gauntlett, 2013).

Many makers position themselves in relation to a vision of the emergence of a decentralized economy that they anticipate and experiment with in their practices (Alvial Palavicino, 2016), for example, in FabLabs. The self-descriptions of makers center around self-determined and creative individuals who creatively and unconventionally use digital technology to make the things that they enjoy doing, that they share this enthusiasm with others and organize online and offline (Gauntlett, 2013; Gershenfeld, 2012). This also ties in into the broader idea of "openness" to indicate values of transparency, collaboration, networking, and public knowledge sharing (cf. Tkacz, 2015). These values of openness are typically not a critique of capitalism per se—although some intellectuals would like to read this into them—but they are a more specific critique of a central tension within contemporary capitalism which is increasingly based on intellectual property monopolies held by big corporations. Against these large organizations making and other fields of practice that emphasize openness place the often voluntary collaboration of individuals and the shared knowledge upon which they draw and that they produce to create technologies and to unfold their technology-centric selves.

In comparison with the post-work coalition, the emancipatory meanings that making assigns to digital technologies are shaped through discourse but also practical engagement. Well aware that many of their practices and organizations are prototypical forms of something to more fully emerge in the future, makers focus on doing and creative work. These doings sit rather ambiguously in relation to capitalism. There is a widely shared critique of intellectual property, proposing open-source approaches as an alternative. However, the maker movement also widely engages in consumer industries selling stuff to making hobbyists and professionals. The start-up discourse has also not left making untouched: During the past years, making and hacking approaches and organizational forms that have been created outside of companies are increasingly taken up into profit-oriented organizations to attract skilled workers or to test new ways of innovating—e.g., Germany's largest maker space at Technical University Munich with direct and strong links to car manufacturers and other companies who send development teams there.[3] Nonetheless, even in these cases one can identify the transformative potential promised through making practices of working more creatively, being able to try things out, to meet others. Making, in short, has been mainly an effort to humanize creative work, to build structures that enable self-determined creativity and to test networked organizational forms that are more flat than the hierarchies of universities and industrial companies. All too easily, making could be dismissed for not taking the transcendence of capitalist relations of production centrally into focus. However, it shows, that we live in times where in the interstices of existing institutions and within them (e.g., in universities and companies) practices and organizational forms are developing in entwinement with digital technologies that by exploring the potentials of digital technologies also explore new ways of working and producing together and individually (Schneider, 2018; Schneider & Lösch, 2019). Making can therefore be read as a particular exploration of the humanization of (creative, technological) work.

Discussion and Outlook

So far, we have outlined two major contemporary currents developing practices of emancipation in relation to digitalization—what we have called concrete utopias. Each of these frames a particular version of digital technology and a version of what emancipation could and should look like, i.e., a particular social construction of technology and emancipation (Fig. 6.1).

We would argue that the conception of emancipation dominant in the respective movements echo, in a one-sided manner, the one by Marx discussed in the introduction. While the post-work discourse is focused on the abolition of work, activists from the maker movement focus their efforts on liberating work from knowledge monopolies and heteronomy, striving to establish working conditions "most favorable to, and worthy of, their human nature." These foci correlate with a specific understanding of work: Within the context of the post-work debate, work is

Understanding of	Post-Work	Makers/Community FabLabs
Emancipation	Emancipation from work	Emancipation within work
Technology and work	Wage labor and (industrial) production technologies as part of class structures	Self-determined work through networked and small-scale digital technologies
Actors	A network of politically active and public intellectuals	A heterogeneous group of 'makers'
Strategy	Build a political vision and coalition (work on discourse)	Experiment with 'openness' in protected spaces (work on technical artefacts)

Fig. 6.1 Emancipation compared

discussed consciously primarily as wage labor, a historically specific form of work which is intimately intertwined with capitalist relations and focuses on the abstract side of work under capitalism: its property to create value; in their longing to transcend this form of work, oftentimes the persistence of socially necessary labor (especially in care) tends to be overlooked. In the context of the maker movement, the objective seems to be to realize the emancipatory potentials contained within digital production technologies, highlighting the concrete dimension of labor as a potentially fulfilling and meaningful activity producing concrete use-value, while oftentimes failing to acknowledge restraints imposed upon this development by the dominant capitalist relations. This one-sidedness repeats itself in the spatial dimension of these movements: While the demands of the post-work activists are aimed abstractly at the whole of society, the activities of many makers are strongly localized.

We are convinced that for work to be self-determined and freed from heteronomy in a comprehensive sense, there needs to be a change in the social relations that determine the social (re-)production process; accordingly, the adaption of a more ambitious stance regarding societal transformation by the maker movement would be appropriate. At the same time, the discourse coalition of post-work could need some more practical engagement with organizational experiments that could inform attempts at broad societal transformation. The postcapitalist economic basis of emancipation within and from work needs to be build—both by policy-making affecting the whole of society (shortening of the working week, democratization of control over the means of production, possibly the introduction of a universal basic income), and by introducing places in which alternative ways to organize ownership of the means of production and the self-organization of work can be experimented with (see also Mason, 2015). Since neoliberalism is collapsing and digitalization speeding up, it is time to find mutual engagements in discourse and practice to enable a further becoming and transformation of these emancipatory practices, potentially leading to transformative experiments that combine visionary discourse, political movements, and experiments with post-neoliberal or even postcapitalist economic structures.

So far many societal debates on the socioeconomic and political implications of digital technologies are caught in a dichotomy between a naïve techno-optimism and a dystopian techno-pessimism. On one side of the spectrum, there is a strong industry that promotes techno-utopianism. Silicon Valley and Co. promote the idea that technology alone—and its assumed unstoppable evolution toward techno-paradise—will solve all human problems, or will even create superhumans (see Harari, 2016; Nachtwey & Seidl, 2017). While this techno-capitalist culture tries to sell "tech" as a transcendental and emancipatory force, it remains within the contemporary logics of capitalist extractivism, exploitation, and corporate control. The other extreme, and not seldom found in left circles, is an aversion of technology and calls to save the "human," the "social" or the "natural" from the cold and powerful techno-rationalizations that are taking place. What is needed from our point of view to transcend these over-simplified cultural extremes and to explore the complex spaces in between, are forums and practices for debates that entwine technology and society and that ask what qualities of change we seek and how different possibilities can enable these changes.

However, such debates, experiments, and coalitions that aim to build better futures need to be actively facilitated. We think that scholars of sociotechnical changes need to become more active in working on the social construction of technology and emancipation. The post-work theorists' role as public intellectuals and their efforts of trying to influence both public discourse in general and the policy-making discourse in particular has been very inspiring to us personally. The time seems to be right, too. Increasingly, there is a strong interest in futures and alternative pathways for societal development both inside and outside of STS and also increasingly, purely analytical approaches are considered too limited when it comes to "future-making" (Adam, 2011; Dobroc et al., 2018).[4]

We believe that such an active stance is appropriate and necessary in the technopolitical fields that our chapter focused on—and that these fields at the same time provide much inspiration for engaged intellectual work. As scientists we are embedded in societal development, for better or worse. Therefore, we want to consciously contribute to societal progress on a normative basis, and we believe that an increased engagement with concrete utopias is a necessary tool of public engagement, enabling debates that confront the current social conditions and their perpetuation with alternative futures that explore what emancipatory potentials there are, what would be possible if they would be redeemed and maybe most importantly, *how* they could be redeemed.

Much is already happening and much more could follow if we collectively regain aspirations for emancipation and for exploring the sociotechnical possibilities that are opening up, appreciating the high uncertainty about the future as an index that the best *might* be yet to come. Engaged scientists working in STS and technology assessment could play a key role in facilitating such societal processes of reflection, providing insight into both technological potentials and the complexities of sociotechnical systems. We hope that this book contributes to transcending a scientific understanding that perceives processes that strive to realize the emancipatory potentials of technology to merely be of a self-referential theoretical interest. Rather, we look forward to engaging with others who also understand the facilitation of such processes as an emerging task of STS and TA scholars and would be happy to get in contact and collaborate in such making of concrete utopias.

Notes

1. For a more detailed discussion of the challenges and opportunities automation presents to emancipatory social actors, see Frey (2017, 2018).
2. Unsurprisingly, Marx took a more nuanced stance: In response to the same quote by Aristotle, he states: "Oh! those heathens! They understood [...] nothing of Political Economy and Christianity," pointing out that under capitalist conditions, "machinery is the surest means of lengthening the working-day," arguing for an anticapitalist, rather than a technodeterminist approach (Marx 1867/1906, p. 446).
3. https://www.unternehmertum.de/makerspace.xhtml.
4. By connecting the reflection of contemporary maker- and post-work discourses with Marx's discussion of emancipation from and within work, we also wanted to make a more general point: That there are existing strands of critical thinking that engaged scientists from TA and STS can draw from to develop their approaches further.

Sources

Adam, B. (2011). Towards a Twenty-First-Century Sociological Engagement with the Future. *Insights, 4*(11), 1–18.

Alvial Palavicino, C. (2016). *Mindful Anticipation: A Practice Approach to the Study of Expectations in Emerging Technologies.* Doctoral Thesis, Universiteit Twente, Enschede. Retrieved from http://dx.doi.org/10.3990/1.9789036540605.

Aristotle. (1999). *Politics.* Kitchener, ON: Batoche Books.

Bloch, E. (1986). *The Principle of Hope.* Cambridge, MA: MIT Press.

Corbyn, J. (2017). *Speech to Labour Party Conference.* Retrieved from https://labour.org.uk/press/jeremy-corbyn-speech-to-labour-party-conference/.

Dickel, S., & Schrape, J.-F. (2017). The Logic of Digital Utopianism. *NanoEthics, 11*(1), 47–58. https://doi.org/10.1007/s11569-017-0285-6.

Dobroć, P., Krings, B.-J., Schneider, C., & Wulf, N. (2018). Alternativen als Programm. *TATuP Zeitschrift Für Technikfolgenabschätzung in Theorie Und Praxis, 27*(1), 28–33. https://doi.org/10.14512/tatup.27.1.28.

Ferrari, A., & Lösch, A. (2017). How Smart Grid Meets In Vitro Meat: On Visions as Socio-Epistemic Practices. *NanoEthics*, 1–17. https://doi.org/10.1007/s11569-017-0282-9.

Frey, P. (2017). Automatisierung - (Alb-)Traum der emanzipatorischen Linken? Zu den gesellschaftspolitischen Implikationen avancierter Produktivkräfte. In P. Buckermann, A. Koppenburger, & S. Schaupp (Eds.), *Kybernetik, Kapitalismus, Revolutionen* (pp. 109–123). Münster: UNRAST.

Frey, P. (2018). Vom Unabgegoltenen der Automation – Einige Gedanken zur gegenwärtigen Automationsdebatte aus Sicht kritischer Technikfolgenabschätzung. In M. Hawel, L. Killius, S. Heinemann, & M. Schröder (Eds.), *Work in Progress. Work on Progress. Beiträge kritischer Wissenschaft* (pp. 81–94). Hamburg: VSA Verlag.

Gauntlett, D. (2013). *Making Is Connecting*. Hoboken: Wiley.

Gershenfeld, N. (2012). How to Make Almost Anything: The Digital Fabrication Revolution. *Foreign Affairs, 91*, 43.

Grunwald, A. (2014). The Hermeneutic Side of Responsible Research and Innovation. *Journal of Responsible Innovation, 1*(3), 274–291. https://doi.org/10.1080/23299460.2014.968437.

Harari, Y. H. (2016). *Homo Deus: A Brief History of Tomorrow*. London: Harvill and Seckler.

Himanen, P. (2001). *The Hacker Ethic and the Spirit of the Information Age*. New York, NY: Random House.

Jasanoff, S., & Kim, S.-H. (2009). Containing the Atom: Sociotechnical Imaginaries and Nuclear Power in the United States and South Korea. *Minerva, 47*(2), 119–146.

Konrad, K., Van Lente, H., Groves, C., & Selin, C. (2017). Performing and Governing the Future in Science and Technology. In U. Felt, R. Fouché, C. A. Miller, & L. Smith-Doerr (Eds.), *The Handbook of Science and Technology Studies* (4th ed., pp. 465–493). Cambridge, MA: The MIT Press.

Labour. (2018). *The New Economics—Previous Events*. Retrieved from https://labour.org.uk/members/new-economics-past-events/.

Lafargue, P. (1883/1907). *The Right to Be Lazy*. Chicago, IL: Charles H. Kerr.

Law, J., & Urry, J. (2004). Enacting the Social. *Economy and Society, 33*(3), 390–410.

Marx, K. (1867/1906). *Capital, Volume I*. Chicago, IL: Charles H. Kerr.

Marx, K. (1894/1966). *Capital, Volume III*. Moscow: Progress Publishers.

Mason, P. (2015). *Postcapitalism: A Guide to Our Future*. London: Allen Lane.

McCray, W. P. (2012). *The Visioneers: How a Group of Elite Scientists Pursued Space Colonies, Nanotechnologies, and a Limitless Future*. Princeton: Princeton University Press.

McDonnell, J. (2015). How Labour Will Secure the High-Wage, Hi-Tech Economy of the Future. *The Guardian*. Retrieved from https://www.theguardian.com/commentisfree/2015/nov/19/john-mcdonnell-labour-technology-tax-economy-of-future.

Nachtwey, O., & Seidl, T. (2017). *Die Ethik der Solution und der Geist des digitalen Kapitalismus* (IfS Working Papers, Nr. 11). Frankfurt am Main: Institut für Sozialforschung. Retrieved from http://www.ifs.uni-frankfurt.de/wp-content/uploads/IfS-WP-11.pdf.

Noble, D. F. (1984). *Forces of Production: A Social History of Industrial Automation*. New York: Alfred Knopf.

Pinch, T. J., & Bijker, W. E. (1984). The Social Construction of Facts and Artefacts: Or How the Sociology of Science and the Sociology of Technology Might Benefit Each Other. *Social Studies of Science, 14*(3), 399–441. https://doi.org/10.1177/030631284014003004.

Pitts, F. H., & Dinerstein, A. C. (2017). Corbynism's Conveyor Belt of Ideas: Postcapitalism and the Politics of Social Reproduction. *Capital & Class, 41*(3), 423–434. https://doi.org/10.1177/0309816817734487.

Sand, M., & Schneider, C. (2017). Visioneering Socio-Technical Innovations—A Missing Piece of the Puzzle. *NanoEthics, 11*(1), 19–29.

Schneider, C. (2018). *Opening Digital Fabrication: Transforming TechKnowledgies*. Karlsruhe: KIT Scientific Publishing. https://doi.org/10.5445/KSP/1000083485.

Schneider, C., & Lösch, A. (2019). Visions in assemblages: Future-making and governance in FabLabs. *Futures, 109*, 203–212. https://doi.org/10.1016/j.futures.2018.08.003.

Schneidewind, U., Singer-Brodowski, M., Augenstein, K., & Stelzer, F. (2016). *Pledge for a Transformative Science: A Conceptual Framework* (Wuppertal Papers No. 191). Retrieved from https://epub.wupperinst.org/frontdoor/index/index/docId/6414.

Söderberg, J. (2014). Reproducing Wealth Without Money, One 3D Printer at a Time: The Cunning of Instrumental Reason. *Journal of Peer Production, 4*. Retrieved from http://peerproduction.net/issues/issue-4-value-and-currency/peer-reviewed-articles/reproducing-wealth-without-money/.

Srnicek, N., & Butler, L. (2018). Technology, Capitalism and the Future of the Left. *RENEWAL, 26*(1). Retrieved from https://static1.squarespace.com/static/58727b5a9de4bbf0b38db631/t/5ac7c00c758d46cd6da2dc77/1523040269065/Snricek+on+automation.pdf.

Srnicek, N., & Williams, A. (2015). *Inventing the Future: Postcapitalism and a World Without Work*. London: Verso.

Tech, R. P. G., Ferdinand, J.-P., & Dopfer, M. (2016). Open Source Hardware Startups and Their Communities. In J.-P. Ferdinand, U. Petschow, & S. Dickel (Eds.), *The Decentralized and Networked Future of Value Creation* (pp. 129–145). Cham: Springer. https://doi.org/10.1007/978-3-319-31686-4_7.

Turner, F. (2006). *From Counterculture to Cyberculture: Stewart Brand, the Whole Earth Network, and the Rise of Digital Utopianism*. Chicago: University of Chicago Press.

Tkacz, N. (2015). *Wikipedia and the Politics of Openness*. Chicago and London: University of Chicago Press.

Wagner, P. (2016). *Progress: A Reconstruction*. Hoboken, NJ: Wiley.

Wright, E. O. (2010). *Envisioning Real Utopias*. London and New York: Verso.

CHAPTER 7

Controlling Labor in Makeathons: On the Recuperation of Emancipation in Industrial Labor Processes

Klara-Aylin Wenten

Introduction: Transforming Labor Processes by Recuperating the Maker Culture

This paper investigates the recuperation of the originally emancipatory principles emerging from the 'maker culture'[1] using the example of a German industrial company. By drawing on Boltanski's and Chiapello's 'new spirit of capitalism' (Boltanski & Chiapello, 2007), the paper examines the relationship between the expectations and demands for emancipation and their adoption by an industrial organization. The paper thereby investigates a short-term event for prototyping ('the makeathon') and argues that originally emancipatory demands from the maker culture were co-opted in the context of organizing labor differently. It finally shows that this co-optation was associated with new (and rather ambivalent) modes of control. Following Boltanski and Chiapello

K.-A. Wenten (✉)
Munich Center for Technology in Society, Technical University of Munich, Munich, Germany
e-mail: Klara-Aylin.Wenten@tum.de

U. Meyer et al. (eds.), *Digitalization in Industry*,
https://doi.org/10.1007/978-3-030-28258-5_7

(2007), 'emancipation' in this paper is primarily understood as the liberation from prevailing power structures and dependencies.

The paper is situated within the larger discourse around the transformation of labor and demands for an autonomous, flexible and entrepreneurial labor force (Briken, Chillas, & Krzywdzinski, 2017; Frayssé & O'Neil, 2015; Mason, 2015). Such expectations and their potential for more team-based labor, creativity or autonomous labor organization are discussed by political, academic and industrial actors (Bauwens & Vasilis, 2014; Harhoff & Lakhani, 2016; Richardson, 2016). In this context, the analysis illuminates the relationship between the expectations or promises and their recuperation by capitalist accumulation rationales in the context of labor organization. By using Boltanski's and Chiapello's (2007) argument of recuperation, the paper seeks to demonstrate the assimilation of the emancipatory critique by capitalism[2] using the example of a car company. Recuperation particularly describes the adoption or repurposing of originally oppositional (emancipatory) voices by capitalism. Therefore, this line of thought can be useful for showing how certain forms of critique get absorbed, thereby achieving legitimation for the capitalist order and its persistence.

Against this background, the paper claims that makeathons can offer an exemplary case for the recuperation of emancipatory principles. Makeathons have emerged as events from the maker culture. With the aim to establish a community without any particular pre-existing expertise, makeathons should offer a place and opportunity for individuals to design and build products, external from any organizational or intellectual hierarchies. As the following paragraphs will show, their major promises concentrate on autonomous physical labor, collaborative communities and personal authority over technological knowledge. They have the particular aim of the emancipation from dominated and controlled production processes. Yet, companies have now started to adopt the idea of makeathons and their attendant promises. This has the primary objective of finding practical solutions to technical or creative problems in industrial development processes. Makeathons can bring together employees from the firm to develop a prototype in very short time frames and within more or less self-organized structures. Thus, these events can provide testing fields for organizing innovation labor differently, by implementing more unconventional practices being inspired by the maker culture.

As follows, the subsequent assessment gives insights into the potential effects of the maker culture on labor processes and on the employees' situation, exemplified by the case of an automobile company. It argues that the relationship between the demands by actors from the maker culture and their recuperation by capitalism is mediated by the introduction of organizational control, collective control and self-control. By this, the industrial company managed to respect the employees' interests and, at the same time, legitimated its own targets. The makeathon can, therefore, be interpreted as a case for the organization's engagement in what Burawoy has called 'manufacturing consent' (Burawoy, 1979) in the labor force.

The paper starts by discussing the theoretical argument of recuperation and a contextualization of the maker culture and its emancipatory critique. Subsequently, the paper introduces a particular makeathon by elaborating on the promises and expectations coming from the car company and its employees. The core sections of this paper examine how the recuperation of three principles of the maker culture is stabilized by the emergence of control. The paper finally demonstrates how the recuperation can produce ambivalent and often conflicting work requirements for the employees.

Conceptual Perspectives on Recuperating the Maker Culture

With reference to Boltanski's and Chiapello's (2007) proposal of a 'new spirit of capitalism,' the paper argues that makeathons are located in recuperation processes of oppositional principles from the maker culture. These principles are based on autonomous physical labor, collaborative communities and personal authority over technological knowledge. Industrial companies now adopt these to (re-)organize internal labor processes. Drawing from Science and Technology Studies (STS) and from the sociology of labor, the following paragraphs discuss both their contributing and missing perspectives for analyzing recuperation in the context of makeathons and innovation labor.

At the core of Boltanski's and Chiapello's argument (2007) stands the recuperation of emancipatory critique, which is related to the social critique and the artistic counterculture of the 1970s. The authors examine management discourses from the 1970s to the 1990s in order to understand the dynamics and conditions under which capitalism maintains its acceptance and legitimation. As both authors clarify:

> The spirit of capitalism is precisely the set of beliefs associated with the capitalist order that helps to justify this order and, by legitimating them, to sustain the forms of action and predispositions compatible with it. (Boltanski & Chiapello, 2007, p. 29)

In this context, Boltanski and Chiapello, however, do not only concentrate on actions that appear '*compatible with*' the capitalist order; they exemplify how capitalism can only sustain and overcome its own inherent barriers by also incorporating viewpoints that are critical toward it: 'it was by recuperating some of the oppositional themes [...] that capitalism was [able] to disarm critique, regain the initiative, and discover a new dynamism' (Boltanski & Chiapello, 2007, p. 168). Thus, Boltanski and Chiapello demonstrate that critical, dissenting and emancipatory beliefs against capitalism were, in turn, co-opted and recuperated by it. They are claimed to be repossessed from the hopes of artists for autonomy, creativity, authenticity and liberation. As the authors note:

> Capitalism attracts actors, who realize that they have hitherto been oppressed, by offering them a certain form of liberation that masks new types of oppression. It may then be said that capitalism 'recuperates' the autonomy it extends, by implementing new modes of control. (Boltanski & Chiapello, 2007, p. 425)

On the one hand, these new modes of control have created new enterprise mechanisms with the aim to re-engage workers and highly skilled employees. On the other, they have led to muting oppositional voices by legitimating the novel spirit of capitalism. Boltanski and Chiapello illustrate how such a process of recuperation resulted in a more flexible, self-responsible and autonomous labor force. Hence, originally oppositional voices were incorporated by capitalism through the emergence of new organizations, enterprise mechanisms and forms of labor or identities. By these means, the capitalist order was able to be maintained and sustained—even when substantial criticism against it arose.

This paper seeks to extend Boltanski's and Chiapello's claims, by arguing that it is likewise the (ideological) principles of the maker culture that are now integrated into the capitalist framework.

The central principles of the maker culture are characterized by beliefs in autonomous physical labor (1), collaborative communities (2) and personal authority over technological knowledge (3).

First, the maker culture calls for the emancipation from controlled, alienated production processes by stressing the importance of autonomous physical labor. Physical labor is here understood as the making and creation of material objects (in contrast to the sole application of intellectual labor). By this development, proponents of the maker culture expect an increase of creativity, self-expression and greater 'satisfaction that comes from [...] physical labor' (Hatch, 2014, p. 12). By performing physical labor in a more self-determined manner, the production process would be less alienated and more personalized. This is why actors from the maker culture anticipate regaining autonomy in the 'making' of physical objects, thereby challenging otherwise controlled production processes (Bauwens & Vasilis, 2014; Harhoff & Lakhani, 2016; Hatch, 2014; Wark, 2004).

Second, the maker culture strongly endorses collaborative communities to produce more networked and sociable qualities in both work and leisure activities. In this regard, the maker culture seeks to present itself as a community that uses different kinds of technology (the Internet, 3D printers, industrial machine tools, etc.) with which every member can connect and distribute knowledge. At the core of this community stands the idea of 'commons-based peer production,' which involves the communalization and sharing of technology, knowledge and expertise (Benkler & Nissenbaum, 2006; Mota, 2011; P2P Foundation, 2012). In so-called shared machine shops,[3] actors from the maker culture aim at a transformation from the hitherto exclusive access to knowledge production, technology and the general workplace into a more collaborative, sharing community with commonly accessible technology.

Third, the maker culture has a more precise claim to personal intellectual authority over technology's functionality. In addition to the claim for autonomous physical labor, the demands also focus on the potential for greater power over technological expertise and knowledge. As Dougherty, the founder of one of the maker culture's main magazines 'MAKE,' underlines in one of his talks: 'makers [...] want to figure out how things work, they want to get access to it, and they want to control it; they want to use it to their own purpose' (Dougherty, 2011). Such a 'do-it-yourself' approach characterizes the principle of understanding and working with technology on your own (Gauntlett, 2011; Hatch, 2014;

Troxler & Maxigas, 2014). The demand for a growing authority and power over technology and its functionality resulted from the lack of transparency and the criticism against state governance over personal data and elite groups possessing expert knowledge over technology's infrastructure (Dougherty, 2012; Stangler & Maxwell, 2012). Thus, the maker movement can be portrayed as an oppositional movement supporting emancipation from prevailing (economic and social) hierarchies in knowledge production and technological development.

However, most of the studies pertaining to STS have already highlighted the ways in which countercultural, often anti-capitalist, viewpoints from the maker culture became integrated into corporate structures. Scholars like Söderberg and Delfanti (2015a) and Turner (2006) indicate how the maker culture's activities have created a substantial impact on working lives. Turner examined the Internet culture in relation to the rise of start-ups and tech companies in Silicon Valley, asserting that

> hierarchies have been replaced by flattened structures, long-term employment by short-term, project-based contracting, and professional positions by complex, networked forms of sociability. (Turner, 2006, p. 239)

Scholars like Drewlani and Seibt (2018), Maxigas (2017) and Söderberg and Delfanti (2015b), argue similarly that this culture is itself 'being hacked' by big companies and capitalist interests. Hence, the maker culture appears to be in the midst of affecting the wider realm of work and industrial production. Consequently, we can observe that the demands for autonomous physical labor, collaborative communities and personal authority over technological knowledge by the maker culture might also enter and affect wider work practices. Irani (2015), Menichinelli, Bianchini, Carosi, and Maffei (2017) and Lindtner and Avle (2017) have begun to focus on the maker culture's potential effects on industrial companies, on labor processes and on the employees. This paper will take these perspectives as its starting point, investigating how certain ideas from the maker culture are recuperated by capitalism when being implemented in a German car company. Assuming that makeathons are applied in the (re-)organization of labor, it needs to be investigated further how they have actually reconfigured it. That is why the paper contributes to the lines of thought in STS by looking more specifically at the labor process.

In this context, the sociology of labor provides a vast literature on the organization of labor in creative industries (Huws, 2010; Lee, 2013; Pfeiffer, Schütt, & Wühr, 2012). These investigations point, for example, to new forms of control. These would stand in stark contrast to demands for autonomy, new resources for greater self-control or the growing importance of craft labor in addition to creativity (Banks, 2010). Yet the present case demonstrates that creative labor and innovation practices are deeply integrated into the industrial context. As follows, it hints at a more complex intertwining of 'creative freedom' (Bennett & Strange, 2015; Huws, 2014), project-based labor organization (Kalff, 2018) and hierarchies or power struggles (Burawoy, 1985; Fuchs, 2014). With regard to makeathons, however, sociologists of labor have only marginally analyzed the implementation of the maker culture into innovation processes. Zukin and Papadantonakis (2017), for instance, investigate the impact of hackathons and (unpaid) labor in platform companies. They focus on software production in IT companies and hackathons that aim at building digital improvements for the company's software. The authors thereby highlight forms of self-exploitation and demonstrate how hackathons can manufacture consent among workers. However, these events taking place in platform companies do not reflect on contemporary conventional labor processes like those used by industrial organizations such as in the car industry.

In summary, this section has argued that the present case of a makeathon is centrally positioned in the tensions between an emancipatory critique and its recuperation by capitalism. Building on Boltanski's and Chiapello's argument, the prevailing dynamics in innovation labor are illuminated by strong and intricate conflicts of power between claims for emancipation and their control. Consequently, the relationship between emancipatory potentials in labor processes and the practices of actually controlling them make for a messy arrangement rather than a diametrically opposed contrast. While autonomous labor might be enabled in the form of practices external from domination, it still remains uncertain whether it could still be applied as control and, thus, another form of domination. It is precisely this interplay between emancipatory demands and their control that will be analyzed more closely in the subsequent analysis.

Makeathons in the Car Industry: Promises and Expectations

This section discusses the promises and expectations articulated by the managers, employees and the organizers of a German automobile manufacturer who were involved in the makeathon. On the one hand, it provides answers to the motives for recuperating principles from the maker culture. It thereby emphasizes how the makeathon contributes to generating consent among the labor force. On the other hand, it can reveal the intricate and ambivalent relationship between the demands by the company and those on the part of a skilled labor force.

The makeathon under investigation was hosted in a shared machine shop that is co-financed by a car company. The makeathon had the general aim of developing a prototype by working at machines. Within a timeframe of less than two weeks, the employees had to start with processes of idea collection and team building. This process was intended to proceed further to the practical manufacturing of prototypes. Educated trainers from the shared machine shop held three-hour courses at machines to help the participants perform the work on their own. Thus, the makeathon sought to create teams and a community, in which employees could collaborate and share their knowledge with each other. The makeathon ended with short presentations to a group of managers who would evaluate the prototypes. Three prizes, ranging from financial rewards to business training, were given to the best prototypes. These would ideally be developed further into professionalized products entering the market, or being applied for the firm's internal use. At the time of this investigation, the makeathon was still in the testing phase but it had been hosted for the fourth time. The examination is based on ethnographic fieldwork undertaken during a makeathon organized by the car company. The fieldwork comprises one and a half months of field observations and 20 interviews being conducted in the period between 2016 and 2018. The data has been analyzed in the form of a content analysis according to Mayring (2010).[4]

With regard to the company's expectations, the makeathon promised to respond to the growing influence of start-ups in the car industry. At one of the biggest fairs for innovation in consumer technology held at the beginning of 2018, start-ups were seen to be growing in importance in the car section. As one article notes:

> ...in the spotlight are start-up founders that generate a plethora of ideas about the possibilities of mobility in the future. Automobile companies have a lot catching up to accomplish in this field. (Kröger, 2018)

The car company therefore emphasized the importance of new and more efficient methods of organizing innovation labor. The general description of the makeathon specifically promises to 'integrate best practices from traditional mechatronic development with methods inspired by lean start-up, scrum and design thinking' into internal innovation processes (Hostettler & Böhmer, 2018). That is why companies are interested in implementing makeathons not only because of the amplification of entrepreneurial thinking, creativity or faster innovation processes. Makeathons also promise being more hands-on and physical labor being established by practical work performed at machines (Böhmer, Beckmann, & Lindemann, 2015; Irani, 2015; Lindtner, Hertz, & Dourish, 2014). Consequently, the makeathon was expected to support the automobile company in keeping up with start-up methodologies that already seem to offer fresh innovation tools in labor organization.

Considering the employees' expectations, they regarded the makeathon as a possibility to regain autonomy over the labor process. One of the interviewed participants mentioned how 'it is important that we work more autonomously and that we organize ourselves, without [...] hierarchies' (Interviewee A). Therefore, the employees expected that these demands especially would be respected and realized in the makeathon. The makeathon promised an exciting workplace since the task of transforming an idea into an actual physical product stood in stark contrast to their everyday practices. According to the makeathon's organizer, it should create an atmosphere where the employees 'don't do Power Points, [have] no meetings and no bosses who interfere' (Interviewee B). Seen from an employee's perspective, the makeathon suggested the opportunity to put their demands for an exciting, diverse and autonomous workplace into practice. Similarly to the employees, the organizers were interested in working in a different, exciting workplace. They engaged in hosting the makeathon because, as the following quote underlines, 'I just really enjoy developing things by myself [...] so I thought: Yeah, awesome, I can work in my own paradise' (Interviewee B). As a consequence, the makeathon was meant for employees and organizers to acknowledge the company's efforts of responding to the demand for autonomy or an attractive workplace.

Consequently, the managers and organizers anticipated a growing motivation among the employees, which seems to have the aim to 'manufacture consent' and acceptance. This describes what Burawoy characterized as the workers' voluntary participation in exploitative labor processes (1979). The makeathon mostly involved engineers and designers with highly skilled backgrounds, or trainees still in apprenticeship. Some of the participants were employees who were formally self-employed but were permanently contracted by the company. In talking to the makeathon's organizers, the company allowed such a hybrid and atypical employment structure since 'before they [employees] get frustrated, they better do something on the side and stay happy' (Interviewee B). In this respect, the car company under discussion seems to react to the growing influence of the start-up culture in the car industry, as well as to the demand for different, more flexible employment structures. Yet, in Boltanski's and Chiapello's reading, the makeathon seemed to embrace the demands for more diverse work practices in order to legitimate and accept even oppositional voices. The makeathon could thereby render opposition in the form of doubts or frustrations at the workplace in ways compatible with the capitalist labor process. As the organizer of the makeathon who was interviewed observed: 'in the end, it turns out that everybody is happy. The employees [...] want reputation and acknowledgment. And if they do everything faster, also the company gets faster results' (Interviewee B). Therefore, while the makeathon should create an exciting atmosphere, it simultaneously functioned as generating acceptance and general consent among the labor force. Consequently, makeathons are not just tools for innovation to provide more enjoyable practices for the company's employees; they can also function as a legitimation for capitalist production processes.

Overall, the makeathon was expected to establish new ways of organizing labor that are inspired and influenced by start-up methodologies. They are further expected to motivate and reactivate the labor force. The makeathon sought to offer an exciting workplace and thereby responded to employee demands. This should ideally contribute to the manufacture of consent among the employees. As a result, the car company could react to potential critique and demands voiced by the employees. Hence, makeathons can provide attempts to realize the recuperation by the integration of new ways of organizing labor. The next section will, therefore, investigate how this is practically realized through the recuperation of three principles by the maker culture.

Recuperating the Maker Culture: The Makeathon Between Emancipation and Control

This section outlines the recuperation of the maker culture's principles of autonomous physical labor, collaborative communities and personal authority over technological knowledge. It exhibits how such a recuperation, however, was stabilized by the introduction of organizational control (1), collective control (2) and self-control (3).

1. Recuperating autonomous physical labor by organizational control

In organizing the makeathon, the car company sought to adopt the maker culture's principle of autonomous physical labor. Such a principle is mainly based on the production of materials without any hierarchical order, which should facilitate self-expression and satisfaction. Yet, paradoxically, it will be shown how the makeathon's promise of hands-on production could only be facilitated by the introduction of organizational control. Organizational control in this context is understood as the company's authority over the employees by formalizing the labor processes.

The makeathon should establish the unfolding of creativity, self-expression and autonomy in the process of generating a physical prototype. It was important to use the machines, to physically create and 'make.' According to the organizer, the physical work was the essential moment when the employees would 'really get a grasp of the material' (Interviewee A). The entire makeathon took place in an external workshop called a 'makerspace.' Such workshops are closely connected to the maker culture as they establish the direct engagement with the production process at the machines and tools. Therefore, the organizers tried to motivate the employees to 'go as creative as you can at the machines' (Field notes ethnography 1). In introducing the makeathon, the organizers emphasized that the workshop was intended as a space for the 'free flow of ideas.' They desired to create an atmosphere in which participants were meant to collect ideas on their own without the imposition of a tangible supervisory context. Therefore, they 'didn't predefine any ideas' (Interviewee C), as one participant mentioned. This should foster creativity and self-expression among the participants: 'we want to create a space for creative and autonomously crafted ideas,' where 'you just organize yourselves and [...] we just leave you by yourselves' (Interviewee A), as the organizer emphasized. Thus, on the one hand, the instructions on how to develop ideas remained very vague in the beginning. On the other hand, the employees were encouraged to abandon long conceptualization phases and, instead, directly start with designing and working with physical material. This can be regarded as the adoption of the maker culture's demand for greater autonomy and the unfolding of creative, self-expressive actions. By focusing on the 'making' of physical objects, the company aimed at implementing the maker culture's call for precisely such elements as self-expression, creativity and autonomous manufacturing.

However, the recuperation of autonomous physical labor was soon accompanied by organizational control. The organizers adopted the call for physical labor and now turned it into the most important imperative of the makeathon. In order to guarantee feasible outcomes in the form of a functioning prototype, they intervened in the ideation process very directly. They tried to ensure that the outcomes of the event exhibited a certain universality and similarity. And this was especially done by stressing the importance of developing a *physical* prototype. More intangible products such as, for instance, software apps were not allowed. The original idea of gaining autonomy and satisfaction through working with material soon turned into formalized organizational control. One employee noted that the participants 'have first gone into the wrong direction a bit, which [they] have found out at the end of the first day' (Interviewee A). These participants began with an idea for a digital software product, but realized later on that it did not match the makeathon's target. Another employee asserted that the organizers 'have bawled us out: "this is a shared machine shop, here you have to create something physical"' (Interviewee C). In this regard, the organizers started to hierarchically arrange a universalization of ideas and outcomes. Thus, the creative and independently crafted thought of the participants was quickly controlled by the firm's expectations and the makeathon's targets. In this manner, the teams were organized solely via a top-down decision imposed by the organizers themselves. By adopting the maker culture's belief in physical labor, the makeathon turned precisely such a demand into the formalization of ideas and their actual outcomes. The possibility of actual self-expression and creativity subsequently remained very limited and determined by the makeathon's main goals.

In sum, the recuperation of the first principle of autonomous physical labor aimed at the generation of creativity, self-expression and autonomous organization of the work practices. However, this section has shown how the recuperation was soon coupled with organizational control. The claim for autonomous physical labor transformed into the main makeathon's imperative and therefore formalized the subsequent stages of prototyping.

2. Recuperating collaborative communities by collective control

The second principle from the maker culture being recuperated by the car company was based on the emergence of collaborative communities. Proponents of the maker culture demand a greater networked community, in which members should collaborate and share their knowledge and practices with each other. Regarding the makeathon, the car company adopted such an approach in the context of innovation labor. The section, however, shows how this came along with collective control.

First, it was the infrastructural construction of the workshop which the car company co-opted in order to establish a collaborative community. In addition to a more direct engagement with the machines, the maker culture has established these workspaces for collectively working at machines. The shared machine shop, in which the makeathon took place, was constructed and built in a very open and transparent manner. Every section of the workshop was visible and accessible due to the use of glass doors. Separated parts of the workshop could be seen from the outside. According to a member of the shared machine shop,

> [the architects] paid a lot of attention [...] that the rooms have windows and [...] that you can see the metal workshop from the main entrance. I think that's pretty important since it nurtures ideas [...]. And by seeing the people, I can immediately help them. (Interviewee D)

Consequently, the participants should feel that they could help and support each other easily. The infrastructure, hence, produced a specific form of collaborative labor based on transparent and thus, perhaps, even more intelligible practices.

Second, the demand for collaborative communities was additionally co-opted in the context of organizing and using the workshop. Employees had to share the machines with the rest of the participants of the makeathon. There were no strict regulations regarding the manner in which the work was accomplished or, for instance, where people stored their material. Therefore, every user interacted on a level playing field. The organizers did not interfere in the allocation schedules or the arrangement systems devised by the users in the workshop.

There were guidelines set by the machine shop, which included principles like 'share all the tools you use with the others' or 'help yourselves when support is needed' (Field notes Ethnography 1). The organizers instructed the participants to fully respect these guidelines. Besides that, however, the organizers seemed to turn invisible and unnoticed during the work in the workshop. Although they always appeared when motivating and encouraging the employees in their work, their role was hardly recognized by the employees. Hence, also the organizers themselves tried to activate a certain community spirit among the employees to permit collaboration and collective regulation of the workshop. Such practices contribute to the unfolding of a novel form of sociability and community. In this respect, scholars such as Dolata and Schrape (2018) or Dahlander and Magnusson (2005) have already underlined the dynamics of 'open innovation' and its economic instrumentalization. They point to the notion of a 'sharing economy' and elucidate the manner in which non-economic, communitarian principles of open, transparent and shared innovation tools have been utilized by larger firms (Hippel, 2005; West, Salter, Vanhaverbeke, & Chesbrough, 2014). Accordingly, this instrumentalization sought to render labor processes more democratic and transparent to a certain (albeit small) extent. In the instance under review, the car company turned the maker culture's tenets into economically feasible attributes for an efficient but collaborative teamwork.

Yet in order to achieve the unfolding of collaborative labor processes, the makeathon transformed the sharing into collective control. Neither the organizers nor other supervisors controlled the organization and use of the workshop directly. By recuperating the idea of a collaborative community, the control over labor processes increasingly shifted to the community itself. The expectation of working collectively and sharing the workspace confronted the employees with another mode of control that was now exercised by the community, that is, is all of the team members. Aspects such as visibility, openness and communalization in the workshop resulted in an atmosphere where everyone was watching everybody. As a consequence, the individual's labor process became supervised and, thus, controlled by the community as a whole. Even though the organizers were not explicitly noticed by the participants, they still played a role in guaranteeing such a collective control. Their 'unnoticed presence' had the effect of motivating and simultaneously intensifying the collaborative workflow. By encouraging the employees' activities, they made sure to keep them working. At the same time, they left the responsibility of organizing the shared machine shop to the community. As a result, the community in the shared machine shop pre-defined and directed everyone's interactions toward a collaborative way of working. This case therefore underpins how the shared machine shop and the organizers contributed to reinforce control among, and also by, the participants themselves. Thus, the recuperation of a collaborative community came along with a collective control over the employees' practices.

The recuperation of collaborative communities in the makeathon sought to address the employees as a community to share their knowledge and personal practices with each other. This, however, simultaneously metamorphosed into specific control coming from the community in the shared machine shop. This collective control was particularly reinforced by the infrastructural setting and the rather subtle influence of the organizers.

3. Recuperating personal authority over technological knowledge by self-control

The third principle of personal authority over technological knowledge was re-purposed by the car company when reinforcing self-responsibility in the development of the prototypes. While the maker culture supports the idea of gaining expertise and knowledge over technology's functionality, it was in this context transformed into the condition of a continuous upskilling and self-marketing. The following paragraphs illuminate how this was stabilized by the emergence of greater self-control.

The significance of the recuperated principles of personal authority over technological knowledge was facilitated by the company's expectation of individual upskilling. Their adoption not only came along with collective control, but the makeathon was also expected to mobilize the self-control among the participants. This was enabled through the courses as well as the final presentations of the prototypes. In addition to the requirement of exercising physical labor, employees had to test the prototypes and to rework them if required. As a precondition of the makeathon, every participant had to take an introductory course on one machine present in the shared machine shop. The taught courses offered by the shared machine shop's trainers were supposed to impart basic knowledge of working at the respective machines. They involved theoretical and practical elements; thus, employees really had to understand how to work at the respective machine. Hence, the makeathon was conceptualized as a means of according individual authority over technological knowledge, an aspiration that is deeply connected to the maker culture's tenets. The manager of the shared machine shop emphasized that the principle of the machine shop was to 'allow you to press the button on your own and to be part of it' (Interviewee E). In doing so, the makeathon was said to facilitate the do-it-yourself principle. In this context, the organizers aimed at motivating the employees by commenting on the current state of the work and pushing the employees' project forward. They served to help the employees to realize the new approach of gaining expertise on prototyping and the machines' functionality. Moreover, the final act of presenting the prototypes in front of the management had the same objective of using the acquired knowledge in the presentation. The employees should use and skillfully display their knowledge and expertise when presenting the final prototype. Consequently, the personal acquisition of technological knowledge should emerge during the work at the machines, as well as during the final presentations. Such do-it-yourself ideals originate from grassroots movements to circumvent consumerism and to gain personal authority and responsibility over expertise (Delfanti, 2014). But in this instance, it has been re-purposed by the industrial company in order to transform the labor process.

The recuperation of the maker culture's claim for gaining greater knowledge on technology required that each of the participants started to control themselves. A closer look at the training sessions demonstrates how the co-opted tenet remained dependent on self-control. This included very important aspects such as the ability to actually understand technology in the first place. As revealed in the fieldwork, the training received did not always actually lead to an easy and comfortable creation of the physical object:

> Our trainer Tim starts introducing me and the other participants into the machines and hands out the manual for each of the machine. […] We are both a bit clumsy and very puzzled. […] Tim gives us some material, explains what to do with it but we are, again, helpless and just start improvising. (Field notes ethnography 2).

The quote indicates that the idea of personal authority over technological knowledge still relies on the usability of technology. Yet, this is quite constrained by the individual's dependence on training material and on the individual's ability to understand it. The dependence on the required experience and knowledge can, thus, intensify the self-control by forcing the employees to manage their own success.

Moreover, the enabling power of makeathons designed to impart individual authority over technology consequently mutated into individual upskilling. The makeathon's organizers did not articulate concrete instructions but they still expected the employees to create value and to contribute to the company's success. One of the organizers of the makeathon asserted: 'You show it to the right people who will immediately say "Make it!"' (Interviewee B). This quote shows how the employees were now confronted with discovering their own internal investor: 'finding the right people' who would then finance their product. The interviewed organizer emphasized further: 'I don't give a shit! You have an idea: Do it! And convince me that your idea is good' (Interviewee B). This resulted in greater self-marketing and self-evaluation according to individual marketing competencies. The employees were forced to control their own work, to hone their capabilities to be the best and to convince the managers that their prototype should win. Obviously, this kind of upskilling became itself a mode of control.[5] It left the employees isolated in evaluating whether their prototype was actually functional, if it was valuable and how it could be promoted to the best effect. Thus, the recuperation of the maker culture's claim for gaining greater knowledge about technology finally engendered and reinforced the self-control among the employees.

To sum up, the recuperation of the maker culture's principle of personal authority over technological knowledge should enable the employees to use their own knowledge and expertise independently. However, it has been shown how the employees became simultaneously confronted by the necessity of continuous upskilling and self-marketing. This expectation set another individual control based on better self-evaluation and on self-controlling the labor process. Hence, the recuperation of the third principle by the maker culture was mediated by intensified self-control.

Conclusion and Discussion

All in all, the analysis has illustrated how the maker culture's principles have been recuperated by capitalist accumulation processes, when being adopted by an industrial company. Originally emancipatory demands for autonomous physical labor, collaborative communities and personal authority over technological knowledge were transformed into the company's approach of organizing labor differently. By studying the specific case of a makeathon, the analysis finally illustrated how the recuperation was stabilized by different modes of control.

First, it identified that the recuperation of autonomous physical labor enabled the employees to self-express themselves and become more creative by 'making' material objects. Yet this was soon constrained by organizational control, when formalizing the makeathon's outputs and teams. As a consequence, the analysis demonstrated how the general framework of the makeathon can put strong limits on the actual realization of originally emancipatory demands. By formalizing the teams and outcomes, it remains questionable to what extent the creativity and self-expression during the labor process can finally develop. Especially due to the strong intervention by the organizers, it seems very difficult to really develop an individually crafted, physically manufactured object that embodies creative—and potentially innovative—qualities.

Second, the paper illustrated how the demand for collaborative communities was integrated by introducing practices of shared knowledge and collective organization. This, however, was soon associated with collective control coming from the community itself. Regarding the appearance of collective control in the introduction of sharing principles, it is, furthermore, rather unlikely to foster an actual community with communitarian and sharing ideals. On the contrary, the integration of collective control in innovation processes could render actual collaboration processes even more challenging. By fostering a mode of collectively monitoring each of the steps in the labor process, it remains to be debated how this might not even lead to an intensified competitive atmosphere. Potential consequences of this new mode of control could lead to a decrease in solidarity and the emergence of even greater individualized identities.

Third, the paper illuminated the incorporation of the demand for personal authority over technological knowledge. This involved greater self-responsibility over the physical work at machines. Nevertheless, also in this context, the paper could demonstrate how the industrial company stabilized the recuperation by implementing another mode of self-control. However, as the collective control has already suggested, the makeathon might reinforce an additional intensification of individuality and a continuous expectation of self-discipline.

As a consequence, the recuperation and the emerging modes of control entail complex and conflicting work requirements. They now alternate between collaborative teamwork and individual self-control. On the one hand, the makeathon allowed the participants to organize their work autonomously and be more self-controlled. On the other hand, however, the demand for collaborative communities turned into the expectation of still collectively organizing the workshop. Hence, encouraged by continuous self-responsibility and autonomy, employees became additionally confronted by the requirement of performing as a team. Thus, the demands for a community increasingly clashed with the ones for more individuality. As a consequence, the combination of organizational control, collective control and self-control can finally turn the new way of working into a very intricate and challenging work requirement. The example of a makeathon can point to the development of new forms of (intensified) pressure, control and internal competition among the employees. Hence, the analysis illuminates how it might become very challenging for the employees to convert their demands into benefits of their own. The emerging modes of control involve highly political implications, considering the fact that playful and self-determined work practices become increasingly monitored and somehow more precarious and vulnerable.

Against this background, the makeathon is interpreted as a case for the organization's engagement in what Burawoy called the manufacturing of consent (Burawoy, 1979). By recuperating the demands from the labor force, the makeathon sought to create a labor process, with which the employees ideally confirmed without opposition. Hence, the industrial company could manage to respect the employee's interests and, at the same time, legitimate its own targets. These involved faster innovation processes, market success, as well as the employees' satisfaction with their working conditions. Even though it remains uncertain how makeathons will fare in the future, they can still exemplify current organizational attempts at mobilizing and maintaining participation in capitalist production processes. This development could, hence, produce different problematic and ambivalent outcomes of newly established labor processes.

Yet, and to conclude, it should be emphasized that the recuperation might still offer the potential for change by the employees themselves. The paper has shown how the recuperation is entangled within heterogeneous demands for emancipation and attempts to instrumentalize them.

Hence, the makeathon can likewise be grasped as a way of organizing labor, in which the potential for emancipation remains integrated—but hidden—in capitalist rationales. Since the makeathon remains a testing field, it could, nevertheless, be potentially re-purposed by those actors that are now the most affected by the emerging control. In Boltanski's and Chiapello's reading:

> Yet the critical approach becomes meaningless if one does not believe that it can serve to inflect human beings' action, and that this action can itself help to change the course of things in the direction of further 'liberation'. (Boltanski & Chiapello, 2007, p. x)

The recuperation of oppositional viewpoints can hence be altered or changed by human actions, which, in the present case, primarily involves the employees. Consequently, it should be stressed that the recuperation is not a fixed matter of fact; it can still be transformed and altered due to the underlying demands for emancipation that capitalism has meant to absorb. The paper, therefore, does not only call for greater attention to the emerging modes of control in attempts to (re-)organize labor processes, but it also seeks to inspire the ongoing debates around recuperation in industrial labor processes. Following Söderberg and Delfanti (2015b), this paper therefore concludes by emphasizing the potential of recuperating the recuperated principles. Such a perspective can become an opportunity for employees to deal with the new modes of control differently. Debating these potentials could be a first step for the controlled actors toward emancipation, instead of simply reproducing the recuperation process by capitalism again.

Index of Interviews and Field Activities

Interviewee A: An employee of the car company; the interview was conducted in December 2017.

Interviewee B: An organizer of the makeathon; the interview was conducted in December 2017.

Interviewee C: An employee at the car company; the interview was conducted in December 2017.

Interviewee D: A team member of the shared machine shop; the interview was conducted in May 2016.

Interviewee E: The manager of the shared machine shop; the interview was conducted in June 2016.

Interviewee F: An employee at the car company; the interview was conducted in December 2017.

Field notes 1: Ethnographic fieldwork undertaken during the course of the car company's makeathon organized in December 2017.

Field notes 2: Ethnographic fieldwork undertaken in the shared machine shop in May–June 2016.

Notes

1. The maker culture assembles a community that is often identified by both its adherents and its external actors as 'makers' or 'hackers.' The term 'maker' connects particularly those individuals and social groups that are interested in self-organized manufacturing processes using technology such as 3D printers, laser cutters or other industrial machine tools. These individuals may espouse various ideologies based on self-sufficiency, anti-capitalism, autonomy, but may also subscribe to commercialization and entrepreneurialism (Dickel, Schneider, Thiem, & Wenten, 2019).
2. Capitalism is here understood as the 'imperative to unlimited accumulation of capital' (Boltanski & Chiapello, 2007, p. 4), which is particularly characterized by the creation of profit through the (re-)investment of capital.
3. The expression 'shared machine shops' functions here as an umbrella term for the great number of different workshops like Makerspaces, Hackspaces, FabLabs, Open Labs or TechShops. This terminology is widely used in current scholarly discourse and best conceptualizes the different forms of decentralized, collectively organized workshops, as well as their diverse orientations ranging from non-commercial to commercial machine shops (Dickel & Schrape, 2015; Smith, Hielscher, Dickel, Söderberg, & van Oost, 2013).
4. The analysis has included periods of coding according to the categories of recuperation and emancipatory critique conceptualized by Boltanski and Chiapello (2007). It has additionally involved a content analysis of different documents (interview transcripts, field notes, newspaper articles and marketing material from the company) in order to establish the main principles of the maker culture. It could finally support the investigation of the different modes of control that emerge during the implementation of the makeathon.
5. This seems to stand in contrast to Braverman's argument of increased managerial control over the labor process by the elimination of skilled labor (Braverman, 1998). Accordingly, workers would lose the ability to apply their knowledge and skills due to the introduction of technology and

the substitution of skilled labor with semi- or unskilled labor (deskilling). The makeathon, however, rather shows how even forms of upskilling can similarly lead to an increase of control, though now concentrating on more self-controlled labor processes.

References

Banks, M. (2010). Craft Labor and Creative Industries. *International Journal of Cultural Policy, 16*(3), 305–321. https://doi.org/10.1080/10286630903055885.

Bauwens, M., & Vasilis, K. (2014). From the Communism of Capital to Capital for the Commons: Towards an Open Co-operativism. *TripleC, 12*(1), 356–361.

Benkler, Y., & Nissenbaum, H. (2006). Commons-Based Peer Production and Virtue. *The Journal of Political Philosophy, 14*(4), 394–419.

Bennett, J., & Strange, N. (Eds.). (2015). *Media Independence: Working with Freedom or Working for Free?* New York, NY: Routledge.

Böhmer, A., Beckmann, A., & Lindemann, U. (2015, December). *Open Innovation Ecosystem: Makerspaces Within an Agile Innovation Process.* Paper Presented at the ISPIM Innovation Summit, Brisbane, Australia.

Boltanski, L., & Chiapello, È. (2007). *The New Spirit of Capitalism.* London and New York: Verso.

Braverman, H. (1998). *Labor and Monopoly Capital: The Degradation of Work in the Twentieth Century* (25th Anniversary ed.). New York, NY: Monthly Review Press.

Briken, K., Chillas, S., & Krzywdzinski, M. (2017). *The New Digital Workplace: How New Technologies Revolutionise Work.* Basingstoke, Hampshire: Palgrave Macmillan.

Burawoy, M. (1979). *Manufacturing Consent: Changes in the Labor Process Under Monopoly Capitalism.* Chicago, IL: University Press of Chicago.

Burawoy, M. (1985). *The Politics of Production: Factory Regimes Under Capitalism and Socialism.* London: Verso.

Dahlander, L., & Magnusson, M. G. (2005). Relationships Between Open Source Software Companies and Communities: Observations from Nordic Firms. *Research Policy, 34*(4), 481–493. https://doi.org/10.1016/j.respol.2005.02.003.

Delfanti, A. (2014). Is Do-It-Yourself Biology Being Co-opted by Institutions? *UC Davis Previously Published Works.* Retrieved from https://escholarship.org/uc/item/4nz3p0hf.

Dickel, S., Schneider, C., Thiem, C., & Wenten, K.-A. (2019). Engineering Publics: The Different Modes of Civic Technoscience. *Science and Technology Studies, 32*(2), 8–23.

Dickel, S., & Schrape, J.-F. (2015). Dezentralisierung, Demokratisierung, Emanzipation: Zur Architektur des digitalen Technikutopismus. *Leviathan, 43*(3), 442–463.

Dolata, U., & Schrape, J.-F. (Eds.). (2018). *Kollektivität und Macht im Internet: Soziale Bewegungen - Open Source Communities - Internetkonzerne.* Wiesbaden: Springer VS.

Dougherty, D. (Author) (2011, January). *We Are Makers* [Television Broadcast]. TED Talk. Retrieved from https://www.ted.com/talks/dale_dougherty_we_are_makers.

Dougherty, D. (2012). The Maker Movement. *Innovations: Technology, Governance, Globalization, 7*(3), 11–14. https://doi.org/10.1162/INOV_a_00135.

Drewlani, T., & Seibt, D. (2018). Configuring the Independent Developer. *Journal of Peer Production, Issue 12: Makerspaces and Institutions* (12). Retrieved from http://peerproduction.net/editsuite/issues/issue-12-makerspaces-and-institutions/peer-reviewed-papers/configuring-the-independent-developer/.

Frayssé, O., & O'Neil, M. (Eds.). (2015). *Digital Labor and Prosumer Capitalism: The US Matrix.* Houndmills, Basingstoke, Hampshire: Palgrave Macmillan.

Fuchs, C. (2014). *Digital Labor and Karl Marx.* New York: Routledge.

Gauntlett, D. (2011). *Making Is Connecting: The Social Meaning of Creativity from DIY and Knitting to YouTube and Web 2.0.* Hoboken, NJ: Wiley.

Harhoff, D., & Lakhani, K. R. (2016). *Revolutionizing Innovation: Users, Communities, and Open Innovation.* Cambridge, MA: The MIT Press.

Hatch, M. (2014). *The Maker Movement Manifesto: Rules for Innovation in the New World of Crafters, Hackers, and Tinkerers.* New York, NY: McGraw-Hill Education.

Hippel, E. V. (2005). *Democratizing Innovation.* Cambridge, MA: MIT Press. Retrieved from http://mit.edu/evhippel/www/books/DI/DemocInn.pdf.

Hostettler, R., & Böhmer, A. (2018). *Experience TAF.* Retrieved from https://taf.expert/experience/.

Huws, U. (2010). Schöpfung und Enteignung: Die Dialektik von Autonomie und Kontrolle in der kreativen Arbeit. *Standpunkte, 38*(38), 1–6.

Huws, U. (2014). *Labor in the Global Digital Economy: The Cybertariat Comes of Age.* New York, NY: Monthly Review Press.

Irani, L. (2015). Hackathons and the Making of Entrepreneurial Citizenship. *Science, Technology and Human Values, 40*(5), 799–824.

Kalff, Y. (2018). *Organisierendes Arbeiten.* Bielefeld: transcript.

Kröger, M. (2018, February 15). Mobileye, Nvidia und Co. Diese Start-ups erfinden die Zukunft des Autos. *Spiegel Online.* Retrieved from http://www.spiegel.de/wirtschaft/unternehmen/autoindustrie-so-treiben-start-ups-daimler-bmw-und-co-vor-sich-her-a-1193319.html.

Lee, D. (2013). Creative Labor in the Cultural Industries. *Sociopedia.Isa*, 1–13.

Lindtner, S., & Avle, S. (2017). Tinkering with Governance. *Proceedings of the ACM on Human-Computer Interaction, 1*(CSCW), 1–18. https://doi.org/10.1145/3134705.

Lindtner, S., Hertz, G. D., & Dourish, P. (2014). Emerging Sites of HCI Innovation: Hackerspaces, Hardware Startups & Incubators. In *Proceedings of the SIGCHI Conference on Human Factors in Computing Systems* (pp. 439–448). New York, NY: ACM.

Mason, P. (2015). *Postcapitalism: A Guide to Our Future.* New York, NY: Penguin Random House.

Maxigas. (2017). Hackers Against Technology: Critique and Recuperation in Technological Cycles. *Social Studies of Science, 47*(6), 841–860. https://doi.org/10.1177/0306312717736387.

Mayring, P. (2010). *Qualitative Inhaltsanalyse. Grundlagen und Techniken* (11., aktual. u. überarb. Aufl). Weinheim/Basel: Beltz.

Menichinelli, M., Bianchini, M., Carosi, A., & Maffei, S. (2017). Makers as a New Work Condition Between Self-Employment and Community Peer-Production: Insights from a Survey on Makers in Italy. *Journal of Peer Production* (10). Retrieved from http://peerproduction.net/issues/issue-10-peer-production-and-work/peer-reviewed-papers/makers-as-a-new-work-condition-between-self-employment-and-community-peer-production-insights-from-a-survey-on-makers-in-italy/.

Mota, C. (2011). The Rise of Personal Fabrication. In *C&C '11 Proceedings of the 8th ACM Conference on Creativity and Cognition.* New York, NY: ACM.

P2P Foundation. (2012). *Synthetic Overview of the Collaborative Economy.* Amsterdam: P2P Foundation.

Pfeiffer, S., Schütt, P., & Wühr, D. (Eds.). (2012). *Smarte Innovation: Ergebnisse und neue Ansätze im Maschinen- und Anlagenbau.* Wiesbaden: VS Verlag für Sozialwissenschaften.

Richardson, M. (2016). Pre-hacked: Open Design and the Democratisation of Product Development. *New Media & Society, 18*(4), 653–666. https://doi.org/10.1177/1461444816629476.

Smith, A., Hielscher, S., Dickel, S., Söderberg, J., & van Oost, E. (2013). *Grassroots Digital Fabrication and Makerspaces: Reconfiguring, Relocating and Recalibrating Innovation?* (SPRU Working Paper Series; No. 2013-02). Brighton: SPRU, Science and Technology Policy Research.

Söderberg, J., & Delfanti, A. (2015a). Hacking Hacked!: The Life Cycles of Digital Innovation. *Science, Technology and Human Values, 40*(5), 793–798.

Söderberg, J., & Delfanti, A. (2015b). Repurposing the Hacker: Three Temporalities of Recuperation. *UC Davis Previsouly Published Works*, 1–22. Retrieved from https://escholarship.org/uc/item/9c86493g.

Stangler, D., & Maxwell, K. (2012). DIY Producer Society. *Innovations: Technology, Governance, Globalization, 7*(3), 3–10. https://doi.org/10.1162/INOV_a_00134.

Troxler, P., & Maxigas. (2014). We Now Have the Means of Production, But Where Is My Revolution? *Journal of Peer Production* (5). Retrieved from http://peerproduction.net/issues/issue-5-shared-machine-shops/editorial-section/editorial-note-we-now-have-the-means-of-production-but-where-is-my-revolution/.

Turner, F. (2006). *From Counterculture to Cyberculture: Stewart Brand, the Whole Earth Network, and the Rise of Digital Utopianism*. Chicago, IL: University of Chicago Press.

Wark, M. (2004). *A Hacker Manifesto*. Cambridge, MA: Harvard University Press.

West, J., Salter, A., Vanhaverbeke, W., & Chesbrough, H. (2014). Open Innovation: The Next Decade. *Research Policy, 43*(5), 805–811. https://doi.org/10.1016/j.respol.2014.03.001.

Zukin, S., & Papadantonakis, M. (2017). Hackathons as Co-optation Ritual: Socializing Workers and Institutionalizing Innovation in the "New" Economy. In A. Kalleberg & S. Vallas (Eds.), *Precarious Work: Research in the Sociology of Work* (31st ed., pp. 157–181). Bingley, UK: Emerald Publishing.

CHAPTER 8

Unpacking Reshoring: The GE GeoSpring Case

ginger coons

Introduction

In 2009, the consumer appliance division of General Electric (GE) publicly pledged to move a subset of its manufacturing from China to the United States (GE Consumer & Industrial, 2009). They would transfer the manufacture of one model of hot water heater from China to a factory in Louisville, Kentucky. The water heater in question, the GeoSpring, was a high-efficiency, high-tech, cost-saving model—perfect for supporting the argument that American workers can benefit from a new generation of advanced manufacturing. Moreover, moving the site of GeoSpring manufacture to Kentucky entailed other important changes: a switch from subcontracting (Bals, Kirchoff, & Foerstl, 2016) to in-house production, and the adoption of Lean manufacturing methodology (Crooks, 2012b).

Articles in popular and trade publications, press releases from GE, and statements from local and regional governments, all positioned the decision to move manufacturing of the GeoSpring as part of a larger movement: bringing manufacturing "back" to the United States, also known

g. coons (✉)
Willem de Kooning Academy, Rotterdam, The Netherlands
e-mail: ginger@gingercoons.ca

U. Meyer et al. (eds.), *Digitalization in Industry*,
https://doi.org/10.1007/978-3-030-28258-5_8

as reshoring. The main action in reshoring is moving manufacturing from a location once perceived as low-cost, and re-situating it in closer proximity to a geographical area and market considered "home." The home market might be one in which the company makes the majority of its sales, or it might be the historical base of a now-transnational corporation. In the case of GE, the move "home" from China also encompassed the renovation of a factory located at a historic GE site: Appliance Park in Louisville, Kentucky.

This chapter uses the case of the GE GeoSpring water heater—an early example of reshoring to the United States—to understand how the process of relocating manufacturing to a developed nation is portrayed to different stakeholders through its description/depiction in a variety of media. Through the GeoSpring example, I question and critique the way various arguments and forms are deployed to make claims about the merits of the reshoring phenomenon. The GeoSpring case is ideal for this purpose because it is a high profile example of the process and has been used as an exemplar to other manufacturers and the public. I outline the history of the GeoSpring case from its inception in 2009, to the reopening of GE's Appliance Park in Louisville and the subsequent news coverage. While the GeoSpring was discontinued in 2016 and GE Appliances was subsequently sold, the focus of this chapter is on discourse concerning the GeoSpring in 2012, the year it first came off the line in Louisville.

This chapter unpacks arguments behind reshoring, as they relate to the use of automation (or not) and novel manufacturing methods. Concerns intersecting work, class, globalization, and national identity are at the heart of my analysis. I use material from trade publications, press releases, popular media, and one Super Bowl advertisement as the basis for an exploration of the way industry and government stakeholders talk about the prospect of reshoring. I particularly focus on the tension between those who are meant to benefit from reshoring and those who are not. I argue that the rhetoric of reshoring acts on an implicit "us and them" dichotomy which places the interests of workers and economies in the developing world in opposition to workers and economies in the developed world. I argue that the rhetoric of reshoring, in addition to treating workers outside of home markets as expendable, treats having domestic manufacturing facilities and jobs not just as an imperative, but as a right. This implied right for American workers means a rhetorical diminution of the capacity and importance of workers elsewhere in the world. Countries which have been sites of offshoring are treated as, at best, markets for the products of newly reshored manufacture. In more cynical moments, those same countries are treated as adversaries from whom jobs and economic growth need to be taken (back). This oppositional relationship between developed and developing nations is a sometimes subtle but always present theme in popular descriptions and representations of reshoring. The GeoSpring case is complicated in this regard by the purchase, in 2016, of GE's Appliance division by Haier, a Chinese appliance manufacturer. However, the purchase of GE Appliances by Haier falls outside of the frame of this chapter, as I am concerned here with the launch of the Louisville-made GeoSpring and the attendant refurbishment of Appliance Park.

This chapter contributes a perspective which is currently underrepresented in the relevant literature. While reshoring has, in the last seven or eight years, been covered extensively in business-focused literature (especially supply chain management), there is a shortage of work which engages critically with the concept and its attendant rhetoric. Early work which uses the term "reshoring" frames it in the context of Obama-era US manufacturing policy (e.g., Levinson, 2012; Livesey, 2012; Paul, 2012; Tassey, 2012). In such contexts, it is leveraged as one portion of innovation-focused arguments about increasing domestic (most often the United States) manufacturing capacity. More recently, the importance of bringing manufacturing jobs to the United States has been leveraged from the other side of the political spectrum, in conjunction with an increasingly home-focused policy toward trade (Ewing, 2018). One notable contribution to the literature assesses the reasoning behind reshoring decisions and even attempts to create a taxonomy which describes and offers an analytic framework for understanding various moves in production (Bals et al., 2016) but does not extend to questioning the motivations behind how reshoring decisions are communicated. My aim in this chapter is to contribute a perspective which treats reshoring not as a business decision which needs to be rationally justified, but as a rhetorical move which allows stakeholders to enact particular kinds of automation, labor relations, and process management.

Methodology

This chapter is based primarily on a close reading of six texts, all published in 2012: (1) a press release from the Lieutenant Governor of Kentucky on the occasion of the grand opening of the GeoSpring manufacturing facility at Appliance Park; (2) an article in the *Harvard Business*

Review (*HBR*), written by Jeffrey Immelt, the CEO of General Electric, on the subject of GE's investments in American manufacturing; (3) an article from *Assembly* magazine on the subject of GE's GeoSpring project, and the broader changes taking place at Appliance Park; (4) an article from the *Financial Times* on the same subject; (5) an article from *The Atlantic* which describes GE's approach to reshoring, aimed at a more general audience; and (6) a 2012 GE advertisement aired during the Super Bowl which showcases GE's efforts at Appliance Park, aimed at an even broader audience.

I have chosen these six texts because they offer a cross-section of communication about the GeoSpring move, from a variety of stakeholders, and for several discrete audiences. The press release from the Lieutenant Governor of Kentucky is of importance because it attempts to communicate something of the public good to be gained from the GeoSpring move. The *HBR* article offers a business-focused view of the initiative, contextualized by Immelt as a call-to-action for other business leaders. *Assembly*'s coverage gives a slight counterpoint: trade journalism which speaks to a broad cross-section of manufacturing stakeholders. The *Financial Times* (*FT*) article offers the story to a business and investing audience, without the gloss that Immelt himself provides in *HBR*. *The Atlantic* packages the story of the GeoSpring and its broader reshoring context for a general audience, characterized as "thinking people" (The Atlantic Monthly Group, 2018). Finally, the Super Bowl commercial does for the public what Immelt's *HBR* article does for a business audience: Sells the story.

In reading the six texts, I employ some of the tactics of critical discourse analysis (CDA). I have chosen to look at the discourse of reshoring through the lens of CDA because of its focus on "the ways discourse structures enact, confirm, legitimate, reproduce, or challenge relations of *power abuse* (*dominance*) in society" (van Dijk, 2015, p. 467). Reshoring in general and the GeoSpring case in particular are politically charged moves which are frequently couched in the language of rational business decision-making. As such, CDA, with its commitment to examining the underlying power structures present in a variety of texts, provides an analytic and methodological magnifying glass through which to scrutinize the particular languages (both textual and visual) which are used to describe and sell GE's reshoring efforts to a variety of publics. Fairclough describes CDA as "analysis of the dialectical relationships between semiosis (including language) and other elements of social practices. Its particular concern is with the radical changes that are taking place in contemporary social life, with how semiosis figures within processes of change, and with shifts in the relationship between semiosis and other social elements within networks of practices" (2001, p. 123). My primary concern in this chapter is how the six texts use various tactics to sell reshoring as an appropriate response to contemporary American economic and social ills. In order to read the texts, I employ van Dijk's "ideological square" (1998), which offers a lens through which to look at how discourse colors in-group attitudes toward out-groups (ibid.).

What van Dijk refers to as the "ideological square" is a "strategy of dominant discourse and mind control [which] often follows the basic intergroup polarization of underlying ideologies: Emphasizing Our good things, Emphasizing Their bad things, Mitigating Our bad things, and Mitigating Their good things" (van Dijk, 2015, p. 474). The construction of this discourse strategy as a square follows from the complementary nature of the four elements, with a conflict between the "us" and "them" at play in a given text (van Dijk, 2011). Van Dijk highlights a variety of strategies which are used in the ideological square, including the kinds of topics broached when talking about "them" and the level of specificity (or not) employed when describing the various actions or attitudes of "us" or "them" (2011). I use the four elements of the square as the codes by which to read the six texts in question. The square is of use in recognizing the ideological choices which underlie things like the portrayal of non-American workers by American news outlets; who has agency in making choices about offshoring, and the importance of heritage and continuity in depictions of reshored manufacturing.

A final concern in this chapter is how reshoring is portrayed to different stakeholder groups. Van Dijk suggests that CDA is concerned with "the way specific discourse structures are deployed in the reproduction of social dominance" (2015, p. 468). With that in mind, one of my primary aims in choosing the GeoSpring case is to look at the different ways in which the four moves embodied in the ideological square are deployed in different contexts and how these differences reflect structures of social dominance. This is why I have chosen texts which are intended for a range of audiences, from business audiences to the general American public.

Reshoring

The GE GeoSpring case is a key example of reshoring. The term is most frequently used to describe the relocation of manufacturing to the country in which a manufacturer or its primary market is based (Gray, Skowronski, Essenduran, & Rungtusantham, 2013). In practice, reshoring means moving manufacturing from locations in the global south and east, "back" to a developed country which has, in recent years, experienced a loss of industrial or manufacturing jobs due to a combination of the offshoring boom of the 1990s and early 2000s (ibid.) and increases to labor productivity brought about by a variety of factors, including automation (ibid.). Whether it's called "reshoring" or "insourcing" (Bals et al., 2016 offer a taxonomy which draws distinctions between these terms), the idea of developed countries seeking out and promoting domestic manufacturing has become a popular talking point (e.g., Northam, 2014). The terminology used to describe the phenomenon is a linguistic counterpoint to the relocation of manufacturing which took place on a large scale in the 1990s and 2000s, known as offshoring (moving manufacturing away from a company's center of activity, to a country perceived as having lower costs) or outsourcing (the act of a given firm undertaking a contracting relationship with another firm in order to fulfill a subset of its business activities—often contracting out manufacturing activities). Received wisdom leveraged in industrial literature and public discourse positions offshoring as the removal of manufacturing work from a developed country and its placement in a developing country with a significantly lower labor cost (e.g., Muro & Kulkarni, 2016; Solis, 2011). China is often presented as the nexus of offshoring, in part thanks to low average wages in manufacturing in the late 1990s and early 2000s, amounting at times to what is generally portrayed as a small fraction of a comparable wage in the United States (e.g., Fishman, 2012). Thus, the decision to move manufacturing to China is often retroactively attributed to an analysis based on the contribution of wages to the cost of per-unit manufacture.

Building on the idea that offshoring decisions were based on per-unit cost calculations, one well-known proponent of reshoring, Harry Moser, positions the logic behind reshoring as a simple reassessment of numbers. Moser advocates that manufacturers should take into account the total cost of bringing a product to market, as opposed to the per-unit price of manufacture (Moser, 2011). This move means that Moser can position reshoring as a good business decision, rather than something primarily patriotic or emotional, a significant rhetorical move when attempting to appeal to capital. In this style of accounting, offshoring needn't be considered *unjust*, when it can instead be *unwise* or *uneconomical*. Moser's rhetorical medium of choice when advancing his arguments, aside from frequent op-eds and media appearances, is an online calculator tool offered through the Web site of his organization, the Reshoring Initiative. The TCO Estimator allows manufacturers to determine what Moser and the Reshoring Initiative call "Total Cost of Ownership" (Moser, 2011), a figure which encompasses not just the cost of manufacture, but of transportation, risk, and other externalities. The TCO Estimator allows industrial stakeholders to understand the prospect of reshoring in relation to their bottom line.

Moser's Reshoring Initiative offers not just its TCO Estimator, but a variety of other tools for companies looking to justify or benefit from reshoring to the United States. Among these tools are a database of articles about reshoring efforts undertaken by American companies, which serve as both case studies and ammunition in the argument for adopting a reshoring strategy. Moser's work is a prominent example of an attempt to communicate to manufacturers the idea that reshoring could have value as a business decision. This kind of logic is repeatedly deployed in the texts analyzed in this chapter.

Efforts to move manufacturing to the United States are not, however, business decisions that exist outside of the political climate. Under the Obama administration, the American Recovery and Reinvestment Act (2009) committed $80 billion to green business activities, including manufacturing (Rodrik, 2014). Products like the GeoSpring and other goods which make a claim to energy efficiency and environmental benefit enjoyed a variety of financial incentives from government during the Obama administration. As I indicate in later sections of this chapter, in the case of the GeoSpring and the recommitment to Appliance Park, these incentives from government proved to be decisive factors.

The GeoSpring Case

Between 2009 (GE Appliances & Lighting, 2010) and 2016 (Alter, 2016), the appliance division of General Electric sold a water heater called the GeoSpring. The GeoSpring was notable in that it incorporated a heat pump into an otherwise traditional electric water heater. The heat pump increased the energy efficiency of the water heater, thus reducing the energy cost of heating water in the home (Merchant, 2012). Initially, the GeoSpring was manufactured in China, by a contractor (Bals et al., 2016). However, in 2009, GE announced that it would begin manufacturing a "new hybrid electric water heater" in Louisville, Kentucky (GE Consumer & Industrial, 2009). The new water heater turned out to be a revamp of the GeoSpring, and the manufacturing facility that would be making it was Appliance Park, the historical base of GE's home appliance manufacturing operations.

Opened in the mid-1950s, Appliance Park was at one time responsible for producing 250,000 domestic appliances a month, according to Fishman (2012). In a history of GE Appliances published on the occasion of its sale to Haier, John Spovieri of *Assembly* magazine indicates that Appliance Park reached its peak employment in 1972, with 23,000 employees "of which two-thirds were members of the International Union of Electronic, Electrical, Salaried, Machine, and Furniture Workers (IUE)" (Spovieri, 2017). Since that peak, the number of employees at Appliance Park has been in decline. By the 1990s, Appliance Park was employing less than half the number of workers, with only 9550 remaining in 1997 (ibid.). While some of these reductions may well have been spurred by the recession of the late 1970s, that was certainly not the only factor in the declining employment at Appliance Park. In the 1980s, GE was a notable force in industrial automation. Kumpe and Bolwijn (1988) describe efforts carried out at Appliance Park to automate dishwasher and refrigerator lines. They indicate that in the decade up to 1988, output at Appliance Park "increased while employment [...] declined from 19,000 to 10,000" (Kumpe & Bolwijn, 1988, p. 76). Spovieri (2017) provides more detail on what the automation of the dishwasher line entailed, including "robotics, ultrasonic plastic welders, point-of-use stamping presses, inventory control systems, bar code scanners and other productivity-enhancing technologies."

Finally, according to Spovieri, the 1990s saw a change in the location of GE's appliance manufacturing, with an emphasis on both other US states and other countries. However, "[e]ven so, in the late 1990s, Appliance Park was selling more than 12 million appliances annually under five brand names to 150 markets worldwide" (Spovieri, 2017). A relevant detail in Spovieri's retrospective of Appliance Park comes in the form of a quote in the *New York Times* contemporaneous with the opening of Appliance Park in the early 1950s, which indicated that "The company expects the concentration of production to make possible more effective management-operation relationships," and that "new product designs should result from closer coordination of engineering and production. Greater economy of operations should arrive out of increased effectiveness of mass production techniques in a 'city within a city'." (quoted in Spovieri, 2017). Similar arguments are offered in the texts analyzed in this chapter.

The move of GeoSpring manufacturing to Appliance Park can be seen as a return to the idea that management at GE were interested in the potential benefits of locating development near manufacturing. Crucially, the GeoSpring move coincided with an adoption of Lean manufacturing methods, a change which GE's own promotional materials at the time gave a sometimes disproportionate amount of attention to (e.g., GE Appliances, 2010). The move to Lean brought product designers, line designers, and hourly waged workers together to not just plan the new manufacturing line for the GeoSpring, but to ultimately redesign the product itself (Fishman, 2012).

In summer 2016, the GeoSpring was discontinued, apparently due to a lack of profitability. The rights to produce the product, as well as the equipment from the production line, were sold to another company, which continued to manufacture the product under a different name (Gibson, 2017). The elimination of the GeoSpring was not the only change to the GE Appliances business in 2016: After a failed previous attempt to sell, GE (the parent company) successfully sold its consumer appliance division to Haier, a leading Chinese manufacturing firm (Lurie & Kellner, 2016). Under the GE Appliances brand, Haier continues to produce a range of goods at Appliance Park.

Messaging Across Media

The first Louisville-built GeoSpring water heaters came off the line at Appliance Park in 2012. To mark that achievement, with the revitalization of Appliance Park, and with the introduction of other Kentucky-made products, a spate of media addressing the GeoSpring and GE's reshoring plans was published across multiple outlets. Below, I use van Dijk's ideological square to interpret six of those texts.

Lieutenant Governor of Kentucky press release, February 2012. (Lt. Gov. Abramson's Communications Office, 2012)

On the occasion of the grand opening of the GeoSpring assembly line at Appliance Park, the office of the Lieutenant Governor of Kentucky issued a press release. The press release emphasized the collaboration and cooperation between multiple levels of government and GE Appliances. The press release contained information about the GeoSpring, about Appliance Park, and importantly, quotes from the Governor and Lt. Governor of Kentucky, the mayor of Louisville, the President and CEO of GE Appliances, and the Senator and House Representative for Louisville.

Notably, a statement from the Representative for Louisville highlighted the historical role of appliance manufacturing in the community. The Representative is quoted as saying: "GE has long played a crucial role in Louisville's past, and this addition further ensures it will be a making a difference long into our future. [...] I was proud to work at Appliance Park for 39 years in-home laundry, and we were always at the forefront of progress. This project follows the same tradition." This statement makes a rhetorical move which is extremely common in messaging surrounding the GeoSpring and the broader Appliance Park revitalization project. It emphasizes the history of Appliance Park in the community, while projecting a bright future. In effect, the quote expresses the hope that residents of Louisville will continue, in the future as they were in the past, to be employed in manufacturing positions at Appliance Park. It expresses this hope while also indicating that technological development is not a new facet of GE's activities in Louisville. That GE has, for decades, employed the people of Louisville is presented as something which goes hand-in-hand with innovation and technological development. It also links the Representative personally to Appliance Park, showing both that a broad cross-section of the local population has direct links to GE and that the Representative understands what it is to work in an appliance factory and endorses it.

The hope that GE will continue to employ people in Louisville (and the importance placed on that employment) is in line with a statement from the Lieutenant Governor, who is quoted as saying that "GE's decision to produce the GeoSpring Hybrid Water Heater at Appliance Park is a shining example of a movement by the United States to get U.S. multinational companies to bring more of their manufacturing back to America." This is the first incidence we see of the word "back" which is prevalent in material about reshoring. While the vast majority of the press release focuses on what van Dijk calls "Emphasizing Our good things," the use of the "back" construction by the Lt. Governor is one of the few indications that something not good has been happening in Louisville specifically and the United States more generally. This is rolled into an example of "Mitigating Our bad things" in a quote from the President and CEO of GE Appliances. Charles Blankenship of GE Appliances is quoted as stating that "To reverse decades of outsourcing by bringing new, industry-leading products and jobs back to Appliance Park takes a tremendous amount of cooperation, imagination, courage and plain old hard work by a lot of people." Blankenship echoes the Lt. Governor in invoking the departure of manufacturing jobs from the United States. He emphasizes the importance of "hard work," a value which sits nicely with a mentality that sees manufacturing as important and relatively high-prestige labor.

It's also relevant that the one quote in the press release which explicitly mentions "decades of outsourcing" is from a representative of GE. While the rest of the text is an exercise in emphasizing the positive aspects of the work being done at Appliance Park, Blankenship invokes the older business strategy which is ostensibly being overturned by a return to American manufacturing. He mentions something which, to an audience based in Kentucky or elsewhere in the United States, would be perceived as negative: The loss of manufacturing jobs which took place in the 1980s and 1990s. He then mitigates this somewhat by applauding the good qualities, including hard work, of all who participated in the GeoSpring project.

Immelt to other business leaders: "The CEO of General Electric on sparking an American manufacturing renewal," March 2012. (Immelt, 2012)

In March 2012, the *Harvard Business Review* published an article by Jeffry Immelt, the CEO of General Electric. The article lays out the rationale and story behind GE's move to increase the amount of manufacturing taking place in Appliance Park.

Immelt starts his article by situating it in the technological history of Appliance Park, recounting how the first computer in commercial use in the United States—a UNIVAC—was installed there in the early 1950s. He contrasts the use of the UNIVAC with the opening of a new data center at Appliance Park, a move he situates as crucial to the success of GE's present-day business. The "$40 million data centre" is described as "just one part of a larger $800 million investment in Louisville," and a larger initiative to "create some 1000 jobs in the United States by 2014." Immelt states that an investment likes the data center "shows that when we invest in our people and our technologies and create new business models, we can bring manufacturing back to the United States and be profitable." The claim of profitability is central to the audience for whom Immelt is writing. In addressing his managerial peers, through the venue of the *HBR*, Immelt must make a clear connection between the ability to gain profit and the decision to manufacture GE Appliances (and jet engines, which he covers later in the article) in the United States.

Immelt strikes a balance between the profit interests of a business audience and the overarching message about American manufacturing with statements like the following: "Our success on the factory floor rests on human innovation and technical innovation—the keys to leading an American manufacturing renewal. When we are deciding where to manufacture, we ask, 'Will our people and technology in the U.S. provide us with a competitive advantage?' Increasingly, the answer is yes." This is one of the many instances in which Immelt invokes the "Emphasizing Our good things" corner of van Dijk's square. This positivity is especially prevalent when talking about the importance of what Immelt refers to as "human innovation," or the capacity of the workforce to contribute to the development of new products and processes. This is also exemplified by the move to a Lean manufacturing methodology.

This positive depiction of workers in the United States is in contrast to Immelt's use of the term "low-cost countries" to describe the countries to which GE manufacturing was previously (and for many product lines, remained) outsourced. Describing factors which influenced the decision to locate some manufacturing in the United States, he suggests that "[s]hipping and materials costs were rising; wages were increasing in China and elsewhere; and we didn't have control of the supply chain. The currencies of emerging markets added complexity. Finally, core competency was an issue. Engineering and manufacturing are hands-on and iterative, and our most innovative appliance-design work is done in the United States. At a time when speed to market is everything, separating design and development from manufacturing didn't make sense." He argues that complexity and non-labor costs outweighed the value of low hourly wages. Here, we see the argument that accompanied the original construction of Appliance Park in the 1950s: that having manufacturing, engineering, design, and marketing functions in close proximity to each other adds value to the product by improving it or simply by shortening time to market.

Describing the value of having centralized American employees, he suggests that the benefit resides not just in having proximity between design and manufacturing, but that a successful "business strategy could no longer rely on having employees literally hand off what they were best at doing." He goes on: "But we could change the environment in which they worked, engaging the entire workforce from design to development to assembly. That is human innovation." What is of interest here is that the capacity of workers to participate in human innovation appears to rely on centralization. It is problematic to imagine that for a global company, such innovation ought or needs to happen in the United States, with the exclusion of other countries in which GE manufactures, and that this innovation is contingent on the reshoring of manufacturing.

The third prong in Immelt's plan for a renaissance in American manufacturing is a new approach to labor relations. He argues that a key factor in bringing manufacturing to Louisville was "the competitive wage agreement between our union workers and management. It wasn't easy for them to find common ground. Both sides had to face new realities, make tough choices, and accept concessions. The union accepted a lower starting wage for new hires; we pledged to create new jobs in Louisville and promised that if the new processes and automation that go along with advanced manufacturing led to redundancy, we would redeploy workers, not let them go." This is one of the few outright mentions of automation in the six texts. It is telling, given the context, that automation is only mentioned when it is in the same breath as a promise to re-assign workers whose functions are made redundant by it. In addition, this promise is couched as one of the concessions made by GE to the union in order to make a lower starting wage for new employees acceptable.

Among the texts analyzed in this chapter, Immelt shows an especially interesting argumentative trajectory. He opens by focusing on the positive by emphasizing the competence and ingenuity of American workers (van Dijk's "Emphasizing Our good things"), transitions into a combination of rationalizing and explaining previous business decisions (an example of "Mitigating Our bad things"), and then moves back to a positive, future-facing attitude. In the course of this trajectory, he runs through making the case for how technologically progressive GE has always been, emphasizes its environmental goals, invokes the history GE has in Louisville, puts the case for why GE offshored in the first place, and emphasizes the importance of people in manufacturing (and thus, American people). Finally (and after also looking at a second case briefly), he issues a call to action: "We need to believe that we can design, develop, and produce here in the United States; that we can do it cost-effectively and efficiently; and that we can win. Then we need to find ways to collaborate and make the necessary investments. If we do, our workers will prove America's potential." This call to action communicates to his readers how they can take the GE examples forward and couches the economics and geopolitics of manufacturing as a game to be won.

Trade press: "GE revives appliance park," June 2012. (Fisher, 2012)

Slightly after the opening of the GeoSpring line, *Assembly* magazine covered the changes which took place at Appliance Park, in a broadly sympathetic way, and for a trade audience.

The author of the article, Seth Fisher, begins by painting an image of the grand opening ceremony at Appliance Park, before contextualizing the position of the GeoSpring line in the history of the facility. He states that "[t]he two facilities [the GeoSpring line and a refrigerator line]—the first new assembly lines at Appliance Park since 1957—are the vanguard of a five-year, $1 billion investment to boost GE's appliance division and create more than 1300 U.S. jobs by 2014." He paints the Appliance Park story as a kind of comeback, recounting GE's previous attempts to sell its Appliance division, before describing its current success: "Less than four years later, GE Appliances & Lighting was featured in a Super Bowl XLVI ad, and politicians, union leaders and executives are calling the company a case study for the future of U.S. manufacturing." Fisher is writing an article which attempts to be engaging and evocative, while also recognizing that its audience is interested in the nuts and bolts of the change taking place.

The *Assembly* article is notable for two reasons: It is one of the few pieces of coverage that mentions that the GeoSpring is not an entirely new product, but one that was previously manufactured in China, stipulating that "Lean manufacturing and a more competitive wage structure for new employees led GE to select Louisville as the production site for the new water heater, instead of China, where an earlier version of the product was made." Indeed, this is a distinction that press releases from GE did not highlight. Fisher is also notable for being concrete about the value and necessity of tax incentives. He writes that "GE estimates that manufacturing the water heater in China would have been approximately 7 percent to 10 percent cheaper, given that country's incentives and labor costs, and specifically credited Abramson for leading the political efforts to make up that difference in federal and state tax incentives for both GE and consumers." The article shows a keen interest in the economic aspects of the Appliance Park project and highlights the knock-on effects on the local economy. Fisher cites a study commissioned by GE, which suggests that the development at Appliance Park makes a major contribution to Kentucky's economy and "directly and indirectly contributes $1.6 billion" while supporting "more than 12,000 jobs in Kentucky, including 5,000 GE employees."

The *Assembly* article predominantly emphasizes what is positive in GE's reshoring efforts, but is also notable for giving some attention to the differences between the earlier, made in China GeoSpring and the new Kentucky-made version (generally unfavorably for the earlier version), which is a very mild example of the "Emphasizing Their bad things" corner of the ideological square. What is visible in this article and others is a propensity to hide critique of overseas manufacturing in assessments of the comparative merits of American-made goods against those produced elsewhere.

Business press: "GE takes $1bn risk in bringing jobs home," April 2012. (Crooks, 2012a)

An article published in the *Financial Times* (*FT*) in April 2012 cites the chief executive of GE Appliances, Charles "Chip" Blankenship, as giving three core reasons for GE's focus on manufacturing at Appliance Park: a change in the wage structure of hourly employees, a major package of incentives from government, and "the adoption of 'lean' manufacturing and design techniques that made the plant more efficient and took labour content out of production" (Crooks, 2012a). These three arguments should by now be familiar, as they are present in both Immelt's *HBR* article and *Assembly*'s coverage of the reopening of Appliance Park. The idea of taking labor content out of production (which we will see more of in the *Atlantic* article) is a key euphemism for a change in the approach to automation and changes to the manufacturing process.

Crooks makes one particularly interesting move in characterizing the aim of the new developments at Appliance Park as to "bring back to Louisville [...] hundred of jobs that had been outsourced to Mexico and China." What is fascinating here is the idea that the *jobs* are what was being outsourced, rather than the manufacturing. In some ways, this article is the most frank of the corpus about the economic and labor reasoning behind reshoring. The process of reshoring is described as "a strategy being tried by many American manufacturers, as rapid wage growth in emerging economies and sluggish pay in the US erodes the labour cost advantage of offshore plants." Crooks backs up that assertion with statistics from the Boston Consulting Group, indicating that wage growth in China between 2005 and (projected) 2015 would drastically cut the pay differential between American and Chinese workers.

As with most of the texts, the *FT* article takes a requisite step into the descriptive, drawing a contrast between areas of Appliance Park that have been renovated and those that haven't: "Untouched areas are still jumbled with old equipment, abandoned when production was moved. Other parts have been transformed: gleaming with white paint, brightly lit and cooled by huge ceiling fans." There is a feeling of contingency in this description, offering the sense that, even though the changes being made at Appliance Park are part of huge investments, the presence of old materials and other unattractive features is a reminder of the previous and potential future misfortunes of the plant.

The *FT* article shows a different treatment of other countries, avoiding the term "low-cost countries" which is frequently used elsewhere, and instead using the phrases "lower-cost plants" and "low-cost centres," along with "emerging economies." While these phrases are of course still marking a difference between the financial status of different potential manufacturing countries, they do take the slightly more restrained position of not referring to a whole country or people as "low-cost." The article's position is, however, slippery in terms of the definition of out-groups and in-groups. Unique among the texts at issue in this chapter, the *FT* is not an American entity. Its own foreignness places it outside of a definition of "Our things" and "Their things" purely based on geography, which complicates the idea of mediating in-group views of out-groups, at least on national lines.

Popular press – The Atlantic "The Insourcing boom," December 2012. (Fishman, 2012)

This December 2012 article by Charles Fishman is an outlier in that it comes nearly a year after the opening of the new line at Appliance Park, and six months after the latest text in the rest of the corpus. It is also an outlier by reason of its length: At nearly 6000 words, it is twice the length of the next longest article, Immelt's *HBR* piece. It attempts to build up a coherent picture of what is happening at Appliance Park and to put it into context. Perhaps unsurprisingly, it takes a far more varied set of positions than the other texts.

Perhaps due to its length and its desire to explain the broader context, the *Atlantic* article makes significant use of "back" and "home" as ways of describing the trajectory of an appliance's manufacture and even goes so far as the personify the GeoSpring as an appliance which looks like the *Star Wars* character R2-D2. The article describes the rise and fall of Appliance Park, swinging from a highly successful version of itself in the 1950s and 1960s, to the early 2010s version of the complex, with far less work and fewer employees.

A particularly interesting move in this article is the assertion that "Low-wage Chinese workers had by [the late 1990s] flooded the global marketplace. (Even as recently as 2000, a typical Chinese factory worker made 52 cents an hour. You could hire 20 or 30 workers overseas for what one cost in Appliance Park.)" There's a jarring mismatch in language in this segment. The "flood"ing of the global market with manufactured goods is attributed to the "Low-wage Chinese workers" themselves, rather than their exploitation by manufacturing firms. Even if it is not intended, the phrasing positions it as the fault of the Chinese workers that the cost of manufacturing an appliance has gone down. While Chinese workers may be described as flooding the market, an older generation of workers at Appliance Park is also treated as problematic. The word "fractious" is used to describe the activities of trade unions at Appliance Park in the 1970s and 1980s. This description is couched in the context of unions "changing their priorities" and accepting measures like the tiered pay scale adopted at Appliance Park in the 2000s. With regard to the connection between labor relations and automation, the *Atlantic* article only goes so far as to address the increase of labor productivity in the United States. The article suggests that "[y]ou simply can't save much money chasing wages anymore." While this alludes to a change in the way different components contribute to the cost of manufacturing a good, it does not attempt to address why labor productivity has gone up.

This article places more weight on "Emphasizing Their bad things" than do the other texts analyzed in this chapter, especially in its characterization of Chinese workers. However, due to the sheer length and scope of the article, there is also ample opportunity to focus on all of the other corners of van Dijk's square (including "Our bad things" which are exemplified by the past relationship between GE and organized labor), with an emphasis on the promotion of "Our good things" and indeed "Mitigating Our bad things." In effect, this article tries to do a thoughtful job of analyzing and reporting the situation, but in so doing, it falls into the trap of painting China, Chinese manufacturing, and Chinese workers as being in opposition to American workers and manufacturing facilities.

Super Bowl advertisement, May 2012. (BBDO, 2012)

In 2012, GE aired two advertisements during the Super Bowl. Super Bowl ads have historically been sought-after and costly, thanks to their perceived ability to speak to a large number of viewers at once and their pop-cultural cachet. In a fragmented media landscape, opportunities to reach a large proportion of the United States all at once are rare. In 2012, airing a 30-second spot during the Super Bowl cost an average of 3.5 million USD (Edwards & Terbush, 2012). GE devoted 45 seconds to promoting the revitalization of Appliance Park.

The ad, titled "Building something big in Louisville," opens on a current GE employee recounting her family's history with GE and Appliance Park—both her father and her grandfather worked there before her. This story situates the factory in the heritage of the community. A second speaker refers to "the people on the line" as "the heartbeat of this place," centering the human, the worker, in the story of Appliance Park and of GE's efforts to produce goods for the American market, using American labor. Even more bluntly, another employee featured in the ad states that "there's a chance to get in [on] the ground floor of something big, something that will bring us back – not only this company, but this country."

Visually, there are two things that are especially striking about the ad. First, there's the sheer number of people. The story of the ad is told entirely through the words of Appliance Park employees, backed by images of people working in the factory. A second crucial feature is the lack of anything that could be popularly perceived as evidence of industrial automation. While shots in the ad show a modern manufacturing facility, the focus is on activities being carried out by humans—someone welding, a woman operating a tool on a moving assembly line, construction work taking place. Thus, the tagline presented at the end of the advertisement has a clear connotation: "GE Works," in the form of American workers employed in manufacturing jobs. In this sense, "GE" is made up of people, a collectivity of individuals who work in order to produce goods that then "work" in a different sense, by being functional.

This ad is the most unmitigatedly positive of all of the texts. It focuses entirely on the good things happening in Louisville and simply does not mention "Our bad things" at all, or "Them." There are only two hints at "bad things," in the entire advertisement, which come in the form of one employee who has joined GE after the factory she used to work at closed, and at the very end, when the final speaker is talking about bringing back "not only this company, but this country" and we thus get the small admission that the country and company may need to be brought back. What's fascinating about those two allusions is how manufacturing is tied to success. GE is bringing success to Louisville by bringing (back) manufacturing jobs.

Analysis

The six texts not only come from different kinds of sources, but are written to serve distinct functions. Thus, particular aspects are made more or less ambiguous to serve the relevant audience and goal. In the same way that there is more clarity in Immelt's piece about the difference between outsourcing and offshoring (a difference which is glossed over elsewhere), the press release from the Lt. Governor of Kentucky unsurprisingly focuses on the benefits that will accrue to the people of Louisville and other towns in the area. It is also unsurprising that a press release might attempt to take some credit for what is happening, couching it in a long-term strategy by the government.

Some features cut across media and audience. Appliance Park is frequently given a kind of mythic character, whether it's being called "storied" by the *Atlantic*, or "famous" by *Assembly*, or being talked about as a cornerstone of the lives of generations of workers and their families in both the Super Bowl ad and the government press release. Clearly, what is meant to matter about Appliance Park is that it is part of a great tradition in Louisville and that such traditions can and should be kept alive into the future.

It is also relevant to notice how automation isn't talked about. There is, in fact, a fetishization of the human in all of the texts. Even though efficiencies are found, technological advancement is discussed, and Appliance Park has historically been a site of automation, it is not discussed in any of the texts, bar a brief mention by Immelt. Instead, a couple of the texts talk about labor productivity. The *Atlantic* piece does so explicitly, and the *Assembly* piece does it implicitly. But the source of those changes to labor productivity is left a mystery.

Immelt picks up on the heritage of technical innovation, uses it to describe new examples of the same, and then offers this as support for claims about the rationality and good business sense of moving manufacturing to the United States. While the Super Bowl ad does not make appeals to rationality and focuses almost entirely on predominantly emotional positive aspects of the work at Appliance Park, Immelt's *HBR* piece emphasizes how reasonable the move is and does so in the context of a changing manufacturing environment in which outsourcing and offshoring have not been unmitigated successes.

"Back" and "home" are recurring features in the majority of the texts analyzed in this chapter. These words are concerned with naturalizing manufacturing work as an essential part of the American experience. The "away" implicit in the "back" is one of the few examples of "Our bad things" that are even approached in the texts. As such, it is perhaps not surprising that the benefits of manufacturing are extolled in glowing terms, both in the emotional language of family histories, and in the political and economic language of employment numbers and contributions to local economies. There is a move in all of these texts to emphasize how government, industry, workers, and community are working together to improve the state of collective prosperity and employment in the region.

Using van Dijk's ideological square as a means of viewing these rhetorical moves, it becomes unsurprising that the "other" or the members of a relevant out-group might be treated unsympathetically, as we see in the few descriptions of Chinese workers and the quality of their outputs. Indeed, the positioning of the American worker in relation to the Chinese worker and the approach to labor relations in the newly revitalized US factory are crucial subtexts in many of the arguments in favor of reshoring to Kentucky. As with the different approaches to the positive treatment of manufacturing jobs in Kentucky, we see that the negative light shed on non-American manufacturing is treated both rationally and emotionally. The importance of the reliability of the factory as a source of work (and work which can be understood as "good") is highlighted over and over again, as a priority of elected officials at all levels, governments, and manufacturing companies themselves. The texts are almost all concerned with attempting to justify why manufacturing was moved abroad, and only some of them seem to feel the need to justify why it is being moved (back) to the United States. This may well be because of the potent association that manufacturing work has for many Americans with boom times and prosperity. With this association in mind, it becomes clearer why the Chinese worker from whom the GeoSpring is being taken needs to remain faceless in stories about Appliance Park: The popular American image of the exploited Chinese factory worker does not fit with the happy, self-sufficient prosperity that an American city might hope to regain through reshoring.

It is possible to see, in the GeoSpring case, how different arguments and rhetorical moves are deployed across media to create a positive image of a decision by a major industrial stakeholder. The rhetoric around the manufacturing of the GeoSpring at Appliance Park serves to show how arguments about reshoring, while frequently couched in rational terms, are an exercise in negating the positive qualities of manufacturing outside of, in this case, the United States and symbolically dominating another people, while extolling the virtues of all the tactics and factors that bring manufacturing "home."

Conclusion

One of the key aims of this chapter has been to examine how different rhetorical positions and strategies are used (in a variety of media) to sell reshoring, as a concept and as a business decision, to a cross-section of publics. I have used van Dijk's ideological square as a lens through which to view the texts analyzed in this chapter, in part because it provides a way to see how communication within a particular group (in the case of the texts in this chapter, Americans) asserts the positive values of the in-group and distances or diminishes the out-group (in this case, Chinese manufacturing workers).

However, van Dijk also notes that "access to specific forms of discourse – for example, those of politics, the media, education, or science

– is itself a power resource" (as cited in van Dijk, 2015, p. 469) and that "if we are able to influence people's minds – for example, their knowledge, attitudes, or ideologies – we indirectly may control (some of) their actions, as we know from persuasion and manipulation" (van Dijk, 2015, p. 470). While it may not be shocking or novel to suggest that a large corporation (or family of corporations) like GE is capable of using its power to advantage, it is relevant to highlight the power relations at play in the production, dissemination, and consumption of media. For example: How does GE sell a story that tells the general American public the good news about jobs coming home, while telling a more nuanced story to other business leaders? My aim in this chapter has been to show that, by emphasizing different parts of the story in different media, GE Appliances was able to present an image of reshoring which manages to be hopeful (jobs are coming back) and non-threatening (almost no mention of automation) to a general public, while presenting a series of business decisions (Lean manufacturing) and contributing factors (concessions by the local union) to an industry audience. With regard to access, it is striking that the GeoSpring case both leverages the largest event in the United States popular culture (the Super Bowl) and produces an inspirational call to action in an influential business journal. Given the sheer influence of the media mobilized to promote the GE version of reshoring, it is unsurprising that the reopening of Appliance Park was seen, at the time, as a key case study in re-emphasizing the importance of manufacturing in the United States.

References

Alter, L. (2016, September 23). *GE Pulls the Plug on the GeoSpring Heat Pump Hot Water Heater*. TreeHugger. Retrieved from https://www.treehugger.com/sustainable-product-design/ge-pulls-plug-geospring-heat-pump-hot-water-heater.html.

Bals, L., Kirchoff, J. F., & Foerstl, K. (2016). Exploring the Reshoring and Insourcing Decision Making Process: Towards an Agenda for Future Research. *Operations Management Research, 9*(3–4), 102–116.

BBDO. (2012). *Building Something Big in Louisville*.

Crooks, E. (2012a, April 2). GE Takes $1BN Risk in Bringing Jobs Home. *Financial Times*. Retrieved from https://www.ft.com/content/21a46546-78f1-11e1-88c5-00144feab49a.

Crooks, E. (2012b, April 2). Lean Cuts Fat Off GE's Production Line. *Financial Times*. Retrieved from https://www.ft.com/content/25ee1d1a-7994-11e1-8fad-00144feab49a.

van Dijk, T. A. (1998). *Ideology: A Multidisciplinary Approach*. London: Sage.

van Dijk, T. A. (2011). *Discourse Studies: A Multidisciplinary Introduction*. London: Sage.

van Dijk, T. A. (2015). Critical Discourse Analysis. In D. Tannen, H. E. Hamilton, & D. Schiffrin (Eds.), *The Handbook of Discourse Analysis* (2nd ed., pp. 466–485). Malden, MA: Wiley Blackwell.

Edwards, J., & Terbush, J. (2012, January 26). *Chart: The Incredible Inflation of Super Bowl Ad Prices Since '67*. Business Insider. Retrieved from https://www.businessinsider.com/chart-the-incredible-inflation-of-super-bowl-ad-prices-since-67-2012-1.

Ewing, J. (2018, October 26). Trump's New Trade War May Create New Auto Jobs. In China. *The New York Times*. Retrieved from https://www.nytimes.com/2018/10/26/business/china-jobs-automobiles-trade-war.html.

Fairclough, N. (2001). Critical Discourse Analysis as a Method in Social Scientific Research. In R. Wodak & M. Meyer (Eds.), *Methods of Critical Discourse Analysis* (pp. 121–138). London: Sage.

Fisher, S. (2012, June 1). GE Revives Appliance Park. *Assembly*. Retrieved from https://www.assemblymag.com/articles/90161-ge-revives-appliance-park.

Fishman, C. (2012, December). The Insourcing Boom. *The Atlantic*. Retrieved from https://www.theatlantic.com/magazine/archive/2012/12/the-insourcing-boom/309166/.

GE Appliances. (2010, May 10). *Less Is More at GE's Appliance Park*. GE Appliances Pressroom. Retrieved from http://pressroom.geappliances.com/news/less-is-more-at-ge-s-appliance-179758.

GE Appliances & Lighting. (2010, March 11). *GE GeoSpring Cruises into Spring with Marketing Momentum*. Business Wire. Retrieved from https://www.businesswire.com/news/home/20100311006258/en/GE-GeoSpring%E2%84%A2-Cruises-Spring-Marketing-Momentum.

GE Consumer & Industrial. (2009, June 1). *GE, State of Kentucky, Louisville, and GE's Union Partner to Create New Jobs, Energy Efficient Products*. Business Wire. Retrieved from https://www.businesswire.com/news/home/20090601005844/en/GE-State-Kentucky-Louisville-GE%E2%80%99s-Union-Partner.

Gibson, S. (2017, February 21). *Bradford White Buys GeoSpring Rights and Equipment*. Green Building Advisor. Retrieved from https://www.greenbuildingadvisor.com/article/bradford-white-buys-geospring-rights-and-equipment.

Gray, J. V., Skowronski, K., Esenduran, G., & Rungtusantham, M. J. (2013). The Reshoring Phenomenon: What Supply Chain Academics Ought to Know and Should Do. *Journal of Supply Chain Management, 49*(2), 27–33.

Immelt, J. R. (2012, March). The CEO of General Electric on Sparking an American Manufacturing Renewal. *Harvard Business Review*. Retrieved from https://hbr.org/2012/03/the-ceo-of-general-electric-on-sparking-an-american-manufacturing-renewal.

Kumpe, T., & Bolwijn, P. T. (1988). Manufacturing: The New Case for Vertical Integration. *Harvard Business Review, 66*(March–April), 75–81.

Levinson, M. (2012). Manufacturing the Future: Why Reindustrialization Is the Road to Recovery. *New Labor Forum, 21*(3), 10–15.

Lieutenant Governor Abramson's Communications Office. (2012, February 10). *Lt. Gov. Abramson Celebrates Grand Opening of GE Appliances' GeoSpring™ Water Heater Plant in Louisville*. Retrieved from http://migration.kentucky.gov/Newsroom/ltgovernor/20120210ge.htm.

Livesey, F. (2012). The Need for a New Understanding of Manufacturing and Industrial Policy in Leading Economies. *Innovations: Technology, Governance, Globalization, 7*(3), 193–202.

Lurie, D., & Kellner, T. (2016, June 6). *Done Deal: GE Sells Its Appliance Business to Haier for $5.6 Billion*. GE Reports. Retrieved from https://www.ge.com/reports/done-deal-ge-sells-its-appliances-business-to-haier-for-5-6-billion/.

Merchant, B. (2012, February 10). GE's New Hybrid Water Heater Is Super Efficient—And Manufactured in America. *TreeHugger*. Retrieved from https://www.treehugger.com/economics/super-efficient-water-heater-first-new-product-roll-assembly-line-ge-appliances-50-years.html.

Moser, H. (2011). Time to Come Home? *Supply Chain Quarterly, Q4*. Retrieved from https://www.supplychainquarterly.com/topics/Manufacturing/201104reshoring/.

Muro, M., & Kulkarni, S. (2016). *Voter Anger Explained—In One Chart*. Brookings Institution. Retrieved from https://www.brookings.edu/blog/the-avenue/2016/03/15/voter-anger-explained-in-one-chart/.

Northam, J. (2014, January 27). *As Overseas Costs Rise, More U.S. Companies Are 'Reshoring'*. NPR. Retrieved from http://www.npr.org/sections/parallels/2014/01/22/265080779/as-overseas-costs-rise-more-u-s-companies-are-reshoring.

Paul, S. N. (2012). Watching Walmart in China. *New Labor Forum, 21*(2), 115–118.

Rodrik, D. (2014). Green Industrial Policy. *Oxford Review of Economic Policy, 30*(3), 469–491.

Solis, H. L. (2011). *Extended Mass Layoffs in 2010*. U.S. Bureau of Labor Statistics. Retrieved from https://www.bls.gov/mls/mlsreport1038.pdf.

Spovieri, J. (2017, March 29). A Century of GE Appliance Manufacturing. *Assembly*. Retrieved from https://www.assemblymag.com/articles/93762-a-century-of-ge-appliance-manufacturing.

Tassey, G. (2012). The Future of National Manufacturing Policy. *Innovations: Technology, Governance, Globalization, 7*(3), 155–178.

The Atlantic Monthly Group. (2018). *The Atlantic—Advertising*. Retrieved from https://advertising.theatlantic.com/.

PART III

Emancipating, Configuring, and Infrastructuring Users

CHAPTER 9

Digital Platforms: Producing and Infrastructuring Users in the Age of Airbnb

Attila Bruni and Fabio M. Esposito

Introduction

How do digital platformsrelate to processes of domination and emancipation?

A huge debate has emerged around this question, represented in two waves. In a first wave, digital platforms are put in connection with concepts such as "peer-to-peer", "digital commons", "online cooperation", "liberation of work", "crowdwork", "crowdfunding", "horizontality", "democracy", "innovation from below", "post-capitalism"

This article is the result of a collaborative effort by the two authors, whose names appear in alphabetical order. If, however, for academic reasons, individual responsibility must be assigned, Attila Bruni wrote the "Introduction", sections "Digital Platforms, Infrastructures and the New Production of Users" and "Hosting: Preparing the Scene, Keeping in Order and Performing the Platform"

A. Bruni (✉)
University of Trento, Trento, Italy
e-mail: attila.bruni@unitn.it

F. M. Esposito
University of Naples "Federico II", Naples, Italy

U. Meyer et al. (eds.), *Digitalization in Industry*,
https://doi.org/10.1007/978-3-030-28258-5_9

and, foremost, the "sharing economy" (Benkler, 2006; Botsman & Rogers, 2010; Bruns, 2008; Gillespie, 2010; Sundararajan, 2016). In other words, platforms are seen as helpful tools that contribute to the pursuit of ideas of freedom and free circulation of knowledge. In fact, one can say that the Internet itself was built on these values, which in past times had found in open software and "hacker ethics" their principal references (Himanen, 2001). This first wave dates to the early days of Web 2.0, when the possibility of users interacting with the World Wide Web and going beyond the original designers' project (by customizing online spaces, uploading content and sharing them in a network of peers) seemed to give concrete support to facilitating commons and commoning (Plantin, Lagoze, Edwards, & Sandvig, 2018). As Van Dijck, Poell, and de Waal (2018, p. 11) put it, it was as if "connectivity automatically leads to collectivity".

More recently, a second wave has stressed how the purest examples of commoning platforms are probably services such as Wikipedia (which exclusively consists of information exchanges), in that "many forms of digital commoning are not purely informational but are entangled within an organizational network of concrete (non-digitalized) economic practices" (Ossewaarde & Reijers, 2017, p. 612). The sharing of a car or an apartment (such as BlaBlaCar or Airbnb), as well as the delivery of food (such as Foodora or Just Eat) and/or a taxi service (such as Uber), is evidently linked to a set of heterogeneous practices, often "material" (such as driving or riding) more than "digital." This second wave thus concentrates on the conditions of those working behind the platform and the ways in which platforms profit from users' labor (Irani, 2015; Jin, 2015; van Doorn, 2016). Platforms are now associated with words such as "precariousness", "fragmentation", individualization", "erosion of workers' rights" and, most of all, "outsourcing". In fact, even if many differences occur between them, Airbnb, Uber, Amazon Mechanical Turk, BlaBlaCar, Foodora or TaskRabbit all share a form of operating "through a hyper-outsourced model, whereby workers are outsourced, fixed capital is outsourced, maintenance costs are outsourced, and training is outsourced" (Srnicek, 2016, p. 95). Together with this outsourcing-based model, platforms seem to display a monopoly attitude, a high degree of institutional isomorphism (due to their

and the "Conclusions"; Fabio M. Esposito wrote sections "Zooming In: The Debate About Airbnb", "Methodology and Empirical Context", "Airbnb: Producing Users, Performing the Platform" and "Becoming Host: Configuring and Producing Users".

graphical layout—Arcidiacono, Gandini, & Pais, 2018), an information architecture that sets the possibilities of interaction among users and the ownership of software and hardware (Choudary, 2015). Through their software, platforms fulfill three main objectives (van Doorn, 2016): (a) They provide a "space" in which users, customers and workers can meet, while the platform itself is positioned as purely intermediary; (b) they create ad hoc (labor) marketplaces, apart from institutional rules and rights; and (c) they optimize labor's flexibility and scalability, articulating a "workforce-as-a-service" model (Starner, 2015). Subsequently, notions such as "algorithmic labor" (Rosenblat & Stark, 2016), "algocracy" (Danaher, 2016) and "algorithmic governance" (Danaher et al., 2017) have been coined to call attention to how algorithms increasingly assess and manage human action.

In other words, if the first wave concentrated on the emancipatory and "horizontal" side of digital platforms, the second highlights issues of power and domination. Despite these differences, both waves display quite a "transparent" if not deterministic idea of technology, in that they assume that platforms will merely act as mediators/facilitators, or that they will directly and automatically "impact" on some broader social dynamics (such as the circulation of knowledge or the labor market).

Notwithstanding this debate, in this chapter we are particularly interested in focusing on how issues of domination/emancipation arise in the relation that digital platforms build and maintain with their users and in the ways in which users give shape to this relation. The pertinent issue from an organizational point of view (still underdeveloped in the ongoing debate) is the relational and performative aspect of platforms, that is, how they "shape the performance of social acts instead of merely facilitating them" (Van Dijck, 2013, p. 29). Mainly inspired by an actor-network approach and the recent "turn to infrastructure" Science and Technology Studies (STS) have witnessed, we will start from the assumption that platforms are not merely intermediaries; instead, they themselves constitute a "set of relations that constantly needs to be performed" (Van Dijck, 2013, p. 26).

To provide evidence for our ideas, we focus on Airbnb, a platform-based company and current leader at the global level in the online hospitality industry, which provides users the opportunity to rent and book accommodations for short-term periods. Since 2007, Airbnb has expanded rapidly throughout the world (but mainly in European and Western cities), representing first an emblematic case of the so-called sharing economy, but being subsequently recognized for disrupting housing and local communities. The platform enables its members to become "Hosts" by listing and renting out their lodgings (with a probably higher yield than a residential long-term rental), while giving travelers ("Guests", as defined by the platform) the opportunity to book accommodation at often lower prices than the hotel industry.

Hence, we focus on the relation the platform tends to establish with the Hosts and on the ways in which Hosts are produced (Hyysalo, Jensen, & Oudshoorn, 2016), as well as the "infrastructure". We then consider how different Hosts translate this relation into practice, thus performing the platform and its infrastructure. From a theoretical point of view, this will help to problematize the domination/emancipation dichotomy through which platforms are often interpreted, showing an apparently contradictory dynamic: Platform-organizations produce and depend on the very subjects they dominate.

Digital Platforms, Infrastructures and the New Production of Users

Looking at digital platforms from an actor-network perspective (Callon, 1984; Callon & Law, 1992; Latour, 2005) means to consider them as the ongoing product of a process of heterogeneous engineering (Law, 1987), insofar as they imply the organization over time and space of human and non-human actors, texts and objects, technologies and knowledge.

Platforms widely rely on an "installed base" (Star & Ruhleder, 1996)—pre-existing and "stabilized" infrastructures (like the Internet or the banking system) and technologies (such as smartphones). In this sense, digital platforms can be seen as the result of the connections between heterogeneous actors, systems and networks, which are able to interact and coordinate thanks to the adoption of standards and interoperability protocols (Plantin et al., 2018; Van Dijck, 2013). Digital platforms operate because they are embedded into a "digital ecosystem" (Peticca-Harris, deGama, & Ravishankar, 2018; Van Dijck et al., 2018), through which they can develop characteristics typical of infrastructures, such as ubiquity, reliability and wide accessibility.

Compared to infrastructures, platforms differ in scale and scope in that they do not seek to internalize their environments through vertical integration, but "are designed to be extended and elaborated from outside, by other actors, provided that those actors follow certain rules" (Plantin et al., 2018, p. 298). At the same time, given the massive diffusion of ICTs and ubiquitous computing, nowadays "platforms can achieve enormous scales, co-exist with infrastructures, ***and in some cases compete with or even supplant them***" (Plantin et al., 2018, p. 302, emphasis in original).

Framing the infrastructural side of platforms allows us to focus on their relational, contingent, incremental, situated and processual aspects, as well as their "transparence" and "invisibility" (Star, 1999; Star & Strauss, 1999). In fact, the architecture of platforms entails a continuous relation, coordination and collaboration between a "programmable, stable core system" with low variability and diverse "modular, variable complementary components" (Baldwin & Woodward, 2009). If it is true that platforms represent a "centrally controlled and designed system (often under corporate control)" (Plantin et al., 2018, p. 302), it is also true that they are built on a modular architecture and would remain "empty boxes" if they are not continuously performed, refined and repaired (Star & Bowker, 2002) through coordination and articulation work (Schmidt & Simone, 1996), which (like the infrastructure itself) remains partly invisible. Therefore, an "infrastructural inversion" (Bowker, 1994) is needed to give visibility to the work and the resources required by the "core system" to enrich it with new complementary components. This means to embrace the relations and the activities that platforms call into question, as well as the (online and offline) work required to fulfill such relations.

By taking into account the "script" (Akrich, 1992) of the platform online interface, it is possible to highlight how it "configures" its users by "setting constraints upon their likely future actions" (Woolgar, 1991, p. 59) and by establishing some standards to adhere to. STS have widely acknowledged the fundamental role users have in technological and innovation processes (Oudshoorn & Pinch, 2003). Since the early experiments of "consumer research" conducted by General Motors in the 1930s, companies, producers and designers have always tried (albeit for different purposes and with different extents) to engage users "as partners in inventing, designing or visioning new products" as well as "testers of early beta and later pilot versions of the technology" (Hyysalo & Johnson, 2016, p. 80).

Nowadays, however, there is a novelty: Companies tend not only to involve users, but also to find strategies to stimulate their activity, while users engage autonomously in creative forms of production. As stated by Hyysalo et al. (2016, p. 2), "the new production of users is thus about users' creativity ***and*** about changing involvement strategies that produce creative users". In other words, if the configuration of users takes place during the design process and "materializes" in the technological script, their production refers to a much wider process, which starts at the design stage but extends to the variety of ways in which the company "activates" users. In this regard, if configuring and scripting usually imply setting limitations to users' actions, the production of users is oriented to making users do more than what is inscripted in the technical object.

Framing the relationship between digital platforms and their users in terms of "production" thus enables us not only to consider how users are configured, but also to explore the activities users perform, the strategies implied by the platform to stimulate their performances and the ways in which users react to these strategies. Users have a significant degree of freedom in giving shape and substance to the platform, so that it becomes important to analyze not only how they decode (Mackay, Carne, Beynon-Davies, & Tudhope, 2000) the platform, but also the concrete practices performed to complete them and keep their relationship with the platform alive.

Given the heterogeneity of platforms (and the services they provide), a shared claim in the ongoing debate refers to the need to concentrate on the features of the specific platform one wants to analyze. Thus, before presenting our data and analysis, we will first zoom in on Airbnb by briefly recalling the main results of the research conducted on it.

Zooming In: The Debate About Airbnb

In "*The Platform Society*," Van Dijck et al. (2018, p. 18) consider Airbnb the epitome of "the invasion of online platforms in the hospitality sector" and of "the many battlegrounds in a society where social and economic interaction increasingly happens through a digital infrastructure that is global and highly interconnected". Guttentag (2015), one of the first scholars to focus on Airbnb, uses the concept of "disruptive innovation" (Christensen, 2006) to show how Airbnb is transforming the market of tourist accommodations (e.g., by differentiating itself from hotels) and attracting different kinds of travelers compared to traditional lodging opportunities. In his conclusions, the author proposes some thematic areas for future inquiry: Airbnb's impact on forms of short-term lodging and on urban areas (e.g., in terms of the perception of local residents or changes in the price and availability of homing solutions); the kind of people it attracts; and factors which affect the choice of the lodging.

It can be said that Guttentag's suggestions mirror today's debate: Ikkala and Lampinen (2015), for example, conceptualize platforms as services that facilitate the offline sharing of material and immaterial resources; Molz (2014) shows how even though most people started their hosting experiences on Airbnb for economic reasons, they continued because of the possibility of meeting and socializing with guests. However, during research conducted in Boston, Ladegaard (2018) develops the concept of "comfortable exotic" to underline how, while getting in touch with diversity constitutes one of the principal added values of the service offered by the platform, Hosts tend to accept bookings made by people who are to some extent similar to them (e.g., by qualification or spoken languages). Cheng and Foley (2018) analyzed the possible forms of discrimination that the platform enables, assuming that having more information about potential guests creates conditions for making discriminatory choices.

With a more economic-oriented analysis, Liang, Schuckert, Law, & Chih-Chien (2017) studied how information gathered and shared on the platform reduces the uncertainty of purchase choices. The authors emphasize how a *gamification* of the service (i.e., "the application of game design elements into non-game contexts"—Liang et al., 2017, p. 456), inscripted in the "Superhost" status and other design elements, can influence consumers' decisions and ratings. Wang and Nicolau's (2017) research follows this path as well: Through a quantitative comparison of 180,000 Airbnb listings in 33 cities, they identify host attributes, site and property attributes, amenities and services, rental rules and online review ratings as the main elements that influence listing prices. Fradkin, Grewal, Holtz, and Pearson (2015) focus in particular on the feedback system, showing how it affects consumers' choices, but also how elements of the system design (e.g., the reciprocity of the feedback) determine a positive bias in ratings. It has also been shown how pre-existing racial biases may lead to negative-biased reviews toward members of certain ethnic groups (Condliffe, 2016), which thereby cause a decrease in the "price" of their offers or demands. In this way, reviews and feedback set an "economy of regard" (Offer, 1997), which (in parallel with the money-economy) contributes to pricing dynamics while amplifying "differences between the 'haves' (those with a solid reputation) and the 'have-nots' (those without a good reputation)" (Ossewaarde & Reijers, 2017, p. 617).

Recently, different research has paid attention to the impact Airbnb has on real estate markets. Horn and Merante (2017), for example, analyzed how Airbnb affects the availability and price of long-term residential rentals in the Boston city area, finding that there are negative effects on availability (which decreases) as well as on the price (which grows) of rentals. Other research (Gurran & Phibbs, 2017; Picascia, Romano, & Teobaldi, 2017) reaches similar conclusions, underlining how in extreme cases Airbnb's impact on the local economy and the real estate market leads to a displacement of the residential population. Consequently, cities like San Francisco ("homeland" of Airbnb), New York, Berlin, Amsterdam, Paris, Barcelona and Tokyo have all adopted policies to regulate the short-term rental market (Dredge, Gyimóthy, Birkbak, Jensen, & Madsen, 2016).

Taken together with research conducted in the broader debate on digital platforms, these studies tend to frame Airbnb as an example of what Srnicek (2016) defines as "lean" platforms: Even if they try to build their identity upon an imaginary linked to the idea of "sharing", these platforms act as capitalist players focused on profit maximization (Ossewaarde & Reijers, 2017). However, studies carried out so far have not taken into consideration the relation the platform establishes with its users and, above all, the practices through which users give shape to this relation and, consequently, to the platform itself. In the rest of this chapter, we will concentrate precisely on these relations.

Methodology and Empirical Context

The data we present are the result of an analysis of the Airbnb platform, together with 20 in-depth interviews held with individuals signed up as Airbnb Hosts in the city of Trento, Italy. A first research step implied accessing the platform, detecting data from the website and focusing on the elements that regulate the relation between the user and the platform (contained in the "terms and conditions of service") and on some processes and mechanisms implied by the platform architecture.

The researcher who conducted the fieldwork was a "participant observer", in the sense that he himself is an Airbnb Host (in a different city). We believe the Host identity of the researcher significantly contributed to the access to the field: Being signed up as a Host since August 2015 and having built an online reputation through received feedback, the researcher was able to use his profile to contact potential interviewees directly through the platform's chat, requesting interviews instead of lodging. In other words, the researcher appeared as a somehow "reliable" and "accountable" person, triggering a reciprocal identification and legitimation between Hosts and interviewer and creating a situation of complicity, which made it easier to approach details and delicate issues (like the Hosts' earnings or the way they managed their fiscal responsibilities). Moreover, an insider knowledge of Airbnb jargon, as well as the procedures and ambiguities connected to the Host role, was very useful in carrying out the interviews.

To deeply investigate Hosts' daily life and practices, we relied on the episodic interview technique (Flick, 2000), asking interviewees to focus on specific episodes and concrete situations. The main criterion used to select the Hosts involved in the research was to balance the number of Hosts who rented out an entire apartment and those who rented out a private room. We started from the premise that different kinds of spaces would imply a different engagement, different starting conditions and a different experience of the Host role. Moreover, this criterion reflects the composition of the population of the examined area, where 48% of the announcements were for private rooms and 51% were entire apartments (the remaining 1% were shared rooms). Thus, after contacting 62 Hosts, we gained access to ten subjects renting out private rooms and ten Hosts offering entire apartments. The average duration of the interviews was 90 minutes; all the interviews were (audio) recorded and transcribed integrally.

Trento, the area in which the research was carried out, is a town in the northeastern part of Italy, well-developed in tourist terms, being the capital city of a region well known for outdoor tourism as well as for the presence of numerous festivals/fairs and the city University (with its related conferences). In the city, the platform's users have grown significantly during the last two years (with an annual growth rate of 57%); however, Airbnb is not diffused as much as in other Italian cities, featuring 343 listings for a total population of 115,000 residents. At the moment of the research, these listings corresponded to 228 active Hosts, with 25% of them having more than one rental. In this regard, it is interesting to notice how this 25% owns 171 lodgings, exactly 50% of the total listings.[1] Finally, and above all, compared to bigger Italian cities (like Rome, Naples, Milan or Florence), delegating the management of the houses rented on Airbnb to a company is not widespread in Trento. Thus, it was possible to reach Hosts who were personally involved in the management of their spaces and to investigate how they concretely gave shape to the role of Host and the tasks required by the platform. We are aware that it is becoming more and more common to find on Airbnb ordinary tourist structures or properties managed by professional agencies that use the platform (together with others, such as Booking.com) simply as a showcase, but we were not interested in looking at the progressive "professionalization" of the platform. On the contrary, we believe that focusing on the experiences of "real people" provides the possibility of considering how issues of domination/emancipation arise in the relationship between the platform and its users.

Airbnb: Producing Users, Performing the Platform

We begin with a description and analysis of the platform's main features and the relation it tries to establish with Hosts; we then consider how different Hosts interpret this relation and put it into practice.

Beginning with the "terms and conditions of service" available on the Web site (Articles 1.1 and 1.2), Airbnb defines itself as:

> online marketplace that enables its registered users ("members") and certain third parties which offer services (the members and third parties who offer services are the "Hosts" and the services they offer are the "Hosts' services") to publish their "Hosts' services" on the Airbnb platform ("listings") and to communicate and negotiate directly with the members who try to book these Hosts' services (the members who use the Hosts' services are "Guests"). [...] Airbnb doesn't own, create, sell, make available, control, manage, offer, deliver or provide listings or Hosts' services, neither it is an organizer or reseller of package travels pursuant to the (EU) Directive 2015/2302. Hosts are exclusively responsible for their listings and services.

Airbnb depicts itself as a place of direct encounter and interaction between offer and demand of short-term rentals, setting out its role as a mere "intermediator" and service provider.[2] As happens with other platforms, the organization is therefore not responsible for platform content and/or listed spaces, nor responsible for the potentially illegal behavior of Hosts (for instance, regarding local short-term rental regulations). A clear division of labor and responsibilities is thus presented, together with the fundamental characters involved with the platform: Airbnb Inc. and its "members" subdivided into Host (provider) and Guest (consumer) roles. These two roles (which are not mutually exclusive) do not have the same strategic importance for the platform: Hosts are those who make their "space" available and build the platform market; moreover, Hosts interact with Guests and are in charge of setting the physical space listed on the platform. In other words, beside the "service fee"[3] the company imposes on transactions between users, Hosts are the main source of value for the platform.

Becoming Host: Configuring and Producing Users

For Hosts (as well as Guests), the first task to enable them to operate on Airbnb is to create an account on the platform. This involves providing an e-mail address and a Google or Facebook account, choosing a payment method (credit card or PayPal) and providing a brief self-description (including a picture) and a phone number (verified by the organization through a code sent by SMS). It should be noted that in this way Airbnb integrates other platforms (Google, Facebook, PayPal) into parts of its infrastructure and verifies that its users: are connected to the most common elements of the global digital communication infrastructure (and therefore have an e-mail address and/or some other type of digital account); possess and can make use of specific technologies (such as a mobile phone); and are equipped for online money transfer (thanks to a credit card or a PayPal account). Thus, in terms of configuration, a basic characteristic that users have to satisfy is "connectivity" and therefore having already been configured by other platforms or digital infrastructures.

From the online procedure one must follow to become a Host (see Table 9.1), the platform approaches users with direct and informal language, trying to frame the relationships that occur in the context of Airbnb into a dimension of "friendship" and peer exchange. At the same time, expressions such as "*earning*", "*successful ideas*", "*being in control*" and "*managing the whole procedure*" are evocative of a more entrepreneurial and managerial dimension. Finally, the platform wants to reassure Hosts by stating that there is continuous "assistance" and a community of "peer experts" to refer to and that the "control" of the rented space is preserved. The first features the platform seems to promote and tries to produce are therefore informality, resourcefulness and trust in the platform itself.

Table 9.1 Become a Host

Become a Host: The online procedure
• On the top-right of the Airbnb homepage, one can find the "button" "*Become a host*": By clicking this, a drop-down window opens, indicating the potential income for accommodations in the city in which the search was made
• The wizard leads to another screen where the platform tells the potential Host that: "*Regardless of what kind of home or room you have to share, Airbnb makes it simple and secure to earn money and reach millions of travellers*"; "*Airbnb offers tools, hospitality tips, ongoing support, and an online community of experienced hosts for asking questions and sharing ideas for success*"; "*you are in full control of your availability, prices, house rules, and interaction with guests. You can set check-in times and handle the process as you wish*"
• The Host must specify the type of accommodation to be rented (full apartment, private room, shared room), its approximate address and the number of people that it can accommodate. Then, further information about the type of accommodation is required: Options range from "*home, apartment, hotel, apartment with hotel service*" to less common possibilities such as "*igloo, boat, train or tree house*". One must specify the number of bathrooms, bedrooms and beds available and declare if the accommodation has been explicitly arranged for guests, or if there are "personal effects". The Host must also specify the address of the accommodation, while the platform ensures that: "*Your exact address will be shared only with confirmed guests*"
• By tackling the boxes of a long list, the Host states which spaces can be used (kitchen, swimming pool, elevator and so on) and which services the guest will find in the accommodation, starting from those defined as "essentials" (towels, sheets, pillow, soap and toilet paper), to Wi-Fi, hairdryer, washing machine, A/C, lock in room or safety devices (such as fire extinguisher or smoke detector). The platform recommends to: "*Provide the main services to make your guests feel at home. Some hosts offer breakfast, others just some coffee or tea. None of these amenities are mandatory, but they can help your guests to feel at home*"
• In the second phase of the listing procedure (what Airbnb defines as "*Preparing the scene*") the platform asks Hosts to upload at least one photo of the rented space, remembering that "*many Hosts have more than 8 photos*", that "*Sometimes taking a picture from a corner instead than frontally makes the image better*", but also that "*if you want, for now you can skip this step*". Then, a description of the space is requested (maximum of 500 characters). Hosts must state if the space is suitable for "*families with children*", "*elderly*" or "*furry friends*", while they are given suggestions about what to describe ("*Describe the furnishings, the lighting, what's nearby,* etc."). It is possible to give further details about the neighborhood or the kind of interaction with Guests: basic and limited to the organization of their stay or more informal and personal. Finally, the listing must be characterized by a short title/slogan (maximum of 50 characters)

(continued)

Table 9.1 (continued)

Become a Host: The online procedure
• The third step concerns the setup of management tools (calendar, payment methods, house rules and booking settings). One can set the criteria potential Guests must meet (such as having uploaded an ID on the platform and/or having been recommended by other Hosts), but the platform reminds Hosts that more criteria to be met could mean fewer bookings. Regarding the acceptance of Guests, for example, the platform sets "*instant booking*" instead of "*booking request*" as the default option. The option is editable, but if one decides to evaluate requests, he/she has to confirm to be aware of the following statements: "*Are you sure you want to receive a booking request from your guests? You will only have 24 hours to answer the request without incurring in a penalty. Your listing will be ranked lower in Guests' search results, so you may receive fewer bookings. You will lose some security and control tools for Hosts, including the option to cancel a reservation without penalty if you do not feel comfortable with it*". The Host is also reminded that: "*In the rare case problems should occur, Airbnb protects you with 24/7 customer service and a Host Guarantee of €800,000*"
• Finally, the platform asks the user to denote how many days shall pass between the booking and the check-in, to set a minimum/maximum number of nights for stays and to set the time-span the lodging will be available for rent (1 month, 3 months), while warning that: "*Keeping your calendar up to date is the starting point for being a successful Host. A cancelation is a big inconvenience for Guests. If you make a cancelation because your calendar is not accurate, you will be charged a penalty and the dates in question will not be available for further bookings*". The Host must set a fixed price or adopt the "smart price" service, which (depending on the market demand) lets the price fluctuate between a minimum and maximum set by the Host
• The last page of the listing procedure states: "*Since you are responsible for your decision to offer your space to rent, you should familiarise with the existing law before starting to rent through Airbnb. By accepting our terms of service and by publishing your listing, you declare that you will follow the laws and norms in force*"

In addition to a personal profile, Hosts must set up a listing to represent the rented space. The listing procedure can be considered the first activity performed by the Host for the platform and, at the same time, the most concrete step in the process of configuration and production of users. During the listing creation, Hosts are stimulated in a variety of ways to fulfill what distinguishes the service/product provided by the platform: making people feel "at home." The platform encourages Hosts in making available to Guests not only "essential" resources but also a whole paraphernalia of household tools and technologies (TV, Wi-Fi, washing machine, hairdryer), as well as some "services" (such as breakfast). Thus, a further feature of the Hosts the platform tries to foster is their capability to recreate a sense of familiarity in their spaces, thanks to the presence of a series of objects, technologies and services.

Through the listing procedure, moreover, the platform enacts selective communication: For instance, it provides Host and Guest with "private" information (telephone number, e-mail address, accommodation address) only after the transaction has occurred. Thus, the platform positions itself as an information hub, while qualifying as a discreet interlocutor: The fact that the Host makes some information available to the platform (such as the exact address of the rented space) does not mean that other users will automatically be able to access it. In this way, a sense of trust toward the platform is reinforced.

Through all these steps, the platform tends to establish a "coaching" relationship with the Host, guiding them through the listing procedure. Most of all, the platform presents a set of options while providing suggestions about the choices to be made and/or examples of what other Hosts usually do. Thus, the Host's action is oriented and somehow controlled by the platform through the suggestion of a variety of possible actions. In other words, and even if it may appear paradoxical, it is exactly by giving Hosts the impression that they are free to do what they prefer that the platform succeeds in setting (and controlling) their concrete possibility of action. In this way, Hosts are "infrastructured" in that they are configured and produced as an integral part of the platform itself. This is quite clear in relation to the message which appears (as a clear "disclaimer") at the end of the overall listing procedure. For the first time since the beginning of the procedure, reference is made to possible sanctions and penalties, and Hosts are addressed as "pieces" of the platform itself, subject to an algorithmic logic ("if A then B"). Depending on various parameters (e.g., the settings of the calendar, prices or the criteria Guests should meet), the Host will be connected to complex algorithms which govern the visibility of the listings and (in the case of "smart prices") the oscillation of prices, and so, of the market itself. Which spaces are available on which dates, for how long and at what price are all essential elements for the correct functioning of a short-term rental market. Consequently, it is essential for Airbnb to infrastructure Hosts' actions as much as possible.

At the very end of the procedure, the platform reminds the Host that roles and responsibilities remain in any case different. In linguistic terms, accepting the terms of service and publishing a listing seem to have a performative power which extends toward the future, since the Host declares the will to follow local laws regarding short-term rental. From an organizational point of view, however, it is worth noticing how even if this message sanctions the end of the procedure of becoming a Host, the Host's actions actually start here. The next section considers how having published a listing practically affects the Hosts' daily life and through which practices they perform the platform.

Hosting: Preparing the Scene, Keeping in Order and Performing the Platform

While narrating their Host experiences, several interviewees focused on the initial investment they made to "prepare the scene". Almost all the interviewed Hosts purchased a new set of linens; some increased the number of glasses, plates and pots in the kitchen; many bought a new mattress; and others repainted the apartment and/or partially renewed the furniture:

> Anyway, we bought a few things: new furniture for the bathroom, a carpet, pillows, lamps, things to let the house look nicer [...] I tried to color the house up a bit... I bought some posters, I removed lots of personal items... I bought some plants... (*Maria, 50, entire apt.*)
>
> Yes, everything is new... I went to buy duvet covers and pillows, for the bed... in fact I left them wrapped in their plastic, so that they [the Guests] know that they are new. Look, I spent €220 for this stuff to put into the room, and I let guests pay only €30 per night, but I want them to have a good service when they come to my home... that they have a good experience... like it happens to me when I go to them [...] now I have to add a new lamp because otherwise they have to get up from the bed to turn the light off or on... (*Marco, 30, private room*)

Both excerpts point to the initial economic investment that the two Hosts (like many others) felt they had to make, but also calls attention to what their Guests will "experience". In many cases, this means going well beyond the "essential" services required by the platform and starting to pay attention to details. In the second excerpt, having already been an Airbnb Guest encourages the Host to refer not only to the platform's requests, but also to his personal experience ("like me when I go to their home"). In other words, almost all of the Hosts, through their previous experience as Guests, witnessed the ways in which their peers "prepared the scene" and, as in the most classic of isomorphic processes, they tried to replicate the average comfort standards they experienced. The "freedom" Hosts have in arranging their space thus resolves in their willingness to do more (and not less) than the platform suggests.

In the first excerpt, the interviewee refers to another practice related to "preparing the scene"—removing personal items. In fact, especially if they rent out an entire apartment, Hosts prefer to take out their personal belongings or at least the objects they are particularly bound to:

> When I decided to start hosting with Airbnb I also decided that my principal home would have become another. [...] In the apartment I have put on the website I only left those things which I wouldn't care about if they get broken or disappear... even if something happens I don't feel that much bad about it. I am really attached to the things I own. In fact, this was one of the reasons why I never did Airbnb before. Like... the idea that someone would come to my home and stain the cover of one of my books... unbearable! Let's say I emptied the house... (*Annibale, 45, entire apartment*)
>
> "Filling" and "emptying" the spaces are two sides of the same process—rearranging the spaces of the house. In several cases, spatial displacements were connected to finding a more appropriate space to host Guests: An interviewee switched his room (which had private access from the outside) with her daughter's room when the latter went studying abroad; one began to sleep regularly in what was previously the guest room, with the aim to leave his (more spacious) bedroom to the Guest; another Host gave up her studio and transformed it in order to make it available to Guests. In situations of shared spaces, Hosts usually gave the priority to Guests in using the bathroom or the kitchen, or they tried to stay at home as little (or as discretely) as possible:
>
> I wake up very early in the morning... at 6:40-6:50 I'm already out of the house [...] but if I have guests I take the shower in the evening, because in the morning it may disturb the guests [...] when there is somebody, I don't use the hairdryer... I pay attention... (*Gianna, 50, private room*)

In situations such as the one above, the possibility given to Hosts to rent out portions of their apartment translates into a rearticulation not only of their domestic spaces but also of the Hosts' presence. Removing (or "limiting") one's own presence is not something required by the platform, but that which Hosts autonomously feel it is opportune to do. In this case, the platform also prefers to rely on Hosts' initiatives (not specifying how should they behave), instead of trying to force them in a particular direction.

As emerged from different accounts, the preparation of the scene never really ends, becoming one of the activities Hosts enact throughout their whole experience:

> A guest comes and asks me... I don't know, if I have an ironing board, and I didn't think about that, so you buy one [...] 'I would need two pillows because I have neck pain'... so you buy pillows [...] All these small things, you know? [...] We also did a few things because the law prescribes it... like the minimum required square footage of the room and bureaucratic things like that. (*Ugo, 50, two entire apartments*)
>
> At the beginning you need to get yourself organized a bit. [...] I had already thought about the bed sheets and towels before I began, so I managed to always run the washing machines when it is full... but for the hair-dryer or the plates, the pans... it took me some time to figure that out... I mean, guests asked me for these things, so I understood I had to get them. (*Monica, 30, private room*)

These two excerpts highlight how preparing the scene becomes an activity that, stimulated by the platform, recurs continuously, aim to provide a sufficiently stable space configuration, which remains an open process. This stems from the fact that new Guests always bring new needs or requests, as well as from the fact that often Hosts decide to invest earnings from Airbnb in improving some aspects of the rented space (for instance, one of the Hosts first renovated his living room, then the kitchen and finally the bathroom). One could argue that Hosts are simply reinvesting profits to make their business grow. By doing so, they contribute to the growth of Airbnb itself, providing their economic resources and their time and energies to the platform-organization. It is as if the Hosts re-invest the profits realized through the platform into the platform itself.

Preparing the scene also entailed two further main practices, "keeping clean" and "keeping in order":

> I separate things a bit... I tend to separate things more... let's put it like this: I myself try not to leave things around when I'm home... I try to keep things in order. (*Annibale, 45, entire apt.*)
>
> Yes, I have to clean up much more... I try to keep everything more in order. [...] I used to leave stuff around, and now... knowing that there are guests, before they arrive I clean everything. If I am in the living room and go to my room I bring my stuff with me... I try to wash the dishes as soon

> as I finish eating... I mean, I have to keep the house clean... it obliges you to do things you normally wouldn't do. Sometimes it's positive, I may also be happy about it, but sometimes I say to myself: 'Fuck! Today I really don't want to...', but I have to! (*Monica, 30, private room*)

As seen in the two excerpts, sometimes "keeping clean" and "keeping in order" coincide, but it is interesting to notice how the latter also means making one's presence in the apartment invisible, thus fulfilling the "emptying" of the spaces. Hosts tend to highlight the positive side of cleaning and tidying up, but in some accounts (as in the final part of the second excerpt above), they underline the "heaviness" of carrying out this activity and how it becomes a duty. Indeed, the same person added:

> The thing that is a bit burdensome is the cleaning issue (...) and then sometimes it's stressing to receive these messages, when I don't want to use or watch my phone. (*Monica, 30, private room*)

Through this excerpt, we begin to see how the platform continues to produce and infrastructure Hosts by keeping the relation with them alive, for example through several "reminders." All Hosts dwelled on this aspect, underlining how sometimes the timing required by the platform does not match their personal attitudes:

> I'm a bit slow in getting things done. [...] Also, for bookings, maybe I read about a reservation and then I tell myself: 'I'll answer in an hour' [...] I don't know why... I could do it immediately, there's no reason to wait an hour. But I've noticed that guests want a fast answer. Also, because otherwise they may book somewhere else... And the site puts pressure on me, there is this countdown... On one hand, the site offers a service to people looking for a place to stay and it wants an answer in a given time... that seems quite fair to me... I mean, it puts pressure on me, but it tries to mediate. (*Maurizio, 35, private room*)

The "countdown" the interviewee talks about refers to the messages Airbnb sends to the Host whenever they receive an e-mail from a Guest or a booking request. Hosts have 24 hours to answer these messages (after this, the booking request will expire) and the frequency of the platform's reminders increases while approaching the deadline. It is interesting to notice how in the interviewee's opinion, the pressure the platform puts on Hosts is justified as a form of mediation between different needs, as if the platform had an impartial position, without having any goal itself.

Thus, we are finally able to acknowledge the web of practices the platform uses to keep its Host infrastructure going and to which Hosts also refer while performing the platform. This web can be found in the e-mails and notifications sent to the Hosts, in the response-rate of the latter and, above all (as with many other platforms), in the rating and feedback system established by the platform:

> I've noticed that when you get negative feedback Airbnb sends you a pre-set e-mail in which they write things like 'try to maintain high standards, anyway you are doing good!'. They write it very informally and put some hearts there... but you still notice it's standardized, because it happened twice to me and it was the exactly same e-mail. And they tell you that listings with low standards get cancelled. That means if you go under a certain rating... I don't remember well, like under two stars out of five... it's practically impossible [...] I lived in that house before starting Airbnb, so I tried to maintain a good standard anyway. Obviously now you notice it more if something is broken, or if something is particularly ugly, you pay more attention [...] because the apartment is still yours, but you need to keep higher standards. (*Giacomo, 27, entire apartment*)

The excerpt highlights a peculiar dynamic. Following negative feedback, the platform reminds the Hosts to fulfill certain standards. Hosts are the first to know that it is "practically impossible" to get below the required standards, given the positive bias that affects ratings between users (Fradkin et al., 2015). Building on Knorr Cetina and Bruegger (2002), it could be argued that the main purpose of the message is to "appresent" the platform and state to the Host that the standards required by the platform are higher than the ones Guests are satisfied with. To be kicked off the platform, one has to reach an average rating of 2/5 stars, but some negative feedback (i.e., inferior to four or five star rating) is enough for the platform to take action toward the Host. This is probably the most concrete and explicit demonstration of the kind of actions (and sanctions) the platform could undertake toward the Host. Again, the platform is not interested in exerting its power explicitly over Hosts; it is much more effective in making Hosts aware of what could happen, so that they "spontaneously" undertake corrective action. As already noted during the user configuration process, the mention of sanctions and penalties reminds the Host that they are part of an infrastructure and that, even if the rented-out spaces remain their private property, the standards to be fulfilled are now the property of the platform.

Hosts also perform the platform not only in relation to potential sanctions, but also by autonomously finding strategies for managing their relationship with it:

> Since there's the app, I use it. [...] Obviously, I pay more attention to my mobile... sometimes it's a source of stress, for example in the daytime I don't use the mobile at all because I'm at work [...] I noticed that the only times I look at it it's exactly because of Airbnb, or in the morning when I'm on the bus... it is a one-hour ride, so I answer to all the... for instance, I write and publish all the reviews... all at once, in the morning during the bus ride, or when I get back home... (*Anna, 25, private room*)

This excerpt is representative of the many ways in which Hosts themselves translate the platform into an everyday practice. As in the case just seen, this commonly happens by linking activities related to the management of the online ad (such as answering requests or publishing guest reviews) into everyday routines. This brings us back to the "new" production of users (Hyysalo et al., 2016): for platform-organizations it is fundamental not only to produce active and creative users, but also to find ways of stimulating users' activity and creativity (e.g., by making a smartphone app available), so that they will keep the platform update and alive.

Concluding Remarks

Coming to the end of this chapter, we would like to provide an answer to our initial question: How do digital platforms relate to processes of domination and emancipation? More precisely, how do issues of domination/emancipation arise in the relation that digital platforms build and maintain with their users and how do users give shape to this relation?

In the case of Airbnb, it seems to us that the answer points to processes that imply "infrastructuring" users and brokering communication and information flows.

We have seen how the platform aims to configure and produce users with specific characteristics: informality, entrepreneurial and managerial attitudes, connectivity and, above all, trust in the platform itself. In becoming Hosts, users are not just configured and produced, they are progressively infrastructured in that they are turned into elements of the platform itself (so that at the end of the process, they become sanctionable by the platform). Users produce a large part of the website content and own, manage, prepare and maintain the listed space (with the associated costs and risks), making available to the company a series of technologies essential for the management of the service (such as smartphones or PCs). Users must perform the contents of the platform, and this performance often coincides with a more general rearticulation of the house spaces, made up of "filling" and "emptying" practices aimed at meeting Guests' expectations and preserving the Host's intimacy. In particular, such "emptying" often implies the removal of the presence of the Host themselves (such as when the Host "gives" to the guests a part of the house previously used by them) or the effort to become invisible in their own home. Also, in keeping the spaces clean and tidy, the idea of "order" often coincides with removing personal effects around the house, while "cleaning" is aimed at eliminating traces of the Host. Thus, Hosts continue the "production" started by the platform, linking its contents to concrete practices and becoming parts of its infrastructure. Airbnb largely relies on Hosts' engagement and activity, turning private time and spaces into productive elements for the platform itself.

Curiously, Hosts seem to voluntarily enter into this relationship and to be willing to maintain it. This result is achieved through a process of "generification" (Pollock, Williams, & D'Adderio, 2016), which gives to users enough autonomy to decide how to perform the requests of the platform. In a way, it is as if control and standardization are exerted not through limiting the possibilities of action but multiplying them. In so doing, the platform can approach Hosts with different local conditions, resources and levels of engagement in a standardized manner. It is here that the management of communication and information by the platform becomes of crucial importance.

In subscribing to the platform, and even more so during the listing procedure, the interaction between the platform and its members shifts and alternates continuously between identification and verification procedures, templates, explanations, advice, clarifications on responsibilities and reassurances. The platform thus manages to gather and distribute selectively detailed information about the Host and their space. Gathering information is of fundamental importance for the platform, in that this data constitutes a large part of its contents and allows the coming-into-being of Airbnb itself. Moreover, detailed and updated information, thanks to Guests' reviews, allow for the monitoring of Hosts' "performances" and their adherence to the standards required by the platform. The platform itself continues to produce the Hosts, maintaining a constant relationship with the latter through a system of notifications sent via SMS and e-mails that reminds them of the tasks to be performed (such as the arrival of guests, a reservation request or the writing of a review). Adopting communication and information to put pressure on Hosts, the process of production and "infrastructuring" of the user is thus articulated into a kind of coercive isomorphism (Powell & Di Maggio, 1991) expressed through suggestions, recommendations and "friendly reminders".

In reference to domination/emancipation processes, we can thus highlight an apparently contradictory dynamic: Airbnb produces the very subject it dominates, so that, at the same time, it totally depends on them. In our view, this is also the main reason why the platform tries not only to produce its members, but also to infrastructure them: if they would leave the platform, it would cease to exist. As with domination or control, emancipation is just to be enacted.

Notes

1. *Source* https://www.airdna.co/market-data/app/it/trentino-alto-adige-sudtirol/trento/overview.
2. Point 7.1.7 in "Terms of Service" declares that the Host signs a legally binding contract with the Guest, not with the platform.
3. The "service fee" represents the income Airbnb earns from every transaction. It covers the 9–12% of the fee paid by the Guest and the 3–5% of the Host's reward. This difference in the "fee" applied by Airbnb to Hosts and Guests further testifies to the crucial role of Hosts for the platform (the platform has an interest in "charging" them less than Guests).

References

Akrich, M. (1992). The Description of Technical Objects. In W. Bijker & J. Law (Eds.), *Shaping Technology/Building Society: Studies in Sociotechnical Change* (pp. 205–224). Cambridge, MA: MIT Press.

Arcidiacono, D., Gandini, A., & Pais, I. (2018). Sharing What? The 'Sharing Economy' in the Sociological Debate. *The Sociological Review Monographs, 66*(2), 275–288.

Baldwin, C. Y., & Woodard, C. J. (2009). The Architecture of Platforms: A Unified View. In A. Gawer (Ed.), *Platforms, Markets and Innovation* (pp. 19–44). Cheltenham, UK and Northampton, MA: Edward Elgar.

Benkler, Y. (2006). *The Wealth of Networks: How Social Production Transforms Markets and Freedom*. New Haven, CT: Yale University Press.

Botsman, R., & Rogers, B. (2010). *What's Mine Is Yours: The Rise of Collaborative Consumption*. New York, NY: HarperCollins.

Bowker, G. C. (1994). *Science on the Run: Information Management and Industrial Geophysics at Schlumberger, 1920–1940*. Cambridge, MA: MIT Press.

Bruns, A. (2008). *Blogs, Wikipedia, Second Life and Beyond: From Production to Produsage*. New York, NY: Lang.

Callon, M. (1984). Some Elements of a Sociology of Translation: Domestication of the Scallops and the Fishermen of St Brieuc Bay. *The Sociological Review, 32*(1), 196–233.

Callon, M., & Law J. (1992). The Life and Death of an Aircraft: A Network Analysis of Technical Change. In W. Bijke & J. Law (Eds.), *Shaping Technology/Building Society: Studies in Sociotechnical Change* (pp. 21–52). Cambridge, MA: MIT Press.

Cheng, M., & Foley, C. (2018). The Sharing Economy and Digital Discrimination: The Case of Airbnb. *International Journal of Hospitality Management, 70*, 95–98.

Choudary, P. S. (2015). *Platform Scale: How an Emerging Business Model Helps Startups Build Large Empires with Minimum Investment*. Boston, MA: Platform Thinking Labs.

Christensen, C. M. (2006). The Ongoing Process of Building a Theory of Disruption. *Journal of Product Innovation Management, 23*(1), 39–55.

Condliffe, J. (2016, September 12). Airbnb Isn't Really Confronting Its Racism Problem. *MIT Technology Review*. Retrieved from https://www.technologyreview.com/s/602355/airbnb-isnt-really-confronting-its-racism-problem/. Accessed 22 September 2019.

Danaher, J. (2016). The Threat of Algocracy: Reality, Resistance and Accommodation. *Philosophy and Technology, 29*, 245–268.

Danaher, J., Hogan, M. J., Noone, C., Kennedy, R., Behan, A., De Paor, A., ... Shankar, K. (2017, July–December). Algorithmic Governance: Developing a Research Agenda Through the Power of Collective Intelligence. *Big Data & Society*, 1–21.

Dredge, D., Gyimóthy, S., Birkbak, A., Jensen, T. E., & Madsen, A. K. (2016). *The Impact of Regulatory Approaches Targeting Collaborative Economy in the Tourism Accommodation Sector: Barcelona, Berlin, Amsterdam and Paris* (Impulse Paper No. 9, European Commission DG GROWTH). Copenhagen, DK: Aalborg University.

Fradkin, A., Grewal, E., Holtz, D., & Pearson, M. (2015, June 15–19). Bias and Reciprocity in Online Reviews: Evidence from Field Experiments on Airbnb. *Proceedings of the Sixteenth ACM Conference on Economics and Computation*. Portland, OR.

Flick, U. (2000). Episodic Interviewing. In M. W. Bauer & G. Gaskell (Eds.), *Qualitative Researching with Text, Image and Sound: A Practical Handbook* (pp. 75–92). London, UK: Sage.

Gillespie, T. (2010). The Politics of 'Platforms'. *New Media & Society, 12*(3), 347–364.

Gurran, N., & Phibbs, P. (2017). When Tourists Move in: How Should Urban Planners Respond to Airbnb? *Journal of the American Planning Association, 83*(1), 80–92.

Guttentag, D. (2015). Airbnb: Disruptive Innovation and the Rise of an Informal Tourism Accommodation Sector. *Current Issues in Tourism, 18*(12), 1192–1217.

Himanen, P. (2001). *The Hacker Ethic and the Spirit of Information Age*. New York, NY: Random House.

Horn, K., & Merante, M. (2017). Is Home Sharing Driving Up Rents? Evidence from Airbnb in Boston. *Journal of Housing Economics, 38*, 14–24.

Hyysalo, S., Jensen, T. E., & Oudshoorn, N. (Eds.). (2016). *The New Production of Users: Changing Innovation Collectives and Involvement Strategies*. London, UK: Routledge.

Hyysalo, S., & Johnson, M. (2016). User Representation: A Journey Towards Conceptual Maturation. In S. Hyysalo, T. E. Jensen, & N. Oudshoorn (Eds.), *The New Production of Users: Changing Innovation Collectives and Involvement Strategies* (pp. 75–100). London, UK: Routledge.

Ikkala, T., & Lampinen, A. (2015, March 14–18). *Monetizing Network Hospitality: Hospitality and Sociability in the Context of Airbnb*. Paper Presented at CSCW Conference, Vancouver, BC.

Irani, L. (2015). Difference and Dependence Among Digital Workers: The Case of Amazon Mechanical Turk. *South Atlantic Quarterly, 114*(1), 225–234.

Jin, D. Y. (2015). *Digital Platforms, Imperialism and Political Culture*. New York, NY: Routledge.

Knorr Cetina, K., & Bruegger, U. (2002). Traders' Engagement with Markets: A Postsocial Relationship. *Theory, Culture and Society, 19*(5–6), 161–185.

Ladegaard, I. (2018). Hosting the Comfortably Exotic: Cosmopolitan Aspirations in the Sharing Economy. *The Sociological Review Monographs, 66*(2), 381–400.

Latour, B. (2005). *Reassembling the Social: An Introduction to Actor-Network Theory*. Oxford, UK: Oxford University Press.

Law, J. (1987). *Technology and Heterogeneous Engineering: The Case of Portuguese Expansion*. Cambridge, MA: MIT Press.

Liang, S., Schuckert, M., Law, R., & Chih-Chien, C. (2017). Be a "Superhost": The Importance of Badge Systems for Peer-to-Peer Rental Accommodations. *Tourism Management, 60,* 454–465.

Mackay, H., Carne, C., Beynon-Davies, P., & Tudhope, D. (2000). Reconfiguring the User: Using Rapid Application Development. *Social Studies of Science, 30*(5), 737–757.

Molz, G. J. (2014). Toward a Network Hospitality. *First Monday, 19*(3). Retrieved from https://journals.uic.edu/ojs/index.php/fm/article/view/4824/3848. Accessed 9 July 2018.

Offer, A. (1997). Between the Gift and the Market: The Economy of Regard. *The Economic History Review, 50*(3), 450–476.

Ossewaarde, M., & Reijers, W. (2017). The Illusion of the Digital Commons: 'False Consciousness' in Online Alternative Economies. *Organization, 24*(5), 609–628.

Oudshoorn, N., & Pinch, T. (Eds.). (2003). *How Users Matter: The Co-construction of Users and Technologies.* Cambridge, MA: MIT Press.

Peticca-Harris, A., deGama, N., & Ravishankar, M. N. (2018). Postcapitalist Precarious Work and Those in the 'Drivers' Seat: Exploring the Motivations and Lived Experiences of Uber Drivers in Canada. *Organization.* https://doi.org/10.1177/1350508418757332.

Picascia, S., Romano, A., & Teobaldi, M. (2017, July 11–14). *The Airification of Cities: Making Sense of the Impact of Peer to Peer Short Term Letting on Urban Functions and Economy.* Paper Presented at the Annual Congress of the Association of European Schools of Planning, AESOP2017, Lisbon, PT.

Plantin, J. C., Lagoze, C., Edwards, P., & Sandvig, C. (2018). Infrastructure Studies Meet Platform Studies in the Age of Google and Facebook. *New Media & Society, 20*(1), 293–310.

Pollock, N., Williams, R., & D'Adderio, L. (2016). Generification as a Strategy: How Software Producers Configure Products, Manage User Communities and Segment Markets. In S. Hyysalo, T. E. Jensen, & N. Oudshoorn (Eds.), *The New Production of Users: Changing Innovation Collectives and Involvement Strategies* (pp. 160–189). London, UK: Routledge.

Powell, W. W., & Di Maggio, P. J. (1991). *The New Institutionalism in Organizational Analysis.* Chicago, IL: University of Chicago Press.

Rosenblat, A., & Stark, L. (2016). Algorithmic Labor and Information Asymmetries: A Case Study of Uber's Drivers. *International Journal of Communication, 10,* 3758–3784.

Schmidt, K., & Simone, C. (1996). Coordination Mechanisms: Towards a Conceptual Foundation of CSCW Systems Design. *CSCW, 5,* 155–200.

Srnicek, N. (2016). *Platform Capitalism.* London, UK: Wiley.

Star, S. L. (1999). The Ethnography of Infrastructure. *American Behavioral Scientist, 43*(3), 377–391.

Star, S. L., & Bowker, G. C. (2002). How to Infrastructure? In L. A. Lievrouw & S. L. Livingstone (Eds.), *The Handbook of New Media: Social Shaping and Consequences of ICT* (pp. 151–162). London, UK: Sage.

Star, S. L., & Ruhleder, K. (1996). Steps Toward an Ecology of Infrastructure: Borderlands of Design and Access for Large Information Spaces. *Information Systems Research, 7*(1), 111–134.

Star, S. L., & Strauss, A. (1999). Layers of Silence, Arenas of Voice: The Ecology of Visible and Invisible Work. *Computer-Supported Cooperative Work, 8*(1–2), 9–30.

Starner, T. (2015). Has 'Workforce-as-a-Service' Arrived? *HR Dive*. Retrieved from http://www.hrdive.com/news/has-workforce-as-a-service-arrived/402237/. Accessed 29 April 2019.

Sundararajan, A. (2016). *The Sharing Economy: The End of Employment and the Rise of Crowd-Based Capitalism*. Cambridge, MA: MIT Press.

van Dijck, J. (2013). *The Culture of Connectivity: A Critical History of Social Media*. New York, NY: Oxford University Press.

van Dijck, J., Poell, T., & de Waal, M. (2018). *The Platform Society: Public Values in a Connective World*. New York, NY: Oxford University Press.

Van Doorn, N. (2016). Platform Labor: On the Gendered and Racialized Exploitation of Low-Income Service Work in the 'On-Demand' Economy. *Information, Communication & Society, 20*(6), 898–914.

Wang, D., & Nicolau, J. L. (2017). Price Determinants of Sharing Economy Based Accommodation Rental: A Study of Listings from 33 Cities on Airbnb.com. *International Journal of Hospitality Management, 62*, 120–131.

Woolgar, S. (1991). Configuring the User: The Case of Usability Trials. In J. Law (Ed.), *Sociology of Monsters: Essays on Power Technology and Domination* (pp. 57–99). London, UK: Routledge.

CHAPTER 10

Governing the Elderly Body: Technocare Policy and Industrial Promises of Freedom

Gunhild Tøndel and David Seibt

Introduction

Demographic forecasts of an increasingly aging society have given rise to widespread fears regarding the end of welfare progress and the collapse of the public health and care sector in many countries of the Global North (Peine, Faulkner, Jæger, & Moors, 2015). For several years, governmental authorities in Norway have been warning citizens that "over the next few decades, society will confront difficult care challenges due to a growing number of seniors, new user groups and a shortage of health care personnel and voluntary caregivers" (Norwegian Ministry of Health and Care Services, 2011: 11, p. 9). Such warnings resemble policy recommendations issued by international stakeholders, such as the OECD (2017), who, among other strategies, advises the Norwegian authorities to make home care affordable for all and better support

G. Tøndel (✉)
Norwegian University of Science and Technology,
Trondheim, Norway
e-mail: gunhild.tondel@ntnu.no

D. Seibt
Technical University of Munich, Munich, Germany

U. Meyer et al. (eds.), *Digitalization in Industry*,
https://doi.org/10.1007/978-3-030-28258-5_10

informal care practices in order to reduce the inequalities in long-term care that a rapidly aging society may generate.

In recent years, policies regarding the management of an aging society have framed these challenges as *opportunities* for building a better society for all, by emancipating the elderly from dependence on state organized care. In line with the policy of the World Health Organization (WHO) (2002) and the United Nations (2002) initiative "A society for all ages," the Norwegian Ministry of Health and Care Services (2018, p. 70) argues that an "age-friendly society" has the potential to benefit all citizens regardless of age. To achieve this goal, extensive efforts have been made to reform and reorganize the health and care sector and promote new perspectives on old age. In Norway, as in the other Nordic countries, an important part of this strategy has been to develop *welfare technology* that can automate care work processes and make the elderly more independent of public services. Or, as the Ministry of Health and Care Services (2018, p. 59) frames this strategy:

> Tomorrow's care service must enable its users to become resources in their own lives. Welfare technology gives older people the opportunity to preserve quality of life, coping and independence longer. It also allows the elderly to stay home longer. Increased use of welfare technology is one of several factors that can contribute to a sustainable care service in the future.

Welfare technology thus implies a reimagining of the elderly as active citizens who, given the appropriate tools, can emancipate themselves from the limitations born of their dependency on assistance from others. The same overall ambition is clearly expressed in the technology optimism conveyed by the term itself: "welfare technology" is technology that produces welfare.

Even though many of the technologies included under the term such as GPS trackers, safety alarms, and feeding robots have existed previously, the idea of implementing them in a care context marks an important innovation that reconfigures the roles and relationships involved in the practice of care. Welfare technology delegates some of the state's responsibility for care to an emerging welfare technology industry; it changes the role of care professionals who must learn how to do care with (and of) technology; and most importantly, it recasts the elderly as active users able to care for themselves by using technology.

In this chapter, we draw on the notion of inscription and description (Akrich, 1992; Latour, 1992) to offer an empirically grounded critique of welfare technology as a *technocare policy* and the promises attached to it in terms of both the social emancipation of the elderly and the rescue of the public welfare system. We base our analysis on publicly available documents on the development of welfare technology as well as data from a mobile ethnography of the use of a safety alarm system in the Norwegian health and care services. On the one hand, this enables us to call into question what Neven (2015) terms the triple-win rhetoric of the aging-and-innovation discourse by tracing the inscription of discriminatory potentials into overtly emancipatory welfare technology. On the other hand, the data allows us to trace how these potentials are enacted and sometimes subverted in the practices of industry, care workers, and the elderly themselves.

Our analysis centers on the ways in which the development, implementation, and use of welfare technology reconfigure the actors, relationships, and responsibilities that are part of elderly care. It contributes to a growing body of work in the field of "user studies" (Hyysalo, Jensen, & Oudshoorn, 2016; Oudshoorn & Pinch, 2003), where the role of technology in the reorganization of care has been garnering increasing attention. For instance, several authors have argued that the large-scale implementation of technology reorganizes care relations toward increased self-care and care by relatives (e.g., Moser & Thygesen, 2015; Oudshoorn, 2011). According to Peine et al. (2015, p. 3), this line of research typically emphasizes the various roles of users and user-producer relationships in innovation processes, as well as the intricate ways in which older persons, their peers, care givers, and family members, transform and articulate ideas about later life through active engagements with technoscientific objects. This includes confronting the existing stereotypes of older persons as passive recipients of technology (Mort, Roberts, & Callén, 2012; Peine, Rollwagen, & Neven, 2014) and bringing into sight older persons as agents that create and develop meaning for later life as they interact with technology (Peine et al., 2015, p. 3). Current literature however frequently leaves out the larger political and industrial context that constitutes the elderly as users of these objects to begin with. While it is important to steer free of a deficit-based understanding of elderly users, tracing their technologically mediated relationship to policy and industry enables us to undertake the equally important task of criticizing larger patterns of domination, which make the creativity or even resistance of the elderly such a vital necessity.

Technological Objects, Scripts, and Users

One of the distinctive features of the Nordic answer to the anticipated challenges of demographic change is its reliance on technology. Yet, in public discourse technologies such as safety alarms, GPS sensors, and smart house systems are usually taken as self-evident or even as quite banal objects. They are considered to be cold, clean, and technical (Roberts, Mort, & Milligan, 2012; Pols & Moser, 2009), the appendages of political decision-making rather than their driving force. By contrast, in this chapter we will use the concepts of "inscription" and "description" (Akrich, 1992; Latour, 1992) to bring technology to the center of attention. In particular, we argue that by opening these black (or rather white) boxes, we are able to analyze the vast networks of actors, relations, and responsibilities they are constituted by and constitutive of. According to Madeleine Akrich, a first step toward this goal is to pay close attention to the representation of the world inscribed into the object by its designers.

> [W]hen technologists define the characteristics of their objects, they necessarily make hypotheses about the entities that make up the world into which the object is to be inserted. Designers thus define actors with specific tastes, competences, motives, aspirations, political prejudices, and the rest, and they assume that morality, technology, science, and economy will evolve in particular ways. A large part of the work of innovators is that of 'inscribing' this vision of (or prediction about) the world in the technical content of the new object. I will call the end product of this work a 'script' or a 'scenario'. (Akrich, 1992, pp. 207–208)

From this perspective, welfare technology already contains a range of assumptions about the world in which it is to be used. When viewed through the lens of *inscription*, the various mundane gadgets define a whole network of actors and relations between them, including a specific "geography of responsibilities" (ibid., 207). For instance, welfare technology presupposes a welfare technology *industry* that develops and manufactures it, but it does not necessarily presuppose a welfare *state*. It does depend on both active old users and tech-savvy care givers, but it may crumble in the hands of traditionally trained care professionals and more fragile old users who insist on practicing care through embodied interaction between humans.

In the case that the world inscribed into the object does not match the world in which it is actually inserted, Akrich proposes two elementary mechanisms of adjustment or *description*. On the one hand, the way an object is designed, labeled, and presented may compel others to act in accordance with its script. Here alignment is achieved as the object (and more often than not its designers) transforms its environment. On the other hand, users may reinterpret or change the object and its script. They may play their roles in ways unintended by the object's designers; they may misuse or break the object, or even worse, they might ignore it entirely, in which case the technical object remains an inconsequential "chimera" subject to oblivion.

For the purposes of this article, we ourselves wish to make three adjustments to Akrich's original argument that relate to the notions of designers, script, and users. The first of these adjustments concerns the idea of *designer*. As we have already argued, welfare technology is a politically based project. That is, its script had already been at least partly written in policy documents *before* the technologist's conceiving of a concrete object. Hence, the "writing" of the welfare-technology-script was distributed as well as sequential. We foreground the policy context, because it was here that welfare technology was fostered and named. Yet, we position it in a longer trajectory of writing. On the one hand, in Norway, the logic of the script's politics extends from a longer line of previous reforms of the public health and care sector. On the other hand, the script as formulated in the welfare policy context was itself meant to enroll future users as well as industrial stakeholders who were supposed to further concretize the policy by developing, producing, marketing, and using specific technologies. While this may appear as a rather specific quality of our own case, we would argue that it is relatively common if one attends closely to the history of technology and the biography of artefacts (Hyysalo, Pollock, & Williams, 2018; Latour, 1987; Noble, 1984; Oudshoorn, 2003).

Our second adjustment relates to the notion of *script* and its relation to technical objects. From what we have advanced so far, it should be clear that the welfare-technology-script is not bound to a single technical object as it is in Akrich's account. The script is first written into policy documents and is then translated into a wide range of various objects ranging from safety alarms to smart house solutions. While all of these embody slightly different scripts, we argue that they have a marked family resemblance, or isomorphism, which makes them recognizable as instances of welfare technology. While classical social constructivist accounts of technology have often been concerned with the stabilization of a single style of object (Latour, 1987; Noble, 1984; Pinch & Bijker, 1987), our argument shifts the focus to the way in which scripts travel (Czarniawska & Sevón, 2005; Igelsböck & Schüßler, 2019) and are embodied in whole landscapes of technical objects.

Finally, with regard to the notion of users, we would like to make salient that welfare technologies do usually imply several different users and the attendant relationships between them. Early welfare technology typically defined users as the elderly, as well as their families, and professional care workers. Given this finding, our focus is less on the direct relationship between the technical object and "the user" (Woolgar, 1991) in the singular. Instead, we focus on the network of relationships which is assumed by the technology and which it requires for its operation. While Akrich's original article provides examples of multiple user roles and relationships inscribed into a single artifact, subsequent adoption of her concept has occasionally overlooked this particular aspect of her work.

The overall goal of these adjustments is to move script analysis beyond the scale of single technologies and their users, and to make it more clearly compatible with a concern for large-scale political and industrial transformation. In this way, we hope to contribute to an understanding of how concrete technical objects, such as those grouped under the label of welfare technology, are simultaneously connected to institutionalized patterns of domination and emerging dynamics of emancipation. In the following section, we will sketch out how we approach this goal from a methodological perspective.

Methodology and Material

Our analysis is grounded in two main sources of empirical material relating to the inscription and description of welfare technology, respectively. In order to understand the world as it is imagined by the writers of the welfare-technology-script, we collected and analyzed publicly available documents such as national policy reports, media coverage of the welfare industry, and material from firms developing and selling welfare technology. We use this data to reconstruct some major ways in which politicians and industry stakeholders *inscribe* welfare technology, weaving together promises of emancipation for the elderly with promises of economic growth. Our analysis follows the development of the Norwegian welfare technology initiative from 2009 to 2017. This period includes the start of the initiative, the first phase of testing and implementation of welfare technologies in Norwegian municipal health and care services and the first renegotiations of the script following its adoption in actual care practices.

The year 2009 was strategically chosen as the starting point for this analysis due to the launch of a policy advising report about technology in care from the Norwegian Board of Technology (2009). Two years later, an official Norwegian report from the Ministry of Health and Care Services (2011) termed "Innovation in the care services" was published, marking the starting point of the welfare technology initiative. We downloaded such national policy documents from the web pages of the national health and care authorities. Additional media documents were located by carrying out a systematic search in the digital media database *Atekst/Retriever*, which contains all Norwegian media material in digital and paper formats. The documents were sorted and organized in accordance with their relevance to the welfare technology initiative and analytically approached both as "containers of meaning" (Prior, 2003) and as "institutional doings" of technology at a discourse level.

On the level of description, our data set consists of interview and observation data collected through a multi-sited ethnography (Hine, 2000; Marcus, 1995), which was undertaken by Tøndel in 2014 and 2015 and then continued in 2017. Originally the fieldwork was designed to explore the construction of "safety" as a tool of governance that materializes in the form of a technocare policy, thereby shaping how old age, technology and care combine in practice. However, Tøndel's main empirical object, a safety alarm system, soon turned out to offer a fruitful point of entry to explore the complex network of human and non-human actants supporting welfare technology more generally (compare Sánchez-Criado et al., 2014). In particular, following the network of social and technical relations inscribed into the safety alarm enabled her to study the description of welfare technology in the interactive use practices of care professionals and service users.

The safety alarm pendant is worn on the bodies of its users, while the end receptor of the alarm is, among other technical devices, often worn on the bodies of health and care personnel. The device's main purpose is to reconfigure the connection between the everyday practices of users and care workers across time and space. It is intended to introduce a safety enhancement that enables the elderly to maintain and prolong independent living conditions in their own homes. By equipping their homes and bodies with these objects, the elderly can call for assistance—either directly to the municipal homecare service, to relatives, or to an alarm central—in case of an emergency. Following this outwardly mundane gadget allows us to study how the various user roles and relationships inscribed into it as part of the welfare-technology-script are enacted in the day-to-day practice of care and how, occasionally, users deviate from the script in the face of ingrained professional values, personal tragedies, and pain. Moreover, the alarm also invites a positioning of the innovation of welfare technology in a longer historical trajectory. It has been utilized in home care service—in most Western countries since the 1990s—while only recently being included under the umbrella of welfare technology and reshaped to fit the ambitions of the new technocare policy.

Tracking the practices connected to the safety alarm involved following people in the municipal services who were constantly "on the run." In order to do this, Tøndel employed methods often referred to as "go-along interviewing," "walk-along interviews," or "walking interviews" (see Kusenbach, 2003). An itinerant methodical strategy is particularly suited to obtaining contextualized perspectives as it allows for the conducting of mobile interviews in which the participant acts as a navigational guide for the activity he/she performs (Carpiano, 2009; Garcia, Eisenberg, Frerich, Lechner, & Lust, 2012; Kusenbach, 2003). Tøndel ended up moving between multiple sites, such as the municipal home care services, private homes of service users, the municipal city-hall and policy and research conferences dedicated to shaping the welfare technology field.

To make sense of these data, they were analyzed using principles from situational analysis (Clarke, 2005) and ultimately articulated through the lens of scripts as a means to focus on the role of technology in ordering this "messy" situation. In what follows, we will zoom in on three sites in which welfare technologies, such as the safety alarm, are negotiated. The first relates to the "writing" of the welfare-technology-script in policy. The second relates to an initial form of description, as the technology is transformed from a policy document into an industrial product. Finally, practices in the third site, the municipal home care services, describe the safety alarm as a means for practical care work. Remarkably, in situated practices of care, welfare technology becomes disconnected from the vocabulary of the active aging policy due to a tiny little, but highly significant detail: At times the oldest among the aging bodies are too tired to be set free.

Transnational Discourses of Old Age: From Greyness to Active Aging

For decades, Western governments have lamented the future of the welfare state, claiming reform as a necessary means to ward off the dangers of an aging society. Such fears are grounded in the idea that the aging society will drown or "overflow" (Callon, 1998) the welfare budgets, as illustrated through commonly used phrases such as "the elderly wave" or the "silver tsunami"[1] (Mort et al. 2012). In this metaphoric language, the increasing demographic gap between the numbers of elderly versus employable citizens is framed as an existential threat to the continued existence of the welfare state. As the elderly become dependent on public health and care services, they will "flood" them beyond their current capacity and thereby constitute a danger for the sustainability of society as a whole.

Interestingly, the water-chaos metaphors used in a policy context are complemented by lay associations of old age with the loss of bodily control or, indeed, the loss of bodily fluids in a literal sense. As one reaches a certain level of function reduction due to biological aging, these fluids can start to run over and become troublesome. Some seniors get diabetics and must monitor and tame their blood with insulin. Some experience incontinence, urinary or excretory, and must solve leakage problems through the use of incontinence products depending on the severity (pads, liners, diapers, briefs). Others may have difficulty coordinating their arms and hands, resulting in a socially embarrassing situation during mealtimes. Some must exert themselves to resist the fluidity of their thoughts or, what is known in medical terms as cognitive decline. Others may become physically passive, sometimes against their own will, in a gradual loss of control over the content of everyday life. These various fluidities are commonly seen to aggravate the elderlies' growing disconnection from society, which finds its expression in their frequent exclusion from the labor market, the reproductive order, as well as from many social activities and spaces, including their own homes.

More recently, an awareness of the systematic discrimination inscribed into this view of the elderly as individually broken and disconnected, yet collectively threatening, has been growing among policy makers. Since the 1990s, Western policy has attempted to replace the historical focus on what older adults can no longer do (i.e., their deficits)[2] with an emphasis on their competence and knowledge (Jacobs, 2005).

This change in orientation is broadly communicated in terms such as "active ageing,"[3] "productive ageing," "healthy ageing," (Boudiny, 2012) or "successful ageing" (Dillaway & Byrnes, 2009).[4] As Asquith (2009) points out, such discourses center on individual autonomy and independence, while simultaneously addressing the material conditions of the elderly and the future sustainability of public senior care. Yet, behind the rhetoric of emancipation from the exigencies of old age lurks the economic disaster awaiting demographically aging nations that are unwilling or incapable of making hard decisions about reducing government expenditure on income, social, and service support for senior citizens (Asquith, 2009; Neven, 2015; Peine et al., 2015; Richardson, 2004).

When translated into a governmental welfare policy context with resource distribution as an important concern, the valuation of positive, active, and successful aging appears not so much as an initiative aimed at the emancipation of the elderly from their dependency on public institutions, but as an attempt to negate public responsibility for senior citizens. From this perspective, the integration of positive, active, and successful aging into welfare policy becomes an articulation of a hyper-individualized neoliberal discourse that asks the elderly to take increased responsibility for their own health and everyday life in order to reduce their burden on the welfare state (Bakken, 2018). Older individuals shall become more responsible for the outcomes of their life choices, and local communities shall provide the social support required for individuals to make better choices over their life course. At the same time, the role of the government is reduced to providing individuals and communities with the necessary infrastructures to facilitate such self-responsible lives (Asquith, 2009, p. 260).

It is exactly this neoliberal twist on the alarmist narrative of "the elder boom" (Christensen, 2018) that is articulated through the rise of the welfare technology initiative. The state fosters the development of technological gadgets and systems to equip senior citizens' homes so that they may uphold their self-responsible lifestyle for as long as possible, thus limiting the necessity of an embodied caring relationship between the welfare state and its aging population. While this move is typically framed as an emancipation of the elderly, the central impetus of the initiative can also be interpreted as an attempt to reduce the financial and organizational expenditure required of the state.

The Welfare-Technology-Script

While the fear of the "Elder Boom" and the trust in a "quick technological fix" (Layne, 2000) are central components of policy development in virtually all Western countries, the social democratic Nordic countries are remarkable for their heavy reliance on technology and therefore industry, to solve their future capacity and quality of care issues. In Norway, part of the success of the welfare technology concept can be explained by situating it in a long line of earlier reforms, including the rise of New Public Management, which popularized the idea of caring (and governing) at a distance (see Hood, 1991; Rose & Miller, 2010). Welfare technology thus emerged at the intersection of various national and transnational discourses that aim to produce welfare through facilitating the cooperation between the state, private companies, and individuals. In the following sections, we will sketch out how the welfare-technology-script was constructed in the Norwegian policy context and how it reconfigures the world of care by fostering a welfare technology industry, by inverting the professional norms of care professionals, and by expecting the elderly to care more for themselves.

From Welfare State to Welfare Industry

The first important aspect of the welfare-technology-script as laid out in policy documents was that it presupposed the development, manufacturing, and marketing of these new technologies. Interestingly, despite some early calls to leave the responsibility for these tasks to the state, the welfare technology initiative extended the neoliberal impetus of the debate around active aging and quickly translated the need for technology into the need to involve private firms. Thus, the welfare-technology-script can be interpreted to move a part of the responsibility for elderly care from the welfare *state* to the welfare technology *industry*.

From the start, the welfare technology initiative included project-based investment programs in this direction. It offered funding opportunities designed to support both the development of welfare technology and the collaboration between private firms, public services, and research institutions. Moreover, by promoting the idea that "welfare technology is the new oil," the government managed to align the emerging welfare technology industry with the state's overall economic strategy, which called for the establishment of a new social economy that could stand in for the reduction of both the public sector and the withdrawal of the primary industry (Norwegian Ministry of Health and Care Services, 2011). In essence, the goal was to turn the care sector as an area with a rapidly growing need for public investment into an area of industry-driven economic growth which would help sustain health care services in the face of an aging society.

In the Norwegian context, this strategy proved successful and attracted a heterogeneous set of new developers, producers, and distributors of welfare technology. User innovators (Shah & Tripsas, 2007) such as health and care professionals have established individual companies offering products designed on the basis of their work experiences. Private entrepreneurs have established small companies out of informal collaborative networks, like those represented by the relatives of service users who have discovered practical solutions to everyday challenges in the private lives of their elderly family members. At the other end of the spectrum, there are medium-sized companies dedicated to welfare technology, which offer a larger repertoire of gadgets and systems, and even large companies such as Apple now compete for a market share. Moreover, in a surprising realization of the "new oil" metaphor, there are even "established companies from the oil industry [who] now turn… towards the production of welfare technology" (NRK, 2016). In sum, with regard to this first reconfiguration of roles and responsibilities, the government managed to create a fit between welfare technology and the world of care not by reconsidering its idea of a technological quick fix, but by fostering and cooperating with an industry that would help realize it.

From Interpersonal Care to Care for the Machine

A second important aspect of the welfare-technology-script concerns the role of care professionals as one kind of user of the new tools. Whereas in a traditional care scenario the focus is on the embodied interaction between the elderly and care workers, the new script advances the ideal of caring at a distance. The elderly should be able to care for themselves using technology, with care workers intervening only in emergency situations. Yet, this vision presupposes tech-savvy professionals willing and able to engage with this new technological reality. In this respect, however, the script and the world in which it was to be inserted did not align so easily. Even in the first official white report launching the

Norwegian welfare technology initiative back in 2011, the committee pointed to the challenges arising from what it framed as a "competence gap" in the care sector:

> [The National Welfare Technology Initiative] shall employ new technology in a sector that is conservative and has had little ability to use new tools, new care technology, smart house solutions and new communication technology ... [The sector] is not well prepared to meet the future preferences, demands and challenges from new user groups and new generations of old individuals ... [and it] has hardly been researched at all. (Norwegian Ministry of Health and Care Services, 2011, p. 9)

This pessimistic account aggregates into a picture of a somewhat reform-unfriendly and worn-out sector that must be rehabilitated accordingly. The sector is "conservative," has "little ability" to adopt technology and is not "prepared" for the future. Nor does it manage to evolve in line with the expressed needs of various groups. It even lacks the experience necessary for attracting a sufficient number of researchers to produce broad knowledge of itself.

There was thus a marked misalignment between the world organized by the municipalities and their care professionals and the world of technological innovation which was inscribed into the vision of welfare technology. Remarkably, the fault for this misalignment was not sought in the idea of welfare technology, but in the deeply ingrained conservativism of care professionals. From the committee's point of view, it was not only that they were unable to carry out the role assigned to them by the welfare-technology-script; in many cases, they were actively resisting it due to their dominant values and professional identities. According to the committee, care professionals were prone to "cultivate" a structural resistance to new impulses, which could "hinder the development of an innovation culture" (Norwegian Ministry of Health and Care Services, 2011, p. 45). The world of welfare technology thus turned the logic of care on its head. Whereas care professionals are traditionally (trained to be) concerned that technology will take up too much space in their relationship with users or patients (Pols, 2010; Pols & Moser, 2009), in the government's vision it is the professionals that will take too much space in the relation between the technology and its user. Within this new logic, the committee frames the profession as a dominating force dedicated to the idea of care as a total institution. Their preference for direct interaction is interpreted as a challenge to be overcome on the way to releasing the elderly from traditional care practices and the control-based knowledge regimes of medicine and health care.

Interestingly, it is once more not the idea of welfare technology that needs to be adapted, but the world of care in which it is to be inserted. In particular, the report advanced a possible scenario in which welfare technology offers an opportunity for "a small number of strong professionals" to "'colonize' the sector and make its challenges into objects for their own professional development" (Norwegian Ministry of Health and Care Services, 2011, p. 133). It is in such formulations that we clearly witness the social construction of technological determinism, together with an idea of breaking up professional hegemony through technology-based upskilling. Upskilling took place, for instance, through the invention of new technology-centered roles for health and care personnel in the services, which often received telling names such as "super users," "technology advisers," and even "techno-pist." Rather predictably, this strategy of upskilling through technology was also thought to attract more men to the traditionally feminine field of care work. In effect, the welfare-technology-script, again, reorganizes the world in a way that reinterprets established roles and responsibilities. Care work is no longer assumed to be limited to traditional forms of care based on direct interaction between the elderly and their care workers. Instead, the elderly must be emancipated, and in order to do this, care professionals must learn how to care for the machine.

From Danger to Resource

The third and perhaps central redefinition implied by the government's welfare-technology-script concerns the role of the elderly themselves. Where ideas such as the "Elder Boom" or the "Silver Tsunami" cast the aging population as a danger to the sustainability of public care services, welfare technology relies on the assumption that the elderly body possesses "untapped resources" that can be mobilized for the sake of its own well-being and to alleviate the financial strain they place on the public welfare budget. As stated in the Norwegian white paper marking the initiative's starting point:

> The largest untapped resource in health and social services is not health personnel, but the users themselves and their relatives. Just as important as recruiting new professionals to the sector, it will be to utilize the users' own resources and develop people's ability to take responsibility themselves. (Norwegian Ministry of Health and Care Services, 2011, p. 57)

What the Norwegian strategy adds to this neoliberal discourse is the notion that *technology* represents the primary means for discovering and unleashing such resources. On the one hand, care is supposed to become more cost-efficient through a reduction of investments in state-sponsored human care work and an equipping of the homes and everyday routines of the elderly with "do-it-yourself" technical gadgets and systems (Bergschöld, 2018) such as safety alarms, GPS sensors, and smart house technologies. On the other hand, it is with the help of technology that the elderly are to emancipate themselves from their dependencies on public care workers and institutions. Through technologized self-care, old age is to become *the new age*,[5] and the traditional approach to care, dependent as it is on professional care work, is increasingly framed as a total institution from which the old must free themselves.

As with the two other redefinitions, the fit between welfare technology and the world of care is achieved by a transformation of the latter. This time it is the elderly, who are to emancipate themselves from their purported dependency on the public institutions of care. The welfare-technology-script assumes that this shift from "passive recipient of services" to "active user of technology" is possible based on the hidden resources possessed by the elderly body. Yet, it is precisely this condition that limits the promise of emancipation through technology to a specific group of "active users," while facing the ones excluded from this category with new forms of discrimination. Some "senior citizens" do indeed meet the physical, psychological, and social conditions necessary to operate welfare technology, enabling them to become active users and to realize an increased degree of independence. Yet, many of the "oldest old" do not fall under this category. In a world which is organized according to the principles of self-care through technology rather than publicly organized interpersonal care services, these people are faced with a peculiar form of discrimination: They are supposed to emancipate themselves using technologies that they cannot operate.

De-scripting Welfare Technology

So far we have shown how the welfare-technology-script as envisioned in a Norwegian policy context gave rise to new roles (e.g., the welfare technology industry), redefined existing ones (e.g., care workers, end-users), and redistributed the responsibilities for elderly care (e.g., from the state to the elderly themselves). Yet, as we will show in the following sections, welfare technology only partly convinces others to play their expected roles. As it enters the arenas of industry and the municipal care services, it is enacted in ways that are at odds with official policy documents.

Welfare Technology as an Industrial Product

As we have outlined above, the Norwegian government has managed to interest a large number of companies in developing, producing, and marketing welfare technology. In doing so, it has transferred a part of its own responsibility for elderly care to the private sector, while hoping that the emerging industry will fuel economic growth. On the one hand, this means that companies are enrolled into the government's technology project and do therefore become dependent on it to some degree. On the other hand, this strategy also means that the technological aspect of welfare technology is not directly under the state's control. Private companies do therefore have some leverage to describe it in ways that can diverge from the script set forth in policy documents. Indeed, when we approach welfare technology as an industrial product rather than an object for policy, we find subtle but important shifts in the roles and responsibilities connected to it.

Companies often sell an image of a self-managing skilled user that blends in well with the vision of the future of old age drawn up in policy documents. However, their vision of the role of municipal care workers is sometimes slightly different, surely owing to the fact that the municipalities are the industry's main customers. In the industry's description, it is by *skillfully facilitating* the introduction of welfare technology that care workers will be able to focus on the central aspect of their job, which remains the direct care for the elderly. In essence, while policy documents focus on the differences between the worlds of interpersonal care and innovation, the industry's goal of selling products for the use of both the elderly and their caregivers makes it necessary to *interface* them (Lipp, 2017).

One example of this tendency can be found in the self-presentation of a company that we call "WelTech" based on our anonymization of the company's real name. WelTech is a large Norwegian company that promotes itself as a nationally leading supplier of smart house and welfare technology, with ambitions to carve out a position on the international market. Founded about a decade ago, WelTech originally offered smart house technology, but has recently moved into the welfare technology industry by providing municipalities with a platform for welfare technology. This platform offers a diverse portfolio of welfare gadgets and digital systems including safety alarms, digital surveillance, and welfare apps for calendars. Thus, WelTech sells flexibility to the municipalities, and it does this with success, as it has "experienced an incredible growth" over the past years.

WelTech defines welfare technology as "a collective term for technical solutions that are developed for making your everyday life easier." Interestingly, this does not only refer to the life of the elderly, but also to their care workers. As the company writes on their Web site:

> [WelTech has] exciting projects underway to simplify and supplement the everyday situation of both every individual citizen in need of assistance and service employees. We want to automatize tasks in everyday life that steal time and resources from nursing procedures and therefore from the relation between humans.

In a section entitled "how welfare technology affects you," the company goes on to explain how welfare gadgets will benefit both the elderly *and* their care workers, precisely by making more time for direct interaction between them.

> If you are in need of assistance, welfare technology offers you more freedom, safety and closeness. Through the easy use of adapted solutions, you can make contact with family, friends and your support network from the sofa – not as a replacement, but as a supplement to the pleasant visits. If you are an employee, your hands will reach more people. The technology will free up space so that you may use time on the important part of the job – the humans. As a facilitator for social welfare technology you will contribute to limiting loneliness by bringing closeness and joy to those you are supposed to help.

In this way, the company promotes the automation of some aspects of care as beneficial for both the individuals in need of assistance and for the health and care workers. Welfare technology is depicted as enabling the former to care for themselves while helping the latter to increase the efficiency of their work by automating away its more tedious aspects.

Even though strategies such as this one do present a variation on the welfare-technology-script as envisioned in policy documents, it is not clear that it diverges from the interests of the Norwegian government.

For one thing, outsourcing part of the responsibility for realizing and concretizing the script has always been part of the government's strategy. For another, the emerging industry has, in many respects, fulfilled its role in the way imagined by policy makers. It clearly shares and supports the government's interest in economic growth, while at the same time reproducing important elements of the active aging welfare policy. WelTech, for instance, did not only reproduce the idea of emancipating the elderly through technology. The company also partly enacts the shift of the responsibility for elderly care from the state to the industry. For example, it frames its rationale for developing the technology as being grounded in a larger concern for society as it declares that "Technology and welfare must be woven close together in order to bear the challenges of the upcoming years." Just as one would expect from the welfare state, the welfare industry expresses responsibility for the future—for us all.

Welfare Technology as an Obstacle to Care

In the final empirical sections, we turn to the way in which welfare technology is enacted by both care workers and the elderly themselves. As will become clear, there is some disconnect between the everyday practices of care and the grandiose promises of emancipation. Both the promise of independence for the elderly, as put forward in official policy documents, and the idea of carving out more time for the more rewarding aspects of care work, as advertized by industrial companies, often deviate from the way in which welfare technology is actually used as a means of care.

When we turn to the care workers, it turns out that in the everyday practices of elderly care, welfare technology is not always as automatic as described by its proponents in industry and policy. Although in some cases welfare technology does indeed benefit the independence of its elderly users (Isaksen, Paulsen, Skarli, Stokke, & Melby, 2017), in other cases it becomes the center of attention, draining care workers' time rather than freeing it up. It is precisely in order to guarantee the continuing fit between the technology's script and the actual world in which it operates that they are forced to "care for" the technology in addition to its not quite so independent users. For instance, they must engage in acts of maintenance as well as following the many prescribed procedures and protocols. A manager in one public district for home care services reported that the testing of an electronic key system in the homes of older service users required the following detailed administrative tasks:

> On a weekly basis:
> Check that all locks have been in use on the web page
> Check that all employees have been active in using the locks on the web page
> Check that all phones are in place
> Train employees how to "knock right" in order to activate the lock on the door
> Train employees concerning login
>
> Monthly:
> Check that "find my iPhone" is activated on all the phones
>
> As needed:
> End/start users and employees
> Update the phones
> Update the list of users who get locks installed on their door
> Create new passwords
> Update apps
> (manager in the municipal health and care services, local memo list).

As reports like this show, welfare technology is not just about enabling care workers to automate the tedious aspects of their work while making more time for interpersonal care. Rather, they—as well as the families of the cared for—often became attendants of the tools produced by industry.

Welfare Technology as a Pathway to Human Care

Similarly, when we look at the use practices of the elderly themselves, we find that the promise of more independence through technology is not fulfilled for all of them. While welfare technology may serve some "skilled users," there are also "fragile users," who are unable to care for themselves as sketched out in the welfare-technology-script. Interestingly, these "fragile users" do not remain passive non-users of the technology. Instead, in some situations they are the ones most visibly re-appropriating the tools for their own needs.

For instance, instead of enacting welfare technology as a way toward greater independence, they may use it as a pathway to access human care.

The safety alarm case is our clearest example of this, highlighting both the creative use practices and the ambivalent consequences that spring from the implementation of welfare technology in concrete contexts of use. Many users receive their needed assistance through using the safety alarm in the prescribed way, and these users do indeed experience it as a tool for safety assurance. Yet, there are some users who "misuse," or reinterpret, the technology, causing alarms in situations that do not qualify as real emergencies in the care service's sense (about "misuse," see also Lopez, Callén, Tirado, & Domenech, 2010). Unable to distinguish between prescribed and "creative" use practices, the home care service workers often experience the safety alarm as an interruption of their practical care work[6]:

> We have to answer the alarm center [who receives the alarm signal first] and consider what they say and whether the user has said anything at all. If there is a silent alarm then we must go … but if anybody calls and says that 'now I want to get up'—because we also have those who call on the alarm and say that—then they just have to wait. … [It can get very stressful] in the morning, at least if you have those users who call many times and who you know are not that … serious. There are many of them, the fake alarms … and that's what is scary. That in the end you might ignore the users because … not that I have experienced that someone has been ignored, but there is a risk for that taking place in the end. (municipal home care nurse)

In this case, the fragile users' alarm use is interpreted as strategic and cynical and as a burden in the context of care work. The technology adds vulnerability to the nurses' decision-making. However, from another point of view, the supposedly fragile users can be seen to subvert the dominant political interpretation of welfare technology. Rather than using it as a means to technology enabled self-care, they are using it as an ally enabling them to "rage" against the automation of care and the care work schedule's tight time regime. Occasionally they succeed in carving out partial victories and strengthening the quality of care for their own benefit. As in the following field note, the technology creates an excuse for care, while at the same time "stealing" time from the caregivers.

Imagine that you quickly walk down a corridor with many doors. You aim for a special door: The door of a service user that has recently pushed the alarm button:

> On the way to the laundry room, the alarm that the nurse has in her pocket calls. It's the alarm center. She answers. We must go to one of the rooms. The alarm had gone off, and the alarm personnel could not hear what the woman was saying. We knock on and go in. The woman is sitting in an armchair by a small coffee table. A plant has been overturned on the table, and water flows down onto the floor and over one of her slippers. The nurse asks, "Hey, was it you who called? Have you got flowers? From whom then? Let's see... you got afternoon coffee, too? No? Is this leftover from the morning and has been sitting here since then? I'll get you a new cup of coffee and dry up the floor for you. I have to go down on my knees then, I don't think I can move you. Like that. Now it's okay for you? Can you manage your flowers then? The woman answers a silent "yes". The nurse continues the talk: "Must fix that too, have a look...?" The woman gives her a glass of water without saying anything, but with clear reference to the nurse being allowed to give the flower the water. The nurse accepts and pours some water into the vase. "Don't need to refill more now, do we? Was it okay? The user again answers a silent "yes".

Giving water to the flowers is not an urgent or dire need, but it is an act that makes sense in the relation between the user and the nurse. In this situation, the safety alarm acts as a pathway to care, by giving the nurse a pretext for visiting a lonely woman and interacting with her in a personal manner (for a further interpretation, see also Tøndel, 2018). Yet, the fact that the nurse used her time in this way is seen as a "human error" from the point of view of the welfare-technology-script since the alarm was not connected to an emergency. Simultaneously, through this error, she enacts a practice of traditional interpersonal care which, in this case, repairs the situation: The nurse could have chosen a different course of action when she discovered that the alarm was "false." Instead, she listened to the silence, the silent "rage" behind the woman's inability to arrange her flowers on her own.[7] The alarm justified the nurse's decision to visit the woman and just engage in some small-talk, thereby freeing herself, albeit momentarily from the service's time regime.

Taming Old Age—Or Releasing It into the Wild?

In this chapter, we have implemented an adapted form of script analysis to explore the sociotechnical dynamics held together by the seemingly mundane objects collectively known as "welfare technology." We have shown that by focusing on a technical solution to the so-called silver tsunami, the welfare technology initiative contributes to legitimizing a shift of responsibility for care from the welfare state to an emerging welfare technology industry and from skilled care professionals to the elderly users themselves. In particular, the script approach has focused our attention on the mutual adaptation between the world inscribed into the technology by its designers and the world in which the object is actually being used. In this way, we call into question several popular ideas about how industrially produced technology relates to dynamics of emancipation and domination.

On the level of inscription, the approach allowed us to cast the welfare technology initiative in a critical light by showing that, despite its adjacent rhetoric of emancipation, welfare technology is inscribed with a range of discriminatory potentials for both care workers and the elderly. These potentials stem from the expectation that it is these two user groups that should adapt to technology, while conversely, Norwegian policy makers have not sufficiently adapted their vision of technology to the world of care in which it was to be inserted. It was in this spirit that the government called for a modernization of professional care work. Professionals were depicted as both unable to continue the provision of high-quality care services and as actively resisting the technological emancipation of the elderly. Unfortunately, the notion of emancipation through technology also proves problematic for some of the elderly themselves. Despite its original intentions, it structurally excludes many of the elderly whose mental and physical condition makes self-care through technology a remote scenario. The welfare-technology-script may therefore open up a degree of emancipation for some while threatening to materialize a structure of domination against those who are unable to operate it.

On the level of description, the script approach helped us to make salient how some of these discriminatory potentials were attenuated or even subverted in practice. As the welfare-technology-script is enacted in the worlds of industry and care, it is adapted to their prevalent practices and norms. For instance, while the emerging welfare technology industry does, on the whole, align with the political thrust of the technocare policy, its mission to sell products may eventually compel it to develop and produce welfare gadgets that facilitate at least some of the needs of municipal care workers (its primary customers). However, for the time being, our study reveals that the misalignment between the vision inscribed into welfare technology and the practical care work currently taking place in the municipal healthcare services and the homes of the elderly has to be repaired by care workers and the elderly themselves. While this may involve large amounts of invisible work (Star and Strauss, 1999) by care professionals, it also involves forms of creative "misuse." Elderly users do not always enact the technology as a means of greater autonomy from their care takers. On the contrary, they sometimes manage to repair distressing situations by using welfare technology as a pathway for accessing human face-to-face care. Ironically, it may sometimes be the most vulnerable who are most efficient in subverting the discriminatory potentials inscribed into welfare technology by the powerful actors in state and industry. In these cases, the elderly body may be too tired to be set free, but it is equally resistant to being enrolled into new structures of domination.

In this sense, we encourage our readers to question the promises of technological emancipation, particularly when they are offered by dominant actors in state and industry, being mindful that even the most powerful alliance between macro-actors cannot persuade the "oldest old" to act against the fragility of their own body.

Notes

1. We assume that the silver color is a reference to the characteristic grey hair of the elderly, which clearly illustrates what Christensen (2018) refers to as the discriminatory discourse grounded in this metaphor.
2. Within gerontology, this is known as the "decline and loss" paradigm (Minkler & Fadem, 2002).
3. The World Health Organization (WHO) (2002) defined "active ageing" in the late 1990s as constituting a broad process of "optimizing opportunities for health, participation and security in order to enhance quality of life as people age."
4. According to Asquith (2009), policy responses to the perceived problem of ageing are predicated on lifelong lifestyle change—social connectedness (successful ageing), social productivity (productive ageing), and good health (healthy ageing). Thus, the different terms for the policy reflect different governmental strategies and responses toward managing ageing.
5. We chose the phrase "new age" with a satirical purpose: To draw a parallel to the "New Age" movement and their grand visions of possibilities for change and fulfillment beyond bodily limitations.
6. This particularly concerns planned tasks and increases the risk of "human error" as a consequence (Svagård, Boysen, Fensli, & Vatnøy, 2016).

7. We are inspired here by Simone de Beauvoir's *Une mort très douce*, which contains a passage about ones' right to rage from a classic poem of Dylan Thomas, originally published in the journal *Botteghe Obscure* in 1951. The poem reads: Do not go gentle into that good night. Old age should burn and rave at close of day; Rage, rage against the dying of the light.

References

Akrich, M. (1992). The De-Scription of Technical Objects. In W. E. Bijker & J. Law (Eds.), *Shaping Technology/Building Society: Studies in Sociotechnical Change* (pp. 205–224). Cambridge, MA: MIT Press.

Asquith, N. (2009). Positive Ageing, Neoliberalism and Australian Sociology. *Journal of Sociology, 45,* 255–269.

Bakken, R. (2018). *Alle vil leve lenge. Men ingen vil bli gamle.* Oslo: Fagbokforlaget.

Bergschöld, J. M. (2018). *Frontline Innovation—How Frontline Care Professionals Innovate Welfare Technology and Services.* Trondheim: Norwegian University of Science and Technology.

Boudiny, K. (2012). "Active Ageing": From Empty Rhetoric to Effective Policy Tool. *Ageing & Society, 33,* 1077–1098.

Callon, M. (1998). An Essay on Framing and Overflowing: Economic Externalities Revisited by Sociology. In M. Callon (Ed.), *The Laws of the Market* (pp. 244–270). Oxford, Malden, MA: Blackwell/Sociological Review.

Carpiano, R. M. (2009). Come Take a Walk with Me: The "Go-Along" Interview as a Novel Method for Studying the Implications of Place for Health and Well-Being. *Health Place, 15,* 263–272.

Christensen, K. (2018). Myten om eldrebølgen. In K. Christensen & L. J. Syltevik (Eds.), *Myter om velferd og velferdsstaten* (pp. 75–97). Oslo: Cappelen Damm Akademisk.

Clarke, A. (2005). *Situational Analysis: Grounded Theory After the Postmodern Turn.* Thousand Oaks: Sage.

Czarniawska, B., & Sevón, G. (2005). *Global Ideas: How Ideas, Objects and Practices Travel in the Global Economy.* Malmö: Liber.

Dillaway, H. E., & Byrnes, M. (2009). Reconsidering Successful Aging: A Call for Renewed and Expanded Academic Critiques and Conceptualizations. *Journal of Applied Gerontology, 28,* 702–722. https://doi.org/10.1177%2F0733464809333882.

Garcia, C., Eisenberg, M. E., Frerich, E. A., Lechner, K. E., & Lust, K. (2012). Conducting Go-Along Interviews to Understand Context and Promote Health. *Qualitative Health Research, 22,* 1395–1403. https://doi.org/10.1177/1049732312452936.

Hine. (2000). *Virtual Ethnography.* London: Sage.

Hood, C. (1991). A Public Management for All Seasons? *Public Administration, 69*, 3–19.

Hyysalo, S., Jensen, T. E., & Oudshoorn, N. (Eds.). (2016). *The New Production of Users. Changing Innovation Collectives and Involvement Strategies*. New York: Routledge.

Hyysalo, S., Pollock, N., & Williams, R. (2018). Method Matters in the Social Study of Technology: Investigating the Biographies of Artifacts and Practices. *Science & Technology Studies*. Published online ahead of print.

Igelsböck, J., & Schüßler, E. (2019). *New Directions for the Concept of the Institutional Script* (Nano-Papers: Institution—Organization—Society, 9).

Isaksen, J., Paulsen, K. B., Skarli, J., Stokke, R., & Melby, L. (2017). Hvilken nytte har hjemmeboende med hjelpebehov av velferdsteknologi? *Tidsskrift for omsorgsforskning, 3*, 117 – 127. http://doi.org/10.18261/issn.2387-5984-2017-02-09.

Jacobs, T. (2005). *Being Old, Feeling Old: Between Autonomy and Dependency in the Area of "Active Ageing"*. Antwerp, Belgium: University of Antwerp.

Kusenbach, M. (2003). Street Phenomenology: The Go-Along as Ethnographic Research Tool. *Ethnography, 4*, 455–485. https://doi.org/10.1177/146613810343007.

Latour, B. (1987). *Science in Action*. Harvard: Harvard University Press.

Latour, B. (1992). Where Are the Missing Masses? The Sociology of a Few Mundane Artifacts. In W. E. Bijker & J. Law (Eds.), *Shaping Technology/Building Society: Studies in Sociotechnical Change* (pp. 225–258). Cambridge, MA: MIT Press.

Layne, L. L. (2000). The Cultural Fix: An Anthropological Contribution to Science and Technology Studies. *Science, Technology and Human Values, 25*, 352–379.

Lipp, B. (2017). Analytik des Interfacing. Zur Materialität technologischer Verschaltung in prototypischen Milieus robotisierter Pflege. *BEHEMOTH A Journal on Civilization, 10*(1), 107–129. https://doi.org/10.6094/behemoth.2017.10.1.948.

Lopez, D., Callén, B., Tirado, F., & Domenech, M. (2010). How to Become a Guardian Angel: Providing Safety in a Home Telecare Service. In A. Mol, I. Moser, & J. Pols (Eds.), *Care in Practice: On Tinkering in Clinics, Homes and Farms* (pp. 71–90). Bielefeld: Transcript.

Marcus, G. E. (1995). Ethnography in/of the World System: The Emergence of Multi-Sited Ethnography. *Annual Review of Anthropology, 24*(1), 95–117. https://doi.org/10.1146/annurev.an.24.100195.000523.

Minkler, M., & Fadem, P. (2002). "Successful Aging": A Disability Perspective. *Journal of Disability Policy Studies, 12*(4), 229–235.

Mort, M., Roberts, C., & Callen, B. (2012). Ageing with Telecare: Care or Coercion in Austerity? *Sociology of Health & Illness, 35*(6), 799–812.

Moser, I. B., & Thygesen, H. (2015). Exploring Possibilities in Telecare for Aging Societies. In M. Barnes, T. Brannely, & N. Wards (Eds.), *Ethics of Care: Critical Advances in International Perspective*. Bristol: Policy Press.

Neven, L. (2015). By Any Means? Questioning the Link Between Gerontechnological Innovation and Older People's Wish to Live at Home. *Technological Forecasting and Social Change, 93*, 32–43. https://doi.org/10.1016/j.techfore.2014.04.016.

Noble, D. F. (2011 [1984]). *Forces of Production: A Social History of Industrial Automation*. New Brunswick and London: Transaction Publishers.

Norwegian Ministry of Health and Care Services. (2011). *Innovation in the Care Services*. White Paper 2011: 11. Oslo: Norwegian Ministry of Health and Care Services.

Norwegian Ministry of Health and Care Services. (2018). *Leve hele livet. En kvalitetsreform for eldre*. White Paper 15 (2017–2018). Oslo: Norwegian Ministry of Health and Care Services.

Norwegian Board of Technology. (2009). *Framtidens alderdom og ny teknologi*. Report 1. Retrieved from December 9, 2015. http://teknologiradet.no/wpcontent/uploads/sites/19/2013/08/Rapport-Fremtidens-alderdom-og-nyteknologi.pdf.

NRK. (2016). Utvikler velferdsteknologi – får ikke solgt den. Retrieved June 22, 2019, from https://www.nrk.no/rogaland/utvikler-velferdsteknologi—far-ikke-solgt-den-1.13019654.

OECD. (2017). *Preventing Ageing Unequally*. Paris: OECD. https://doi.org/10.1787/9789264279087-en.

Oudshoorn, N. (2003). *The Male Pill: A Biography of a Technology in the Making*. Durham and London: Duke University Press.

Oudshoorn, N. (2011). *Telecare Technologies and the Transformation of Healthcare*. Basingstoke: Palgrave Macmillan.

Oudshoorn, N., & Pinch, T. (Eds.). (2003). *How Users Matter: The Co-Construction of Users and Technologies*. Cambridge, MA: MIT Press.

Pols, J. (2010). Caring Devices: About Warmth, Coldness and "fit". *Medische Antropologie, 22*(1), 143–160.

Pols, J., & Moser, I. (2009). Cold Technologies Versus Warm Care? On Affective and Social Relations with and Through Care Technologies. *ALTER, European Journal of Disability, 3*(2), 159–178. https://doi.org/10.1016/j.alter.2009.01.003.

Peine, A., Faulkner, A., Jæger, B., & Moors, E. (2015). Science, Technology and the 'Grand Challenge' of Ageing—Understanding the Socio-Material Constitution of Later Life. *Technological Forecasting and Social Change, 93*, 1–9.

Peine, A., Rollwagen, I., & Neven, L. B. M. (2014). The Rise of the "Innosumer"—Rethinking Older Technology Users. *Technological Forecasting and Social Change, 82*, 199–214.

Pinch, T., & Bijker, W. E. (2012 [1987]). The Social Construction of Facts and Artifact: Or How the Sociology of Science and the Sociology of Technology Might Benefit Each Other. In W. E. Bijker, T. P. Hughes, & T. Pinch (Eds.), *The Social Construction of Technological Systems: New Directions in the Sociology and History of Technology* (pp. 11–44). Cambridge, MA: MIT Press.

Prior, L. (2003). *Using Documents in Social Research*. London: Sage.

Richardson, J. (2004). *Ageing and Health Care: Inexorable Costs Versus Modest Adaption*. Melbourne: Centre for Health Economics.

Roberts, C., Mort, M., & Milligan, C. (2012). Calling for Care: 'Disembodied' Work, Teleoperators and Older People Living at Home. *Sociology, 46*(3), 490–506. https://doi.org/10.1177/0038038511422551.

Rose, N., & Miller, P. (2010). Political Power Beyond the State: Problematics of Government. *The British Journal of Sociology, 43*, 173–205.

Sánchez-Criado, T., Lopez, D., Roberts, C., & Domenech, M. (2014). Installing Telecare, Installing Users: Felicity Conditions for the Instauration of Usership. *Science, Technology, & Human Values, 39*(5), 694–719. https://doi.org/10.1177/0162243913517011.

Shah, S. K., & Tripsas, M. (2007). The Accidental Entrepreneur: The Emergent and Collective Process of User Entrepreneurship. *Strategic Entrepreneurship Journal, 1*(1–2), 123–140. https://doi.org/10.1002/sej.15.

Star, S. L., & Strauss, A. (1999). Layers of Silence, Arenas of Voice: The Ecology of Visible and Invisible Work. *Computer Supported Cooperative Work (CSCW), 8*(1–2), 9–30. https://doi.org/10.1023/a:1008651105359.

Svagård, I., Boysen, E. S., Fensli, R., & Vatnøy, T. (2016). *Responssentertjenester i helse- og omsorgstjenesten: Behov og fremtidsbilder*. Report 1-2016. Trondheim: SINTEF.

Tøndel, G. (2018). Omsorgens materialitet: trygghet, teknologi og alderdom. *Tidsskrift for omsorgsforskning, 4*, 287–297. https://doi.org/10.18261/issn.2387-5984-2018-03-11.

United Nations. (2002, April). *Report of the Second World Assembly on Ageing*. Madrid, 8–12. Retrieved June 7, 2019, from https://documents-dds-ny.un.org/doc/UNDOC/GEN/N02/397/51/PDF/N0239751.pdf?OpenElement.

World Health Organization (WHO). (2002). *Active Ageing: A Policy Framework*. Geneva: WHO.

Woolgar, S. (1991). Configuring the USER: The Case of Usability Trials. In J. Law (Ed.), *A Sociology of Monsters: Essays on Power, Technology, and Domination* (pp. 57–103). London and New York: Routledge.

CHAPTER 11

The Digitalization of Musical Instruments and Musical Practice

Andreas Möllenkamp

Introduction

The process of digitalization has both affected and transformed the musical instruments industry as well as the way that music is made. Facing the possibilities of digital music production and the Internet, the "digital revolution" promised to bring about new aesthetic possibilities as well as a democratization of music culture. How did digitalization affect music making and the work of musicians? How did the promises of democratization and emancipation play out in the experience of musicians? This article traces the main developments in the musical instruments industry in the course of digitalization and discusses its effects on artistic strategies and musical practice. It provides a survey of the main innovations in the fields of electronic musical instruments and music software and describes the transformation of business models in the musical instruments industry. The study draws on three kinds of sources and corresponding methods: a discourse analysis of magazines for musicians, an analysis of music software applications and their

A. Möllenkamp (✉)
Universität Hamburg, Hamburg, Germany
e-mail: andreas.moellenkamp@uni-hamburg.de

U. Meyer et al. (eds.), *Digitalization in Industry*,
https://doi.org/10.1007/978-3-030-28258-5_11

human-computer interaction design as well as interviews with musicians, developers and experts.

On the way to a cultural history of music technology and musical practice (Braun, 2002, 2016), I argue for a differentiated view of the effects of digitalization for musicians. On the one hand, the computer expanded the artistic possibilities of musicians while it facilitated the precarization of working conditions on the other.

With the computer as a musical instrument, new ways of sound production developed and the use of existing musical material was simplified and became cheaper to access. Musical strategies and genres like algorithmic composition and generative music developed as well as new ways of performance like video jockeys (VJs) and live coding. In contrast to traditional musical instruments, the separation of sound production and control opened up new possibilities for the interface design of musical human-computer interaction. Next to tangible user interfaces, tablets and smartphones are used for new ways of music creation that are no longer limited to simulating analog instruments. Besides these extensions of musical possibilities, the computer challenges the very idea of musical creativity and gains technical agency by formalizing and simulating not only other instruments, but composition styles and music cognition itself.

Looking at the themes of democratization as well as emancipation, I argue for a more critical assessment of the effects of digital media on the work of musicians. By providing possibilities previously limited to specialized staff (like producers, audio engineers, etc.), music software facilitated the "outsourcing" of these tasks and musicians were faced with increased expectations for self-marketing as well as precarious working conditions. For most musicians, digitalization did not lead to a process of professional differentiation, but instead to de-specialization and precarization.

The Digitalization of Musical Instruments

As a key development in contemporary societies, digitalization affects all aspects of our daily life, economy and culture. Computers, smartphones, tablets and other digital media have become an integral part of our life, material culture and symbol systems. In music culture, digitalization has not only led to a comprehensive transformation of the music industry and the everyday use of music, but also transformed the musical instruments and the way music is made (Bovermann, de Campo, Egermann, Hardjowirogo, & Weinzierl, 2017; Stange-Elbe & Bronner, 2008). The development of electronic musical instruments and music software has become one of the most dynamic fields in the history of musical instruments and the creative economy. The historical and systematic research on musical instruments so far concentrated on material and technical developments, famous composers and their innovations for composition techniques and musical aesthetics. Using technical developments as the basis for historical periodization, the history of musical instruments was divided into the three stages of mechanization, electrification and digitalization. Correspondingly, the dominant classification system for musical instruments is oriented toward the material type of sound production. It goes back to Erich Moritz von Hornbostel and Curt Sachs (1914) and distinguishes between idiophones, membranophones, chordophones and aerophones. With the advent of electric musical instruments, the system was extended in 1940 to include the fifth main group of electrophones. In 2011, a consortium of European museums of musical instruments published a further revision of this classification (MIMO Consortium, 2011). The music computer in this classification system is understood as a sub-form of the electrophone, since sounds can only be heard via electrical signals and loudspeakers. This categorization according to the physical origin of sounds already reached its limits with the electrification of instruments, since electricity and loudspeakers do not produce specific sounds. Without further differentiation, neither the specifics nor the variety of making music with the computer can be mapped with this system. The next step therefore should be not only to extend the Hornbostel–Sachs system to cover the functional and design principles of music software, but also to foster research on the related musical cultures and practices.

Igor Kopytoff (1986) and Eliot Bates (2012) argued that musical instruments like other objects also have something like a social life or a cultural biography. Instrumentality is thus subject to culturalization and historical change (Großmann, 2010). Sarah-Indriyati Hardjowirogo (2017, p. 10) notes the blurring of the boundaries between the traditional understanding of a musical instrument and other categories such as medium, system, configuration or machine. She argues that not every sound-generating object (such as a smartphone) is an instrument, but its artistic-creative use can make it one. Whether or not we perceive an object as an instrument depends not only on the intended use of the manufacturers, but also on the intention and skill of the musicians as well as the recognition by the audience.

Before sketching the history of the computer as a musical instrument, I will give a short overview of the sources and methods used in the underlying research project.[1]

Sources and Methods

Three kinds of sources and corresponding methods are used here:

1. A discourse analysis of magazines for musicians;
2. An analysis of music software applications and the human-computer interaction design;
3. Interviews with musicians, developers and experts.

Magazines for musicians play a central role in creating a discourse on music software as well as a consumer culture for musical instruments. They serve as a forum for the musicians and their interest in information and entertainment as well as the musical instruments industry generating attention for their products (Théberge, 1997). The analyzed magazines include the English and German magazines Computer Music Journal, Leonardo Music Journal, Keyboards, Keys, Sound and Recording and Beat. The magazines were selected as musicians are their main target group and because they cover both the development of music software and musicians' approaches and experiences.

Following on from material culture studies and artifact analysis, my *analysis of music software applications* concentrated on the questions how the human-computer interaction is designed and how the implicit user can be characterized.[2] This involves describing how the interface is designed and which way of music making the developers sought to create.

Finally, I conducted 12 *interviews with musicians, developers and experts* between 2012 and 2017 (cf. Table 11.1). The interview partners were chosen and invited following a theoretical sampling used in the grounded theory methodology. The sampling aimed to cover different musical genres, ages, musical education, levels of professionalization, software applications as well as gender.

The interviews include a biographical as well as a thematic part. As far as possible, the interviews were conducted in the (home) studio

Table 11.1 Interviews

Date	*Interview partner*	*Role*	*Place*
October 15, 2012	Tim and Puma Mimi	Musician	Zurich
December 27, 2012	Johannes Kreidler	Musician	Berlin
December 27, 2012	Peter Kirn	Expert, Musician	Berlin
February 2, 2013	Robert Henke	Musician, Developer	Berlin
February 18, 2013	Derek Holzer	Musician	Berlin
May 31, 2013	Marek Brandt	Musician	Leipzig
July 14, 2013	Maya Consuelo Sternel	Musician	Berlin
October 4, 2013	Jeremy Bernstein	Developer, Musician	Lüneburg
May 2, 2014	Joachim Heintz	Musician, Developer	Karlsruhe
May 3, 2014	Miller Puckette	Developer, Musician	Karlsruhe
March 16, 2016	Karl Steinberg	Developer, Musician	Hamburg
December 4, 2017	Joachim Stange-Elbe	Expert, Musician	Hamburg

or working environment of the musician or artist and include a discussion of one or more works or projects. A central theme of the interviews revolved around the role of the computer in the everyday life and work experience of the musicians.

History and Culture of the Computer as a Musical Instrument

How did the computer and other digital media develop into a musical instrument? In the following, I will briefly survey important developments in the fields of electronic musical instruments and music software in the course of digitalization. In my argument, this survey provides the background to understand the construction of the implicit users of music software applications. This history is very diverse and manifold. It covers the development of electronic and hybrid analog-digital instruments, protocols and industry standards like MIDI as well as diverse music software applications, hardware controllers and apps.

As a rough historical periodization, one can differentiate an early phase of musical experiments on mainframe computers and a later phase of personal computers which has been further expanded through smartphones, tablets and corresponding apps (Möllenkamp, 2017b). To provide an overview of the history of music software, I distinguish between five paradigms (Möllenkamp, 2014). A paradigm in the sense of Thomas Kuhn (1996) is a basic way of thinking and a practical approach shared

Table 11.2 Paradigms of music software development

Paradigm	*Software applications (examples)*	*Implicit user*
Score paradigm	MUSIC, Finale, Sibelius	Composer
Studio paradigm	Cubase, ProTools, Logic	Audio engineer, Producer
Patching paradigm	Max, Pure Data, Reaktor	Technician, Tinkerer
Coding paradigm	SuperCollider, ChucK	Programmer
Live paradigm	Ableton Live, Bitwig Studio	Performer

by a group of actors, a community or even a whole field. In the narrow sense, a paradigm refers to an application or central metaphor that provides a model for subsequent development. In the design of technologies like music software, programmers use metaphors to transfer central ideas of musical interaction into code. For the user, metaphors help to read, understand and use the software. Music software thus may be seen as inscriptions of musical ideas, theories and interactions into an application (Akrich, 1992). Similar to an implicit reader of a text, I speak of an implicit user of the software (Table 11.2).

In the following, I will briefly elaborate on these paradigms by putting them into their historical context. I will concentrate on music software development from the 1950s onwards. The history of electronic musical instruments may of course be traced further back (Ruschkowski, 2019). In the 1920s and 1930s, a number of electric instruments like the *Ondes Martenot*, the *Theremin*, the *Trautonium* and the *Hammond Organ* were developed and publicly presented.

Since 1950: MUSIC on Mainframes

Musical experiments in the computer development of the 1950s and 1960s were performed on the mainframes of American and Australian universities as well as private companies such as Bell Laboratories. Subsequently, the new field of computer music emerged. In Europe, similar developments in public broadcasting studios and other institutions took place using the more general terms electronic and electroacoustic music. In this context, only a limited number of experts had the possibility and the qualifications to use this relatively expensive technology. The first program for digital synthesis was MUSIC. It was developed by Max Mathews from Bell Laboratories in 1957 and was presented with a 17-second-long piece of music using an IBM 709 computer (Neukom, 2005, p. 21). In his essay, "The Digital Computer as a Musical Instrument", Mathews (1963) described how the computer not only generates sounds, but also can be used as a composition aid. Further developments which were based on MUSIC were MUSIC 360 and MUSIC 11, Csound, CMix and Real-time Cmix, CMusic and the Structured Audio Orchestra Language (SAOL), respectively. The development of these programming environments used the notation of a musical score as the central metaphor and thus may be subsumed as applications of the *score paradigm*: Initially, the orchestra with its instruments had to be defined and then notes as well as playing instructions (mostly in the form of lists) had to be programmed before, following several calculation phases, a corresponding audio file could be saved and finally played (Lazzarini, 2013).

From the discovery that computers can be used for music up to the present variety of different musical styles as well as internationally successful music software companies, this development followed manifold steps in technical and cultural formation. Especially in the field of computer music, new procedures of algorithmic composition, sound production and processing could be tried out. While software on mainframe computers mostly was programmed to run on a specific machine for a specific task, machine-independent software in the 1970s made it possible to transfer programs from one computer to the next. Hardware, software and service thus became commercially independent products and computer science became an academic discipline (Gugerli, 2018).

Since 1980: MIDI, Virtual Studios and Software Synthesizer

The probably most widespread paradigm of music software is the *studio paradigm*. It offers a virtual studio environment to the musician and enables him or her to record, edit and mix songs. The Musical Instrument Digital Interface (MIDI) was a very influential innovation in the development of music software and an important point of departure for companies like Steinberg, Emagic, MOTU, Cakewalk and others to develop multitrack sequencers. MIDI was published in 1983 by a panel of music industry representatives and is maintained by the MIDI Manufacturers Association (Diduck, 2018). While Cubase, Logic or Digital Performer started with MIDI functionality, others like ProTools, published 1991 by Digidesign, started as Digital Audio Workstations (DAW). In the 1990s, MIDI and digital audio were increasingly integrated in music software applications. Furthermore, the studio paradigm was successfully expanded by the introduction and establishment of plug-ins. The Virtual Studio Technology (VST) promised to increasingly integrate the outboard equipment found in analog recording studios into the computer and became a successful standard for plug-ins. Companies like Native Instruments and others began to offer software synthesizers both as standalone and plugin versions that could be played in real time. *Virtualization* in the sense of simulation of existing instruments by using techniques like physical modeling was one central strategy in this domain (Bense, 2014).

As personal computers became affordable by average musicians, music software companies diversified their product range to address more specific target groups like DJs or guitarists. Programs like VirtualDJ, Traktor, Serato or Mixxx tried to bring turntables and DJ-mixers into the computer and expanded DJing with specific functions (Grote, 2016). Companies like Antares and Celemony developed the ability to analyze and synthesize audio further allowing for differentiated editing of individual voices and instruments in an existing recording. Immanuel Brockhaus (2017, pp. 393–402) as well as Ragnhild Brøvig-Hanssen and Anne Danielsen (2016, pp. 117–132) describe Antares Auto-Tune as a characteristic "signature sound". German music software company Celemony also offers digital audio pitch correction software. Their software Melodyne is a tool to tune and manipulate audio signals like a singer's vocals. It also allows for time-stretching, rebuilding melodies and the creation of backing vocals from an existing lead vocal. The Direct Note Access (DNA) technology allows independent manipulation of individual notes within chords and polyphonic recordings.

Music software applications of the *patching paradigm* follow the idea of working with modular synthesizers or studio equipment. To produce a desired sound or effect, musicians used patch cables to connect separate modules or outboard equipment. Similarly, artists using a patching software are able to set up their own music production environment. The most prominent examples of this kind of software are Max, Pure Data and Reaktor. The user of patching programs is enabled to combine sound generation, processing and control in a flexible way. Miller Puckette (2002) and David Zicarelli (2002), two of the main developers of Max and PureData respectively, see this relative openness or absence of a given structure as a central feature of the patching approach.

Applications like SuperCollider and ChucK that belong to the *coding paradigm* have the programmer as the implicit user. Sounds can be produced directly by entering code.

Whereas the recording studio paradigm puts the user into a studio, the *live paradigm* puts him on the stage. The most prominent examples of this kind of software applications are Ableton Live and Bitwig Studio. One basic innovation in this field was the ability to edit digital audio in real time. This allowed the workflow to change from a recording studio setting to a session orientated setting.

In 2015, Ableton introduced *Link*, a functionality for synchronizing devices over a local network, initially developed by the Berlin-based start-up *Coire*. Link is part of Ableton Live and comes as a built-in feature of other software and hardware for music making like iOS apps and desktop software. Unlike other synchronization technologies, "Link does not require master/client roles. Automatic discovery on a local area network enables a peer-to-peer system, which peers can join or leave at any time without disrupting others" (Goltz, 2018).

Since 2008: Smartphones, Tablets and Apps

The introduction and popular use of *smartphones, tablets and apps* have been a further step toward the diversity and affordability of music tools. After the first iPhone launched in 2007 without any third-party apps, Apple announced that it was opening up its platform to third-party apps. The app store launched July 2008 with 500 apps, a number that has grown fast and has reached more than 2 million. Google made its Android Market available to users in October 2008. In March 2012, the Android Market was re-branded as Google Play. Until October 2017, Google Play offered more than 3.3 million apps. In 2019, more than 80,000 apps in the Apple app store belonged to the category of music and the Google Play Store offered more than 148,000 apps in the category music and audio (Statista, 2019). Matthias Krebs (2018) proposes four categories of music apps as a rough orientation:

1. Apps for music consumption, including player and streaming apps that can be used to play music stored on devices or available on the Internet, including concerts or tutorials.

2. Apps that support music making as a tool like a metronome or automatic accompaniment, including learning and training apps.
3. Apps for composing and producing music, including audio recording, arranging and sound editing apps as well as effects, samplers, drum machines, etc.
4. Instrumental music-making apps that transform the mobile device into a musical instrument and provide functions for playing and modifying rhythmic, melodic, harmonic and tonal structures in real time.

In addition to the touch display, smartphones and tablets mostly are equipped with microphones, cameras, GPS, a gyroscope and other sensors that can be used musically in innovative ways. New interface concepts and possibilities for location and situation-based applications, personalization and real-time interaction with others are explored within these apps.

In contrast to traditional musical instruments, the separation of sound production and control opened up new possibilities for the *instrument and interface design*. Designers of both software and hardware electronic musical instruments developed a big variety of control elements and concepts: from hardware elements like pads, wheels, benders, joysticks, touchstrips, xy-controllers and sensors to concepts like step-sequencing, matrix-editing, gestural control as well as virtual and mixed reality (Bjørn, 2017).

Like in other fields of application, software companies started to develop and experiment with *artificial intelligence* applications and services. Examples are Amper, IBM's Watson Beat, Google's Magenta and Artificial Intelligence Virtual Artist (AIVA). Created in February 2016, AIVA is an artificial intelligence application that specializes in classical and symphonic music composition. Its algorithm is based on deep learning and reinforcement learning architectures. By reading a collection of existing works of classical music, AIVA is capable of detecting regularities in music and on this base composing on its own. US-based company Amper as well provides a system that utilizes artificial intelligence for a music composition platform that helps to produce music in a desired style, length and structure. Music software thus promises to remain a dynamic field of techno-cultural development.

How is music software actually produced? Scholars in the field of material culture have pointed to the importance of the modes and contexts of production to understand the investigated artifacts and practices. The following part therefore looks at the organizational and economic aspects of music software development.

Economy of Music Software

Music software is developed, disseminated and applied in various contexts and in different ways. Commercial music software applications are digital media products on a globalized market while open-source communities understand and develop their applications as a common good. Looking at the history of music software companies and the market for music software, both general phenomena of a capitalist market economy as well as specific characteristics of music software as a product and of software markets can be observed. This section therefore explores the main organizational and economic aspects of music software development to provide a better understanding of the characteristics of commercial as well as open-source software applications. Copyright, cracked software and digital rights management (DRM) are rarely discussed in the literature on musical practice, but can play a relevant role for the appropriation and artistic use of music software.

The specific *characteristics of software* in general include low reproduction costs as software can be copied as often as desired without any loss of quality. However, this also means that copyright and property rights are difficult to enforce when non-copy-protected versions spread over the Internet. “The software industry is more international in nature than practically any other sector”, Peter Buxmann, Heiner Diefenbach, and Thomas Hess (2013, p. 3) claim. Both the development and distribution of software can be organized globally at low prices. However, this also leads to global competition between software vendors, both for customers and employees. Another advantage of software is that you can easily create different versions or bundles to sell at different prices to different audiences. Most music software companies offer versions of their software that address different target groups like professional users (studios, radio, etc.) as well as amateurs and home studio owners. In addition, time-limited or functionally limited demo versions are offered as well as educational versions for students and teachers.

A strategically relevant question in software development is whether and how the software provides interfaces and standards for connecting or integrating hardware or software from other manufacturers. If a software application provides interfaces such as MIDI or VST, its functionality may be extended by external controllers, effect plug-ins as well as software synthesizers or samplers. The presence of a programming interface (API) may be a competitive advantage for a software or hardware product, as offering additional third-party programs increases the functionality and attractiveness of the source system. For closed systems that only allow products from one manufacturer on the other hand, it is easier to protect itself from the competition and to develop a stable system.

Due to the *network effect*, software markets are often so-called *winner-takes-it-all markets*. The network effect means that the benefit of a good increases with the total number of users. If many musicians use the same software or the same file format, they can communicate and work together more easily and cheaply. If new users also tend to use the same software, positive feedback will be created and the value of the network will continue to increase (Varian & Shapiro, 2002). As a result, a market may emerge that is dominated by one winner, while small software companies and startups find it hard to establish themselves in the market, even if they offer a better software solution. In addition, the principle of complementarity plays an important role in the *network economy*, since decisions for hardware, operating systems and application software depend on each other or may be mutually exclusive. For many musicians, it has been a crucial question whether they opt for an Apple, Windows or Linux system. Once a user has decided on a system and becomes accustomed to it, the likelihood of switching to another system is low. In economics, linking a user to a system of lock-in as well as switching costs contribute to consumer loyalty and revenue security. New versions of programs that are already widely used are often considered cash cows by software companies because of their relatively predictable revenues.

Because of the network effect, *cooperations, mergers and acquisitions* can have economic advantages for the companies involved and therefore regularly occur on the music software market. Whether and to what extent cooperations, mergers and acquisitions have advantages or disadvantages for users depends to a large extent on the respective objectives, the structure of the acquisition and the broader product policy. After the acquisition of the German software and hardware manufacturer Emagic by Apple in 2002, the development of product versions for Microsoft Windows was discontinued and only the development for Apple iOS continued. The aim was not only to make Apple's music software more attractive, but also to persuade Windows users to buy an Apple computer. In addition, there are also acquisitions whose primary goal is to remove competing products from the market, which for their users means that their application will no longer be developed and supported.

Compared to traditional industrial companies, the *number of employees* in software companies is often significantly lower. As the International Music Software Trade Association (2017) writes on its website, "With just a few exceptions the vast majority of our members have less than 20 employees, quite a few are 2 and 3 person operations". The *revenues* of software companies can fluctuate strongly due to seasonal factors, depending on whether and how many new products or updates are released. From a historical perspective, following Jörg Pflüger (2004), one can distinguish between three *concepts of software development* that can also be found in the field of music software: From the early, individual programming that resembles the writing of a text to the factory-like, hierarchical organization of the programming process (building) to the current, self-organized bottom-up concepts of agile software development (growing).

Since software can be developed all over the world, software companies often pursue strategies of *outsourcing or offshoring*, as this may save labor costs or enable them to acquire well-trained employees. In 2006, for example, US software and hardware manufacturer Avid acquired London-based Sibelius Software Ltd, which specialized in music notation software. In 2012, Avid announced that it was closing Sibelius headquarters in London dismissing its employees as part of extensive restructuring measures to develop the program further in California and Ukraine (Kirn, 2012). In early 2013, it became known that the old Sibelius development team was working on new music notation software for Steinberg, which was released in October 2016 under the name Dorico.

The main *distribution* channels of musical instruments are specialized music retail shops that focus on musicians as their target group. Next to this distribution channel, music software companies started to distribute their software directly over the Internet as well as using the app stores of the most common operating systems for smartphones and tablets (Apple App Store for iOS, Google Play Store for Android). Some music software companies like Ableton or Propellerhead also use a platform model to sell additional software, samples or sounds.

In order to protect intellectual property and to prevent illegal copies, providers of digital goods resort to so-called *digital rights management* (DRM) systems (Hess & Ünlü, 2004). These provide protection procedures through implementations in the hardware or software, which make it possible to control access and use, identification via metadata, the application of copy protection or a specific payment system. Tarleton Gillespie (2007) argues that copyright enforcement in the digital world has tacitly shifted from regulating copying to regulating technology design. While the logic of copyright law so far has been to set rules for users and allow the author to legally pursue a violation of these rules, DRM already restricts access to the work at the technological level.

In addition to commercial software production, the field of *open-source software* production has also developed dynamically and plays an important role in many segments of the IT market. A large part of the open-source music software development takes place at technical universities, art schools and music academies. While open-source software was already a widespread principle in the hobbyist culture and in academic hacker circles, it was not legally secured until the end of the 1980s with new licensing models such as the GNU Public License (GPL). Free Software became a utopian alternative to capitalist economic structures in 1983 through Richard Stallman (2002) and the Free Software Foundation. At the turn of the millennium, open source became more and more a standard method of software production, partly due to the marketing efforts of the Open Source Initiative founded in 1998. Examples such as the open-source operating system Android for smartphones and tablets, developed by the Open Handset Alliance founded by Google, show that open source has also become an integral part of the strategies of commercial software companies. They usually do this to increase the distribution of their software environment and to make it more relevant for other developers (Schrape, 2016, p. 73).

How did digitalization affect music making and artistic strategies? In the following section, I will switch the focus from the developers of music software to the musicians.

Digital Innovations in Music Culture and New Artistic Strategies

Which artistic strategies, genres and musical practices have emerged in the course of digitalization? The following part looks at new artistic strategies and digital-born innovations in the field of musical practice. Musicians that used the computer for music making faced a couple of questions and problems how to integrate the computer into their artistic work and live performance. Artists started to explore and extend the boundaries of how to make music with a computer and how this would sound and look. The appropriation and domestication process of computers and music software by artists is a particularly interesting phenomenon since there are hardly any obligatory agencies of socialization or control that one necessarily has to go through. In addition to the journals, there is a big range of practically oriented books, DVDs and online courses as well as companies offering workshops and training courses for music software applications. Nevertheless, the appropriation process of music software is highly context-dependent and contingent. This has contributed to the diversity of musical styles and artistic strategies developed in the digital domain.

Apart from the effects of digitalization on the music industry and the everyday use of music, the probably most discussed topic in cultural journalism and musicology is the question of aesthetics. Which new musical styles, aesthetics and genres did musicians create using the computer and other digital media?

Algorithmic composition and *generative music* are phenomena that go back to the early mainframe era of *Push Button Bertha* (1956) and the *Illiac Suite* (1955–1959) (Ames, 1987; Collins, 2008). Composers not only used the computer for automatic music transcription, but also as a composition aid as well as for computer-composed scores. Brian Eno (1996) used and coined the term *generative music* to describe music that is created by a system, but may be changing every time it is played. Eno used SSEYO's Koan generative music system to create the hybrid album *Generative Music 1*, which was published in 1996. German composer Johannes Kreidler (2012) has used COIT, a self-designed graphical interface, for his compositions. The title not only alludes to (musical) effusions, but is also the acronym for calculated objects in time. It is based on Pure Data and serves above all to compose pieces faster in which live instruments as well as samples or electronically generated sounds are combined. It allows him to generate notes automatically and then edit them manually.

In addition to the algorithmic generation of music, the computer has also expanded the artistic possibilities in the field of *interactive media art* and *sound installations*. Interactive media art and installations often operate with a playful approach to involve the audience. As Jacob Sello (2014) writes, visitors of sound art installations are not passive consumers as in the classical concert hall, but move at their own pace through the sounding rooms and become protagonists of their own aesthetic experience. Stefan Poser (2016, p. 11) observes in the field of technical games the creation of new possibilities for game design and an increased number of game subjects, but also a pre-formation of games that requires a cultural–historical observation and analysis. In the field of video and computer games, musical games from Toshio Iwai's *Otocky* (1987) to *SingStar* (2004) and *Guitar Hero* (2005) became part of popular entertainment (Custodis, 2013). Interactive music systems like *Voyager* by George E. Lewis (2000) provide a virtual interactive orchestra that analyzes the performance of a musician in real time, generating both responses to the musician's playing and independent behavior.

With works like these, the computer challenges the very idea of musical creativity and gains technical agency by formalizing and simulating not only other instruments, but also composition and improvisation styles and music cognition itself (Rowe, 1993).

Musicians not only used computers as a tool for the composition and production process, but also integrated robots in performances and installations. Belgian composer, performer and instrument maker Godfried-Willem Raes founded the Logos Group in 1968, from which the M&M Orchestra with over 40 robots emerged. The *Logos Robot Orchestra* works within collaborative concert projects involving interactive robots and musicians. Singer-songwriter Taryn Southern produced a full album that was co-written and co-produced by different artificial intelligence systems. For her album *I Am AI*, published in May 2018, she used four different AI systems: Amper Music, IBM's Watson Beat, Google's Magenta and AIVA.

Interestingly, technical and practical problems are a recurring phenomenon, even for professional users. Musicians with many years of computer experience therefore often developed a high frustration tolerance or technical perfectionism in dealing with computers or have put their artistic interest precisely on these errors and their effects. Especially in media art, the production and its artifacts are often reflected upon or even form its starting point. Aesthetic developments and discussions about errors, artificiality or authenticity may therefore be seen as central themes in the discourse on the aesthetics of the digital (Warnke, 2011).

Since all kinds of data may be used to control or modify a musical performance, artists experimented with *sonification* as well as algorithmic *visualization* as artistic strategies. This includes new ways of performance for *video jockeys* (VJs) and *livecoding* (Collins, McLean, Rohrhuber, & Ward, 2003). In the twentieth and twenty-first centuries, concerts have been extensively mediatized through diverse audiovisual forms such as films, visualizations or live broadcasts. Digital technologies have expanded the possibilities of concerts and live performances that include the joint performance of spatially separated musicians over the Internet or the interaction with the audience using their mobile phones.

To take one example, Hatsune Miku, a character developed by the Japanese media company Crypton Future Media, has become a successful pop star in Japan since 2007. Her visual appearance is a manga figure designed by the illustrator KEI, and her voice is based on the software synthesizer Vocaloid2 developed by Yamaha. As a collaboratively constructed "cyber celebrity", she appears at concerts as a 3D projection.

Democratization and Emancipation of Musical Practice?

The "digital revolution" in music culture was associated with a set of promises and utopias about new musical worlds, new ways of music making, of music distribution and about a new relationship between musicians and audiences. In the history of music technology, new musical instruments often were charged with futuristic images and utopias. Constructed by its producers, the media as well as popular musicians, these images are part of the dreamscapes of their time and shape the diffusion and appropriation of these instruments. As recurring topos in techno-cultural discourses about the computer, ideas of democratization and emancipation also spurred the imagination of many musicians: The computer would create aesthetically unlimited possibilities and new musical worlds. The means of music production (music software, samples, etc.) would be easily accessible to everyone via the Internet. In addition, the Internet would offer the opportunity to reshape the relationship between musicians and audiences independently from the music industry. In Germany and other countries, these hopes resonated with the so-called New Cultural Policy, which claimed the right for every citizen to access, participate in and make culture (Hoffmann, 1979).

English sociologists Richard Barbrook and Andy Cameron (1996) described the worldview of these utopias as the "Californian Ideology", the "heterogeneous orthodoxy" of the information age, which emerged from a mixture of the liberal individualism of the hippies with the entrepreneurial drive and technological determinism of the yuppies. Sascha Dickel and Jan-Felix Schrape (2015) understand this digital utopia as a technical media utopia in contrast to classical social utopias, because their point of departure is not located in society, but in the new communication and information technologies.

What has become of the promise of democratization and emancipation? In this final part, I argue for a differentiated analysis and critical assessment of the effects of digital media in the field of musical practice. While the effects of digitalization on the music industry have been extensively discussed and investigated (Tschmuck, 2008), a corresponding analysis of the effects on musicians is still largely lacking (Möllenkamp, 2017a). How have musicians' musical practices and artistic strategies changed in the course of digitalization?

On the level of *accessibility of music*, digitalization has led to a significant expansion. The catalogs of the most common music download and streaming platforms cover music from all periods and areas of the world. Did the social participation in musical life also increase as a result of using computers for making music? Unfortunately, it is very difficult to answer this question. This is mainly due to the fact that sales and download figures for music software and apps say little about the actual use. There is also little independent information on the effects of cracked software. Another interesting question in this context is to what extent people have started to make music with music software without a preceding music education. Here, it can only be said that music software has opened up or expanded the possibilities of sound generation, processing and control as well as the use of sample libraries for musicians, which previously were only possible with analog equipment at a much higher price.

Regarding the claim of the *computer as a universal instrument* and its *unlimited aesthetic possibilities*, digitalization enabled musicians to develop a wide range of new artistic strategies and aesthetics. As Max Mathews (1963) claimed: "There are no theoretical limitations to the performance of the computer as a source of musical sounds, in contrast to the performance of ordinary instruments". Music software is not only used to record and edit existing analog instruments or to develop virtual instruments that simulate existing acoustic or electronic instruments. Any kind of data can be used to generate or manipulate sounds with a computer in real time. Sherry Turkle (1984, p. 165) argued that "the computer is a particularly rich and varied tool for serving so wide a range of purposes" that it works as a projective medium. Both musicians and music software companies used this medium to devise new artistic strategies, instruments and aesthetics. Composer and writer Curtis Roads (2015) writes enthusiastically about the unlimited possibilities of electronic musical instruments: "Electronic music evokes new sensations, feelings, and thoughts in both composers and listeners. Opening the door to an unlimited universe of sound, it engages spatialization as an integral aspect of composition and focuses on sound transformation as a core structural strategy. [...] The power of algorithmic methods amplify the capabilities of music technology. Taken together, these constitute game-changing possibilities". In this sense, music software helps to translate and transport visions and ideals of music making, to allow or at least promise musicians to take a role they probably would not be able to play otherwise.

The role of the computer in music practice has changed and expanded several times: from an aid to notation and composition to a virtual studio and flexible production environments to an instrument that can be played live. In the course of economization, however, digitalization has also contributed to the development of what Andreas Reckwitz (2012) has called a "creativity dispositive". As studies on the economic situation of artists as well as my research shows, digitalization did not lead to the emancipation from the music industry, but played a role in the continuation of precarious working conditions. Online platforms for music did not solve the problem of generating attention for the musicians but led to increased competition and growing expectations for self-promotion. With the advent of online streaming platforms, most musicians earn less than by selling downloads, CDs or LPs. As music software allowed musicians to work on tasks previously reserved to specialized staff in the music industry (like audio engineering and mastering), these tasks could be outsourced by the music industry to the musicians. Instead of an ongoing process of differentiation of professional tasks, musicians experienced the *de-specialization* of their work and were faced with increased expectations for self-marketing. Looking at independent musicians, Hracs (2016) describes that the freedom over how and where to work forced musicians in practice to take on technical, business and managerial tasks. This may be seen as an example of the exploitation of free labor in the cultural sector, as musicians largely remain dependent on the dominant infrastructures for music distribution of the music and media content industry.

From this perspective, the ideas of democratization and emancipation appear more as a point of departure than the effect of music software development. Digitalization thus expanded the artistic possibilities of musicians on the one hand, while it facilitated the precarization of working conditions on the other.

Notes

1. The Ph.D. project has two main goals: It aims to write a history of the computer as a musical instrument and analyzes the effects of digitalization on music making.
2. On the construction as well as production of users cf. Friedewald (2003) and Hyysalo et al. (2016).

References

Akrich, M. (1992). The Description of Technical Objects. In W. E. Bijker & J. Law (Eds.), *Shaping Technology/Building Society: Studies in Sociotechnical Change* (pp. 205–224). Cambridge, MA: MIT Press.

Ames, C. (1987). Automated Composition in Retrospect: 1956–1986. *Leonardo, 20*(2), 169–185.

Barbrook, R., & Cameron, A. (1996). The Californian Ideology. *Science as Culture, 6*(1), 44–72.

Bates, E. (2012). The Social Life of Musical Instruments. *Ethnomusicology, 56*(3), 363–395.

Bense, A. T. (2014). *Musik und Virtualität. Digitale Virtualität im Kontext computerbasierter Musikproduktion*. Osnabrück: Electronic Publishing.

Bjørn, K. (2017). *Push Turn Move: Interface Design in Electronic Music*. Copenhagen: Bjooks Media.

Bovermann, T., de Campo, A., Egermann, H., Hardjowirogo, S., & Weinzierl, S. (Eds.). (2017). *Musical Instruments in the 21st Century: Identities, Configurations, Practices*. Singapore: Springer.

Braun, H.-J. (Ed.). (2002). *Music and Technology in the Twentieth Century*. Baltimore: John Hopkins University Press.

Braun, H.-J. (Ed.). (2016). *Creativity: Technology and Music*. New York: Peter Lang.

Brockhaus, I. (2017). *Kultsounds. Die prägendsten Klänge der Popmusik 1960–2014*. Bielefeld: Transcript.

Brøvig-Hanssen, R., & Danielsen, A. (2016). *Digital Signatures: The Impact of Digitization on Popular Music Sound*. Cambridge, MA: MIT Press.

Buxmann, P., Diefenbach, H., & Hess, T. (2013). *The Software Industry: Economic Principles, Strategies, Perspectives*. Heidelberg and New York: Springer.

Collins, N. (2008). The Analysis of Generative Music Programs. *Organised Sound, 13*(3), 237–248.

Collins, N., McLean, A., Rohrhuber, J., & Ward, A. (2003). Live Coding in Laptop Performance. *Organised Sound, 8*(3), 321–330.

Custodis, M. (2013). Playing with Music—Featuring Sound in Games. In P. Moormann (Ed.), *Music and Game* (pp. 159–170). Wiesbaden: Springer.

Dickel, S., & Schrape, J. (2015). Dezentralisierung, Demokratisierung, Emanzipation. Zur Architektur des digitalen Technikutopismus. *Leviathan, 43*(3), 442–463.

Diduck, R. A. (2018). *Mad Skills: MIDI and Music Technology in the Twentieth Century.* London: Repeater.

Eno, B. (1996). Generative Music. *Motion Magazine.* Retrieved from http://www.inmotionmagazine.com/eno1.html.

Friedewald, M. (2003). Die fortwährende Konstruktion des Computernutzers. Leitbilder in der Geschichte der Mensch-Computer-Interaktion. *Technikgeschichte, 70*(4), 255–276.

Gillespie, T. (2007). *Wired Shut. Copyright and the Shape of Digital Culture.* Cambridge: MIT Press.

Goltz, F. (2018). Ableton Link—A Technology to Synchronize Music Software. In H. von Coler, F. Neumann, & D. Runge (Eds.), *Proceedings of the Linux Audio Conference 2018* (pp. 39–42). Berlin. Retrieved from https://lac.linux-audio.org/2018/pdf/LAC2018_proceedings.pdf.

Großmann, R. (2010). *Distanzierte Verhältnisse. Zur Musikinstrumentalisierung der Reproduktionsmedien.* Retrieved from http://www2.hu-berlin.de/fpm/popscrip/themen/pst09/pst09_grossmann.html.

Grote, F. (2016). Interfaces for Sound: Representing Material in Pop Music Production. In R. Großmann & G. Hajdu (Eds.), *SMC 2016 Proceedings: 13th Sound & Music Computing Conference* (pp. 193–196). Hamburg: Zentrum für Mikrotonale Musik und Multimediale Komposition (ZM4). Retrieved from https://smc2016.hfmt-hamburg.de/wp-content/uploads/2016/09/SMC2016_proceedings.pdf.

Gugerli, D. (2018). *Wie die Welt in den Computer kam. Zur Entstehung digitaler Wirklichkeit.* Frankfurt am Main: S. Fischer.

Hardjowirogo, S. (2017). Instrumentality: On the Construction of Instrumental Identity. In T. Bovermann, et al. (Eds.), *Musical Instruments in the 21st Century: Identities, Configurations, Practices* (pp. 9–24). Singapore: Springer.

Hess, T., & Ünlü, V. (2004). Systeme für das Management digitaler Rechte. *Wirtschaftsinformatik, 46*(4), 273–280.

Hoffmann, H. (1979). *Kultur für alle. Perspektiven und Modelle.* Frankfurt am Main: Fischer.

Hracs, B. J. (2016). Working Harder and Working Smarter: The Survival Strategies of Contemporary Independent Musicians. In B. J. Hracs, M. Seman, & T. E. Virani (Eds.), *The Production and Consumption of Music in the Digital Age* (pp. 41–55). New York: Routledge.

Hyysalo, S., Jensen, T. E., & Oudshoorn, N. (Eds.). (2016). *The New Production of Users: Changing Innovation Collectives and Involvement Strategies.* New York: Taylor and Francis.

International Music Software Trade Association. (2017). *Myths*. Retrieved from http://www.imsta.org/myths.php.
Kirn, P. (2012). *Avid's Sibelius Scoring Tool Marches on, but Without Its Creators, as Users Protest*. Retrieved from http://cdm.link/2012/08/avids-sibelius-scoring-tool-marches-on-but-without-its-creators-as-users-protest/.
Kopytoff, I. (1986). The Cultural Biography of Things: Commoditization as Process. In A. Appadurai (Ed.), *The Social Life of Things: Commodities in Cultural Perspective* (pp. 64–91). Cambridge: Cambridge University Press.
Krebs, M. (2018). Digitales Instrumentarium. Die Musikapp als zukünftiges Instrument in der Musikschule. *üben & musizieren, 1*, 40–43.
Kreidler, J. (2012). *Musik mit Musik. Texte 2005–2011*. Hofheim: Wolke.
Kuhn, T. (1996). *The Structure of Scientific Revolutions*. Chicago: University of Chicago Press.
Lazzarini, V. (2013). The Development of Computer Music Programming Systems. *Journal of New Music Research, 42*(1), 97–110.
Lewis, G. E. (2000). Too Many Notes: Complexity and Culture in Voyager. *Leonardo Music Journal, 10*, 33–39.
Mathews, M. V. (1963). The Digital Computer as a Musical Instrument. *Science, 142*(3592), 553–557.
MIMO Consortium. (2011). *Revision of the Hornbostel-Sachs Classification of Musical Instruments*. Retrieved from http://www.mimo-international.com/documents/Hornbostel%20Sachs.pdf.
Möllenkamp, A. (2014). Paradigms of Music Software Development. In T. Klouche & E. R. Miranda (Eds.), *Proceedings of the 9th Conference on Interdisciplinary Musicology—CIM 14* (pp. 61–63). Berlin: Staatliches Institut für Musikforschung.
Möllenkamp, A. (2017a). Musiksoftware und die Demokratisierung der Musikkultur. Zu den Effekten der Digitalisierung für Musiker. In *Samples* 15. Retrieved from http://gfpm-samples.de/Samples15/moellenkamp.pdf.
Möllenkamp, A. (2017b). The Computer as a Musical Instrument: Music Software and Musical Practice in Transformation. In C. Restle, B. Brilmayer, & S. Hardjowirogo (Eds.), *Good Vibrations: A History of Electronic Musical Instruments* (pp. 55–59). Berlin: Deutscher Kunstverlag.
Neukom, M. (2005). *Signale, Systeme und Klangsynthese. Grundlagen der Computermusik*. Bern: Lang.
Pflüger, J. (2004). Writing, Building, Growing: Leitvorstellungen der Programmiergeschichte. In H. D. Hellige (Ed.), *Geschichten der Informatik* (pp. 275–320). Berlin and Heidelberg: Springer.
Poser, S. (2016). *Glücksmaschinen und Maschinenglück. Grundlagen einer Technik- und Kulturgeschichte des technisierten Spiels*. Bielefeld: Transcript.
Puckette, M. (2002). Max at Seventeen. *Computer Music Journal, 26*(4), 31–43.

Reckwitz, A. (2012). *Die Erfindung der Kreativität. Zum Prozess gesellschaftlicher Ästhetisierung*. Berlin: Suhrkamp.
Roads, C. (2015). *Composing Electronic Music: A New Aesthetic*. New York, NY: Oxford University Press.
Rowe, R. (1993). *Interactive Music Systems: Machine Listening and Composing*. Cambridge, MA: MIT Press.
Ruschkowski, A. (2019). *Elektronische Klänge und musikalische Entdeckungen*. Stuttgart: Reclam.
Schrape, J. (2016). *Open-Source-Projekte als Utopie, Methode und Innovationstrategie. Historische Entwicklung - sozioökonomische Kontexte - Typologie*. Glückstadt: Hülsbusch.
Sello, J. T. (2014). *Die Klanginstallation. Ein interdisziplinäres Versuchslabor zwischen Kunst, Musik und Forschung*. Hamburg: Kovač.
Shapiro, C., & Varian, H. R. (2002). *Information Rules: A Strategic Guide to the Network Economy*. Boston, MA: Harvard Business School Press.
Srnicek, N. (2017). *Platform Capitalism*. Cambridge, UK: Polity.
Stallman, R. M. (2002). *Free Software, Free Society: Selected Essays*. Boston, MA: Free Software Foundation.
Stange-Elbe, J., & Bronner, K. (2008). Musikinstrumentenindustrie im digitalen Paradigmenwechsel. In G. Gensch, E. Stöckler, & P. Tschmuck (Eds.), *Musikrezeption, Musikdistribution und Musikproduktion. Der Wandel des Wertschöpfungsnetzwerks in der Musikwirtschaft* (pp. 311–334). Wiesbaden: Deutscher Universitäts-Verlag.
Statista. (2019). *App Stores*. Retrieved from https://de.statista.com/statistik/studie/id/23703/dokument/app-stores-statista-dossier/.
Théberge, P. (1997). *Any Sound You Can Imagine: Making Music/Consuming Technology*. Hanover, NH: Wesleyan University Press.
Tschmuck, P. (2008). Vom Tonträger zur Musikdienstleistung - Der Paradigmenwechsel in der Musikindustrie. In G. Gerhard, E. M. Stöckler, & P. Tschmuck (Eds.), *Musikrezeption, Musikdistribution und Musikproduktion. Der Wandel des Wertschöpfungsnetzwerks in der Musikwirtschaft* (pp. 141–162). Wiesbaden: Deutscher Universitäts-Verlag.
Turkle, S. (1984). *The Second Self: Computers and the Human Spirit*. New York: Simon & Schuster.
von Hornbostel, E. M., & Sachs, C. (1914). Systematik der Musikinstrumente. Ein Versuch. *Zeitschrift Für Ethnologie, 46*(4–5), 553–590.
Warnke, M. (2011). Ästhetik des Digitalen. In H. Graber, D. Landwehr, V. Sellier, P. Haber, & C. Rosiny (Eds.), *Kultur digital. Begriffe, Hintergründe, Beispiele* (pp. 145–160). Basel and Zürich: Merian.
Zicarelli, D. (2002). How I Learned to Love a Program That Does Nothing. *Computer Music Journal, 26*(4), 44–51.

Index

U. Meyer et al. (eds.), *Digitalization in Industry*,
https://doi.org/10.1007/978-3-030-28258-5

The manufacturer's authorised representative in the EU is Springer Nature Customer Service Centre GmbH, Europaplatz 3, 69115 Heidelberg, Germany. If you have any concerns regarding our products, please contact ProductSafety@springernature.com

Printed and bound by CPI Group (UK) Ltd, Croydon, CR0 4YY

30/09/2026

02225649-0009